MW00570494

CHICKEN SOUP FOR THE TEEN'S SOUL II COLLECTION Volume II

Jack Canfield
Mark Victor Hansen
Kimberly Kirberger

Health Communications, Inc.
Deerfield Beach, Florida

www.hcibooks.com
www.chickensoup.com

We would like to acknowledge the following publishers and individuals for permission to reprint the following material. (Note: The stories that were penned anonymously, that are in the public domain, or that were written by Jack Canfield, Mark Victor Hansen or Kimberly Kirberger are not included in this listing.)

A High School Love Not Forgotten. Reprinted by permission of Diana L. Chapman. ©1996 Diana L. Chapman.

Practical Application and *Pay Attention.* Reprinted by permission of Dan Clark. ©1998 Dan Clark.

My Angel Has a Halo. Reprinted by permission of Amanda Johnson. ©1998 Amanda Johnson.

Starting a New Path. Reprinted by permission of Jessie Braun. ©1998 Jessie Braun.

Discovery. Reprinted by permission of Eugene E. Beasley. ©1998 Eugene E. Beasley.

Library of Congress Cataloging-in-Publication Data
is available from the Library of Congress

ISBN 0-7573-0386-2

Publisher: Health Communications, Inc.
3201 S.W. 15th Street
Deerfield Beach, FL 33442-8190

Cover re-design by Kevin Stawieray
Inside formatting by Lawna Patterson Oldfield

Contents

1. RELATIONSHIPS

2. FRIENDSHIP

3. LOVE

4. ACTS OF KINDNESS

5. FAMILY

6. LEARNING AND LESSONS

7. TOUGH STUFF

8. OVERCOMING OBSTACLES

9. MAKING A DIFFERENCE

10. SELF-DISCOVERY

11. GROWING UP

12. LETTERS FROM READERS

1

RELATIONSHIPS

Love means each person is free to follow his or her own heart.

Melody Beattie

A High School Love Not Forgotten

When they saw him walking across our high school campus, most students couldn't help but notice Bruce. Tall and lanky, he was a thinner replica of James Dean, his hair flipped back above his forehead, and his eyebrows always cocked upward when he was in deep conversation. He was tender, thoughtful and profound. He would never hurt anyone.

I was scared of him.

I was just breaking up with my not-so-smart boyfriend, the one you stayed with and went back to thirty times out of bad habit, when Bruce headed me off at a campus pass one morning to walk with me. He helped me carry my books and made me laugh a dozen times with giddiness. I liked him. I really liked him.

He scared me because he was brilliant. But in the end, I realized I was more scared of myself than of him.

We started to walk together more at school. I would peer up at him from my stuffed locker, my heart beating rapidly, wondering if he would ever kiss me. We'd been seeing each other for several weeks and he still hadn't tried to kiss me.

Instead, he'd hold my hand, put his arm around me and send me off with one of my books to class. When I opened it, a handwritten note in his highly stylized writing would be there, speaking of love and passion in a deeper sense than I could understand at seventeen.

He would send me books, cards, notes, and would sit with me at my house for hours listening to music. He especially liked me to listen to the song, "You Brought Some Joy Inside My Tears," by Stevie Wonder.

At work one day I received a card from him that said, "I miss you when I'm sad. I miss you when I'm lonely. But most of all, I miss you when I'm happy."

I remember walking down the street of our small village, cars honking, the warm lights from stores beckoning strollers to come in from the cold, and all I could think about was, "Bruce misses me most when he's happy. What a strange thing."

I felt deeply uncomfortable to have such a romantic spirit by my side, a boy—really a man at seventeen—who thought his words out wisely, listened to every side of an argument, read poetry deep into the night and weighed his decisions carefully. I sensed a deep sadness in him but couldn't understand it. Looking back, I now think the sadness stemmed from being a person who really didn't fit into the high school plan.

Our relationship was so different from the one I'd had with my prior boyfriend. Our lives had been mostly movies and popcorn and gossip. We broke up routinely and dated other people. At times, it seemed like the whole campus was focused on the drama of our breakups, which were always intense and grand entertainment for our friends to discuss. A good soap opera.

I talked to Bruce about these things and with each story, he'd respond by putting his arm around me and telling me he'd wait while I sorted things out. And then he would read to me. He gave me the book *The Little Prince,* with the words underlined, "It's only in thy mind's eye that one can see rightly."

In response—the only way I knew how—I wrote passionate letters of love and poetry to him with an intensity I never knew before. But still I kept my walls up, keeping him at bay because I was always afraid that he'd discover I was fake, not nearly as intelligent or as deep a thinker as I found him to be.

I wanted the old habits of popcorn, movies and gossip back. It was so much easier. I remember well the day when Bruce and I stood outside in the cold and I told him I was going back to my old boyfriend. "He needs me more," I said in my girlish voice. "Old habits die hard."

Bruce looked at me with sadness, more for me than himself. He knew, and I knew then, I was making a mistake.

Years went by. Bruce went off to college first; then I did. Every time I came home for Christmas, I looked him up and went over for a visit with him and his family. I always loved his family—the warm greetings they gave me when they ushered me into their house, always happy to see me. I knew just by the way his family behaved that Bruce had forgiven me for my mistake.

One Christmas, Bruce said to me: "You were always a good writer. You were so good."

"Yes." His mother nodded in agreement. "You wrote beautifully. I hope you'll never give up your writing."

"But how do you know my writing?" I asked his mom.

"Oh, Bruce shared all the letters you wrote him with me," she said. "He and I could never get over how beautifully you wrote."

Then I saw his father's head nod, too. I sank back in my chair and blushed deeply. What exactly had I written in those letters?

I never knew Bruce had admired my writing as much as I had his intelligence.

Over the years, we lost touch. The last I heard from his father, Bruce had gone off to San Francisco and was thinking about becoming a chef. I went through dozens of bad relationships until I finally married a wonderful man—also very smart. I was more mature by then and could handle my husband's intelligence—especially when he'd remind me I had my own.

There's not one other boyfriend I ever think about with any interest, except for Bruce. Most of all, I hope he is happy. He deserves it. In many ways, I think he helped shape me, helped me learn how to accept the side of myself I refused to see amid movies, popcorn and gossip. He taught me how to see my spirit and my writer inside.

Diana L. Chapman

Practical Application

He's teaching her arithmetic,
He said it was his mission,
He kissed her once, he kissed her twice and said,
"Now that's addition."
And as he added smack by smack
In silent satisfaction,
She sweetly gave the kisses back and said,
"Now that's subtraction."

Then he kissed her, she kissed him,
Without an explanation,
And both together smiled and said,
"That's multiplication."
Then Dad appeared upon the scene and
Made a quick decision.
He kicked that kid three blocks away
And said, "That's long division!"

Dan Clark

My Angel Has a Halo

You always were a daredevil. Flying eight or more feet through the air on your bike (your pride and joy), swinging high on a rope swing or flipping head first into the lake below.

I think that is what gives you both your wonderful character and your extraordinary inner strength. What amazes me most about you is the fact that no matter what, your determination pushes all your fears away. You never let fear stand in the way of accomplishing your goals.

But despite all your dangerous stunts, I never thought that this day would come. (Maybe in the back of my mind I did, but only there.)

You were away on a trip to the coast and I eagerly awaited your call. It came the morning of the third day of the seven days you'd be gone. Your voice was normal—but your words were not—"I broke my neck."

Right then every fear in the world hit me. My mom quickly reminded me that I needed to stay strong for you. I didn't talk much. I just quietly cried as you explained to me your ordeal and the halo you would have to wear for two months to keep your neck stabilized as it healed.

You seemed okay considering the situation, but in pain

and in low spirits. I hung up the phone and finally the tears could, and did, flow freely. Throughout this whole day I came to terms with the fact that you would be in a cast, with the exception of your arms, for two entire months. At first I was selfish and thought of how this would affect me. *He can't drive, so we'll see each other less often. He can't take me to school on the first day. I can't even give him a real hug.* But then I remembered and told myself: *Amanda, be glad that he's still alive and here for you to hug at all, no matter what form it's in. And be thankful for the fact that he can walk.*

I went and saw you tonight. You looked good but no smiles—no smiles, that is, until you saw a video of your biking stunts. I saw the determination in your eyes and it brought tears to mine. I know you're scared, but I also know that you're going to be okay. Because that determination inside of you is once again going to push those fears away, and you'll be 110 percent. You helped me be less afraid for you. I stopped thinking about what you cannot do and concentrated instead on what you can do, or what you will do again. Two months is a very short time in exchange for a lifetime of living.

I want to thank you. You have taught me more about inner strength and determination in this one day than I've learned in my whole life. I love you, Logan. We all do. Don't ever lose heart. Just let your wonderful self shine through. You're going to pull through this with flying colors, pushing yourself all the way, because that's who you are: a fighter. I feel so much better now that I'm not thinking about what I won't have and what I won't get from you. Instead, I feel grateful and so happy that you are who you are.

All I have for you now is faith and determination. I always knew that you were a blessing to me, my angel. Now, for two months, you'll have a halo to prove it.

Amanda Johnson

Starting a New Path

"But I love you, Jessie," he says as we sit on the couch in my living room, his voice quivering and unstable. His pleading eyes look directly into mine, begging my forgiveness. I don't recognize these eyes that once provided me with a sense of comfort and security. The warm blue of his eyes that used to reassure me of a love that would last forever is replaced with a colder gray. I shiver and look away.

Tears cloud my eyes as I feel him breathing next to me on the edge of the couch. My mind wanders to a time a year earlier, a happier time, when I had also been acutely aware of his breathing as we sat in silence on that same couch. My heart had pounded that day as I glanced nervously into his eyes, unable to hold my stare, yet unable to look away. It was that particular day that my heart decided to surrender itself to the magic of first love. And as I sat beside him, overwhelmed by the certainty of my love for him, I struggled to say the words out loud for the first time. I wanted to scream to the world that my heart felt bigger than my whole body, that I was in love and nothing could ever take away that feeling, but no sounds came out of my mouth. As I fidgeted with the edge of a pillow, he gently placed his hand on my arm and looked directly into my eyes. His soft stare soothed my nerves. "I love you, Jessie," he told me, his eyes holding my stare. A small smile formed on my face as my heart began to beat quickly and loudly. He had known that night, just as I had—and he had felt the power of the realization of love, just like I had.

But that power is gone now, I remind myself. That returns me from that distant memory to the present moment like a slap in the face.

"Doesn't it mean anything to you that I love you?" he asks. "Please, I'm so sorry." His hand reaches for my face to brush the hair out of my eyes. I duck my head to avoid his touch. It has become too painful since I found out. He had told me two days before that he had kissed another girl. I had sat in stunned silence, unable to move or speak.

I sit now in silence, not because I don't know what to say, but because I am afraid that my voice will deceive me and begin to quiver. As I start to speak, I look into his eyes and stop myself, wondering if I will be making a mistake. *Maybe it can work,* I think, and I imagine his arms around me, hugging my head tightly to his chest, making everything okay like he had done so often in the past when I was in need of his comfort. Now, more than ever, I ache for the comfort of his arms and for the reassurance of his warm blue gaze. But it is not possible, for the trust is gone and our love has been scarred. His gaze is no longer a warm blue and his arms no longer provide comfort.

Now I struggle to find the words that I know must come out of my mouth, not like before when I knew the words would lead us to a place of magic on the path of our relationship. I now struggle to find the words that will end that path. It's not that my love for him has been taken away, it's just that I know my heart can never again feel bigger than my whole body when I am with him. When he gets up from the couch to leave, the pain in my heart feels too strong to endure, and I have to stop myself from calling after him. I know that I have done the right thing. I know that I am strong, although at this moment I feel anything but strong.

I sit frozen on the couch for a long time after he has left; the only movement in the room is the tears that run down my cheeks and soak the thighs of my jeans. I wonder how I can possibly go on when it feels like half of me is missing. And so I wait. I wait for time to heal the pain and raise me to my feet once again—so that I can start a new path, my own path, the one that will make me whole again.

Jessie Braun

Discovery

My class was two weeks away from the opening night of our play when Sherry walked into my classroom and in a hesitant voice announced that she would have to quit.

Hundreds of reasons for such a declaration rushed through my mind—tragic illness, death in the family, a terrible family crisis.

The expression on my face prompted a further explanation. Sherry stammered, "My boyfriend Dave wants me to quit. The rehearsals are taking too much time away from our being together. I bring him sandwiches after football practice."

Her boyfriend was a football player who later went on to play in the pros. He was the opposite of his brother Dan, who also played on the high school team. While Dan was easygoing, had a terrific sense of humor and was liked by nearly everyone, Dave seemed to always be angry and in need of someone to boss around.

"Sherry," I said, "we're only two weeks from opening. You're outstanding in your role. I'd never be able to replace you."

"Really?" She beamed.

"Really," I said, and I meant it. "Everyone should be

allowed to do the things they are good at. You're a good actress. Dave should realize that. I know you know how much he loves football."

"Yes," she agreed. "But I still have to quit."

"I'll bet you're his best fan."

She measured the words. "I am," she said.

"Has he ever been to a Saturday morning rehearsal to see how good you are?"

"No."

"He should," I told her. "He should be your number one fan."

The next day after sixth hour, my door flew open with a thud. Dave thundered toward me, looking twice as big as his 260 pounds. His arms dangled by his side, his large fists clenched as if around my neck.

He leaned across my desk, veins popping, face red as a beet. "You . . . you . . . you . . ." he stammered.

"Can I help you, Dave?" I asked, hoping that my voice wouldn't shake the way my knees were.

He never got beyond "you" before he turned and stomped out the door. I listened until the heavy footsteps started down the stairs to the first floor.

Sherry did continue with the play, and I can honestly say starred in her art. I also noticed that she smiled more, and I occasionally saw her interacting with other students with a great deal of poise.

Dave, I heard, found another girlfriend.

Eugene E. Beasley

Inside

Bottled up inside
Are the words I never said,
The feelings that I hide,
The lines you never read.

You can see it in my eyes,
Read it on my face:
Trapped inside are lies
Of the past I can't replace.

With memories that linger—
Won't seem to go away.
Why can't I be happier?
Today's a brand-new day.

Yesterdays are over,
Even though the hurting's not.
Nothing lasts forever,
I must cherish what I've got.

Don't take my love for granted,
For soon it will be gone—
All you ever wanted
Of the love you thought you'd won.

The hurt I'm feeling now
Won't disappear overnight,
But someway, somehow,
Everything will turn out all right,

No more wishing for the past.
It wasn't meant to be.
It didn't seem to last,
So I have to set him free.

Melissa Collette

Lost Love

Love is the extremely difficult realization that something other than oneself is real.

Iris Murdoch

I don't know why I should tell you this. I'm nothing special, nothing out of the ordinary. Nothing has happened to me my whole life that hasn't happened to nearly everybody else on this planet.

Except that I met Rachel.

We met at school. We were locker neighbors, sharing that same smell of fresh notebook paper and molding tennis shoes, with clips of our favorite musicians taped inside our locker doors.

She was beautiful and had that self-assurance that told me she must be going with somebody. Somebody who was somebody in school. Me—I'm struggling, trying to stay on the track team and make good enough grades to get into the college my folks went to when they were my age.

The day I met Rachel, she smiled and said hello. After looking into her warm brown eyes, I just had to get out and run like it was the first and last run of my life. I ran ten miles that day and hardly got winded.

We spent that fall talking and joking about teachers, parents and life in general, and what we were going to do when we graduated. We were both seniors, and it was great to feel like a "top dog" for a while. It turns out she wasn't dating anybody—which was amazing. She'd broken up with somebody on the swim team over the summer and wasn't going out at all.

I never knew you could really talk to somebody—a girl, I mean—the way I talked with her.

So one day my car—it's an old beat-up car my dad bought me because it could never go very fast—wouldn't start. It was one of those gray, chilly fall days, and it looked like rain. Rachel drove up beside me in the school parking lot in her old man's turquoise convertible and asked if she could take me somewhere.

I got in. She was playing the new David Byrne CD and singing along to it. Her voice was pretty, a lot prettier than Byrne's—but then, he's a skinny dude, nothing like Rachel. "So where do you want to go?" she asked, and her eyes had a twinkle like she knew something about me I didn't.

"To the house, I guess," I said, then got up the guts to add, "unless you want to stop by Sonic first."

She didn't answer yes or no, but drove straight to the drive-in restaurant. I got her something to eat and we sat and talked some more. She looked at me with those brown eyes that seemed to see everything I felt and thought. I felt her fingers on my lips and knew I would never feel any more for a girl than I did right then.

We talked and she told me about how she'd come to live in this town, how her dad had been a diplomat in Washington and then retired and wanted her, all of a sudden, to grow up like a small-town girl, but it was too late. She was sophisticated and poised and always seemed to know what to say. Not like me. But she opened up something in me.

She liked me, and suddenly I liked myself.

She pointed to her windshield. "Look," she said, laughing. "We steamed up the windows." In the fading light of day, I suddenly remembered home, parents and my car.

She drove me home and dropped me off with a "See you tomorrow" and a wave. That was enough. I had met the girl of my dreams.

After that day, we started seeing each other, but I wouldn't call them dates. We'd get together to study and always ended up talking and laughing over the same things.

Our first kiss? I wouldn't tell the guys this, because they would think it was funny, but she kissed me first. We were in my house, in the kitchen. Nobody was home. The only thing I could hear was the ticking of the kitchen clock. Oh, yeah, and my heart pounding in my ears like it was going to explode.

It was soft and brief; then she looked deep in my eyes and kissed me again, and this time it wasn't so soft and not so brief, either. I could smell her and touch her hair, and right then I knew I could die and be happy about it.

"See you tomorrow," she said then, and started to walk out the door. I couldn't say anything. I just looked at her and smiled.

We graduated and spent the summer swimming and hiking and fishing and picking berries and listening to her music. She had everything from R&B to hard rock, and even the classics like Vivaldi and Rachmaninoff. I felt alive like I never had before. Everything I saw and smelled and touched was new.

We were lying on a blanket in the park one day, looking up at the clouds, the radio playing old jazz. "We have to leave each other," she said. "It's almost time for us to go to college." She rolled over on her belly and looked at me.

"Will you miss me? Think of me, ever?" and for a nanosecond I thought I saw some doubt, something unlike her usual self-assurance, in her eyes.

I kissed her and closed my eyes so I could sense only her, the way she smelled and tasted and felt. Her hair blew against my cheek in the late summer breeze. "You are me," I said. "How can I miss myself?"

But inside, it was like my guts were being dissected. She was right; every day that passed meant we were that much closer to being apart.

We tried to hold on then, and act like nothing was going to happen to change our world. She didn't talk about shopping for new clothes to take with her; I didn't talk about the new car my dad had bought for me because that would be what I drove away in. We kept acting like summer was going to last forever, that nothing would change us or our love. And I know she loved me.

It's nearly spring now. I'll be a college sophomore soon.

Rachel never writes.

She said that we should leave it at that—whatever that meant. And her folks bought a house in Virginia, so I know she's not coming back here.

I listen to music more now, and I always look twice when I see a turquoise convertible, and I notice more things, like the color of the sky and the breeze as it blows through the trees.

She is me, and I am her. Wherever she is, she knows that. I'm breathing her breath and dreaming her dreams, and when I run now, I run an extra mile for Rachel.

Robby Smith
As told to T. J. Lacey

David's Smile

David could make me deliriously happy or crazy with anger, quicker than anyone I'd ever known, and when he smiled everything else disappeared and I could not help but smile back. He had a million smiles, but there was one in particular that I could even hear in his voice across the phone from miles away. It was playful and knowing and cynical and sincere and secretive and assertive and a thousand other paradoxical things all at once. That smile made me laugh when I was hurting, forgive him when I was angry and believe him even when I knew he was lying. That smile made me fall in love with him—and that was the last thing I ever wanted to do.

When he was mad or hurting or thinking or listening, his face was stone. When he smiled, though, I felt like I was looking right into his soul, and when I made him smile, I felt beautiful inside and out.

David was the first guy I ever really loved. Sometimes when he held me and my head was resting on his broad shoulder I felt that he could hear my deepest, darkest thoughts. He always knew how to say exactly what I needed to hear. He would touch my face and look into my eyes and say he loved me with such warmth that I couldn't help believing.

From the first time we touched, he dominated my thoughts. I would try to concentrate on school, church, my family or my other friends, but it was no use. I would tell myself over and over again that he wasn't the kind of guy I needed in my life, but with each passing day, I only wanted him more. I felt so out of control, so scared and so excited. I would fall asleep at night thinking about his kisses and wake up in the morning with his soft, magical words ringing in my ears. Sometimes when I was near him I trembled. Then, he would put his arms around me and I would relax and feel safe again.

My instincts were in constant conflict. *Trust him. Don't trust him. Kiss him. Don't kiss him. Call him. Don't call him. Tell him how you feel. No, it will scare him off.* And then finally I would wonder if maybe that would be the very best thing that could happen.

If he was scared or insecure, I only saw it once or twice. Like the rest of his emotions, I could never tell how much was an act for my benefit and how much he really felt. He fascinated me. I would stare into his brown eyes and wonder if he had any idea how much control he had over me. If he knew, he never let it show.

Then, one day it all came crashing down around me. He was gone and, as I hurt, I wondered if he had ever really loved me. I had so many questions—and so much to tell him. It was like an alarm had gone off too soon and now my dream was over. He was gone, and all that was left of all we had shared were a few letters and some memories that I was too proud to dwell on. My heart cried out for him, but my mind warned me to move on. In the end, that is what I did.

I learned more from David than from any other guy, with the single exception of my father. When the time and the strength finally came, I was forced to take those lessons and move on without him. Time passed, life continued and I think of him less and less. But, sometimes my mind drifts back to the sweet dream of my first love, and I am haunted by images of his smile. I loved his smile.

Cambra J. Cameron

One of Those Days

For of all sad words of tongue or pen, the saddest are these: "It might have been."

John Greenleaf Whittier

Today is one of those days that I miss him—the lonely I-wonder-what-he-is-doing days. I don't have them often, hardly at all, but once in a while I do when I hear a song he used to sing or drive past his neighborhood. I am not sure why it is that I sometimes still miss him. It's been nearly eight months since we broke up for the second time. Maybe losing him bothers me a lot more than I let myself believe. Sometimes, I hate myself because I know that I am to blame.

The first time I met Justin I was completely infatuated with him. I just knew that I had to be with him, and two months later, I was. For a while, I thought my life was perfect. He was older and more mature than previous boyfriends were; he knew how to have a real relationship that meant something. I was always happy, and I always felt beautiful around him.

Eventually, my immaturity began to surface. Three and

a half months into the relationship I started to feel like my freedom was dwindling. I still cared about him a lot, but I was feeling exhausted. I needed a break. He wasn't ready to let me go, but I wasn't going to let that stop me. Tearfully, I chose to take the road of independence and broke his heart in the process.

I dated other guys, but he would creep into my thoughts at least once a day. None of the guys measured up to him; none of them gave me the special feelings that I longed for day after day. Then, one day, about eight months after our breakup, he called out of the blue. Until then we had barely spoken, and I realized just how much I really missed him. We decided to get together and catch up. We went out to dinner, and he talked about his new girlfriend . . . a lot. I thought I was going to have to dump my glass of water on him to get him to shut up about her. After a long conversation he revealed that he wanted me back. And I wanted him back. So, after his breakup and a few more emotionally charged talks, we got back together. It almost felt as if no time had passed since we were last a couple. We were happy, and I felt complete again. I had matured a lot and could now handle committing to him. Sometimes my adoration for him would overwhelm me. Never before, and never after, have I cared about a boy so strongly.

After a while, though, I became too busy with my after-school activities to be able to put so much energy into the relationship. He felt like I was betraying everything that we had, everything we had worked for. And in a moment of anger, I felt like he betrayed my trust in the worst way. We broke up. I held a grudge for a long time. My pride was wounded and my feelings torn.

With time we were able to be friends again. We had given it two tries, and it seemed it wasn't meant to be. What I learned from him and the relationship was worth all the painful times we went through. There were many happy memories, too. I heard a quote once that rang loud and true: "You always believe your first love to be your last, and your last to be your first." For me, he's been both. We shared secrets and laughs, rainy nights and sunny days. Though we experienced many storms together, we taught each other valuable lessons about life and love. The way that I was able to look at myself through his eyes was one of the most amazing feelings I've ever had. But, there comes a time when the feelings start to fade and the memories become bittersweet. A time where all that you can do is hope that somehow he will realize what a difference he made in your life and how he contributed to the person that you've become.

I can't ignore the feelings that once were. I can, however, let go and remember.

Cassie Kirby

Experience Is a Teacher

The true test of character is not how much we know how to do, but how we behave when we don't know what to do.

John Holt

I was shaking when I heard the car pull into the driveway. I blamed it on the chill in my house, although most likely it was because of my uncontrollable nerves. When I opened the door, Becca was standing on my porch with a smile plastered on her face.

"Hey," she said. As she stepped inside the doorway, the guys behind her became visible. "Oh, ya," she added. "This is Dan, Josh and Kevin."

"Hi," I said, and they replied the same in unison. They looked kind of like deer in headlights, standing outside the door, hands jammed in pockets, mouths half-open. As Becca made her way into the house, the guys followed her, and I felt awkwardly lost, unsure of what to say. To avoid forced conversation, I took the opportunity to jot a note to my mom, explaining where I was going.

Eventually, we made it out of the house, and I found

myself in the back seat of a navy-blue truck, wedged between Josh and Kevin, two older guys from a different school. Becca was chattering away in the passenger seat, changing the radio station and singing along. My legs began to shake, a sure indicator of my nervousness, and I had to put my hands on my thighs to steady them. We soon reached the restaurant, and I was thankful for the chance to get out of the truck.

Dan was toying with the miniature coffee creamers at the end of the table. "I don't trust these," he announced. "They've probably been sitting here since 1982."

At the opposite end of the table, next to Kevin, I giggled, probably for the eighth time since we'd sat down. I wanted to smack myself. Between my legs shaking and my ridiculous giggling, my immature nervous habits were driving me crazy, and I prayed that nobody else noticed.

Suddenly, Becca stood up. "I have to call my mom. Dan, come with me."

"Um, I'll come, too," I said. Feeling the need to elaborate, I continued, "I have to call my mom, too." I felt stupid following Becca and Dan out to the lobby, like a girl in elementary school who can't go anywhere without her best friend.

As we waited while Becca called her mom, Dan nudged me and said, "So, what do you think of Josh and Kevin?"

"Josh is pretty cute," I said, figuring that honesty was the best way to go.

"Not Kevin?" Dan's eyes sparkled, and I knew what Becca had been talking about when she said how wonderful he was.

"No . . ." I looked out the window. "But don't tell him that I said that."

"I won't." Of course he wouldn't. What did I think this was, elementary school? I felt like a child in a world of adults, unsure how to act or what to say.

"Josh thinks you're really hot," Dan continued.

His statement immediately grabbed my attention. "Oh, really?" I was flattered.

Becca hung up the phone and caught the end of our conversation, saying excitedly, "You have to sit by him when we go back to the table!"

"No," I protested. "That'll look dumb."

"No it won't," she insisted, and Dan agreed.

"Yeah, we'll just move stuff around or whatever." It was obvious that this was an argument I was not going to win.

When we returned to the table and assumed our new seats, Josh didn't say anything. I wondered if he had figured out our juvenile plan, and then I wondered if he even cared. But I quickly tried to brush the thoughts out of my head and proceeded to giggle at everything Dan said.

Next we went to the movies. Without Becca next to me in the theater, I felt completely defenseless. I gripped my knees for support, angry at myself for being nervous. Why couldn't I have more self-confidence and be as charming as other girls are? I leaned my head back against the headrest, watching Dan and Becca out of the corner of my eye. No contact yet, I noted. I didn't know what to do with my hands, and it seemed like they took on a life of their own as they repetitiously roamed from my knees to my thighs and eventually gripped the edge of my purse.

I felt a nudge on my right arm. I looked over at Dan and watched as he mouthed the words, "Make a move." He then grinned at me and raised his eyebrows in Josh's direction.

"No!" I whispered emphatically.

"Why not?" he replied with a kind of urgency.

I half-shrugged my shoulders. "I don't know." How could I explain to him the way my mind works? I could never "make a move" on anyone; I didn't have the nerve.

My fear of rejection was too intense. Out of the corner of my eye, I saw that Becca was leaning on Dan's shoulder, and his hand was resting on her knee. I sank farther into my seat.

On the way home from the movies, Becca asked Dan if he had a piece of paper. I knew immediately what she was doing and wanted to object, but couldn't. When she handed me Josh's number on a torn piece of paper, I didn't even look at it. I just played with it between my fingers, bending the edges and running it along the folds of my jeans. Josh's reaction to the piece of paper in his hand was similar.

We pulled into my driveway, and I thought that I was finally safe at home as I said good-bye to everyone and sauntered up to my porch. But as I turned around to give a final wave good-bye, I found Josh standing on the lawn.

"Hey," he said, in a way only older guys can. "When are you going to be home tomorrow?"

"Probably all day," I managed and immediately thought of how dumb I sounded.

"Okay, then. I'll, um, call you around one."

I flashed a slight smile. "Okay. Bye!" I stepped inside my house, allowing myself to breathe only when I had closed the door and was safe inside.

I washed my face, wondering if he would think that I was "really hot" without makeup. As I curled up in bed, the phrase "If only I had . . ." crossed my mind so many times that I became exhausted. But then I remembered that experience, even if awkward and uncomfortable, or in the form of a guy named Josh, is always a teacher. With that, I gradually fell asleep, knowing tomorrow was a new day, and I could rest assured there would be more lessons to learn.

Julia Travis

Living Without You

I keep looking in all the places,
Where you are supposed to be.
But I never seem to find you,
And you're all I long to see.

I just can't seem to understand,
What it was that changed your mind.
All this time I thought I knew you,
When really, I was blind.

But know that I do not hate you,
And I know I never will.
Because I cared about you then,
And I care about you still.

Even though you hurt me,
I can't seem to let you go.
But I will go on without you,
And I want to make sure you know.

It will take some time to mend,
The damage that you've done.
But broken hearts do heal,
That's where strength comes from.

For now, the tears may be falling,
And my thoughts keep circling to you.
But soon, things will get better,
If you have hope, then they always do.

Kristy Glassen

Kiss

Point your lashes down
  and you can picture my face—
    I'm smiling . . .

Open your mouth, speak with your heart
  and you can see my soul—
    I'm waiting . . .

Place your arms around my waist
  and you can embrace my uncertainty—
    I'm shaking . . .

Press your lips against mine
  and try to catch me—
    I'm falling . . .

Emily Crane

He Finally Said, "I Love You"

As I looked into his eyes
And found his longing stare
I stopped myself from saying words
That would show how much I care
I put my hand up to his face
To hold my feelings in
I wouldn't say the words again
To show my love for him
The last time I had told him
How much he meant to me
He put my hands away from his
And said to leave him be
I never spoke the words again
For fear of his deep fright
I thought it was the last time
Until that blissful night
His fingers traced around my face
Pushing hair away
And I was quite unprepared
For what he was to say
My heart beat quickly, my head raced on

I thought that I might cry
He looked as if he might faint—
Imagine this strong guy
But never would I be more impressed
With anything he'd do
Than when he took that heartfelt leap
And told me, "I love you."

Jennifer Orendach

My Childhood Sweetheart

Love can sometimes be magic. But magic can sometimes . . . just be an illusion.

Javan

I met Jake when I was eleven. To me, he wasn't just "my older brother's friend." He was a thirteen-year-old—an older man. Jake and my brother would sit in my brother's room, door closed, and shake their heads to the music of Guns 'n Roses. I would desperately try to think of excuses to knock on my brother's door, just to get a peek or a quick smile at Jake. I found something attractive in this geeky computer whiz. But I was just "Phil's baby sister," so the lines were drawn: He was the friend, and I was the annoying little sister, two seemingly incompatible titles.

Jake went away to private school, and I missed his presence in the house, even if it had just been behind my brother's locked door. A few months after he left, Jake wrote a letter to Phil, and at the end of the letter, in barely legible script, he scribbled, "Say hello to your sister for me. Is she still cute?" I lived on that line for months; it was enough to give me a constant flutter in my stomach.

In the summer of 1993, Jake came home. One evening, the phone rang. When I answered it, the voice on the other line responded, "Hi, Leesa, is Phil around?" I searched my memory, trying to remember the familiar voice on the other line. After a few seconds, I realized it was Jake. JAKE!

"Actually, he's not here. Where are you?" My voice shook. I couldn't believe it when he replied, "Cranbrook." He was home.

Our friendship began the instant he spoke again and said, "Well, if Phil isn't around, I guess *you* are going to have to talk to me." That night, we got together and sat in the park for hours.

I brought a friend along, with the intention of setting her up with the friend who accompanied Jake. I watched as Jake talked and laughed with my friend, Mel. I realized I wasn't going to be the one setting anyone up. Jake was obviously interested in Mel.

When Jake and Mel became a couple, my heart sank. To my selfish pleasure, I felt smug later that month when they broke up, and Jake called me to complain. We ended up talking again, and my anger toward his dating Mel wore off rather quickly. It was hard to stay mad at him.

Although he left for school again soon after that, his letters were now addressed to me, with side notes that read, "Say hi to Phil for me." Our friendship was growing stronger and stronger.

He left his school two years later, only to move farther away. I thought we would both move on, since we were so far apart, but we only grew closer. It wasn't long before I realized that I was officially in love with him. Whenever he came to visit, it was like a whole new adventure. We felt free to act like kids, but at the same time, we had endless conversations. We laughed and shared our secrets, and I always dreaded the day he had to go back home.

Every time he visited, I told myself, *This is it. I am going to tell him how I feel.* I promised myself that I would before he left, but I never got the guts to confess my true feelings.

Jake came home again a few days ago. I swore to myself that there was no more next time, that it was now or never, and that I couldn't hold it in anymore. While we had hinted at our feelings, we had never talked about them. I worked up the nerve to tell him how I felt, that I loved him and had for some time. The words just flowed out of me. He cut me off, leaned over and kissed me. I expected to feel complete bliss, but, surprisingly, I didn't. *This is Jake,* I reminded myself. *Remember? You love him!* Still, I felt nothing. When he looked at me, I could tell he felt the same. I believed that kissing Jake would be the last piece of the puzzle to complete my perfect fantasy. Yet somehow, the puzzle pieces just didn't match up.

Jake left again today, and for once, his leaving doesn't feel like a tragedy. We are best friends, nothing more, and always will be.

So maybe this isn't a storybook ending. Perhaps my childhood sweetheart will not become my fairy-tale prince, but we can still live happily ever after.

Leesa Dean

Late-Night Talk

His name came up
On the caller ID
At exactly
Eleven forty-three.

I answered it
In my cheery fashion
For our late-night talks
Were always my passion.

But his voice told me
That something was wrong
Like a horror movie's
Foreshadowing song.

As he took a deep breath
And told me the phrase
"We need to talk"
I was put in a daze.

"We have a connection
And get along fine
There's nothing you've done
The problem is mine.

"You understand, don't you?
Are you still there?"
I tried to answer
As I felt my heart tear.

"We're gonna stay friends,
We'll talk every day.
Nikki, do you have
Anything to say?"

A thousand thoughts were
Ready to spill
But my mouth wouldn't talk
As my eyes began to fill.

Thoughts raced through my head
Old memories played
The thought of being alone
Made me feel so afraid.

"I'm not expecting you
To understand.
You're a sophomore,
Life holds different demands.

"Still one day
When your life is SATs'
College applications
And activities,

"You'll realize why
I made this choice.
Talk to me, Nikki,
Do you have a voice?"

I would if I hadn't
Hung up so quick
To comfort myself,
I was feeling quite sick.

So then this is it,
This is the end.
What more can I say then?
I'll miss you, my friend.

Nicole Hamberger

I Had to Let Him Go

"I'm sorry, I just don't really remember . . ."

His words tore through me, piercing every inch of my body and cutting jaggedly through to my heart. Just one week earlier, we had watched the sun set and held each other. He comforted me while I asked him why my best friend and I just couldn't get along anymore. But tonight, his mind was somewhere else; he couldn't remember that special night.

Why was he so distant? Was he so lost in the pain that had been haunting him for so long?

There were nights he cried himself to sleep, remembering the harsh words of his mother. He told me how much he dreaded the weekends spent with her, because it meant another seventy-two hours of being blamed for everything that went wrong. The nagging didn't stop—she harassed him because his grades were lower than his brother's and he wasn't the perfect son she wanted him to be. She said he was dumb; that he wouldn't get into college, wouldn't succeed in life. She called him a loser, a disappointment to her. His gift at art was undeniable, yet her criticism caused him to believe he had no talent, when actually, he was winning prizes for his work.

What kept him alive, he told me, was our love. Friends for years, and now dating, he needed me. He counted on me. In one letter I received from him, he said, "You're like my family. Just you. We can be a family. Do you need anyone else? I don't. Just keep loving me," he wrote, "and I'll be okay."

For a while, I believed him. I promised I would never hurt him like she had, never leave him, never stop loving him. I would be his family; the one he needed in good times and in bad, the one who held him when he was sick and cheered for him at track meets. I thought that if I held him tightly enough, his pain would disappear.

It was like a roller coaster, though, our relationship. Sometimes, he was the happiest kid I knew—laughing, joking, smiling and kissing. I always knew if he was happy by his eyes. Crystal clear and blue, they told me no lies. If he was happy, they sparkled. But if he was sad, they seemed more gray than blue. On those sad days, he didn't joke. When I tried to cheer him with a kiss, he would refuse. He wouldn't let me touch him. I couldn't show him how much I loved him. When he was hurt, all he knew was to return the hurt to those undeserving. He said things he knew were cruel, apologizing the next day. The cycle never ended—the cruelties, the apologies. Yet I knew why.

Though I loved him, I couldn't take away his pain. It stemmed from events that occurred long before I knew him. Soon I realized my love couldn't compete with his inner pain. Though it hurt, I realized that I couldn't help him; rather, he had to seek professional help. I had to let him go.

The night I told him this couldn't continue, the tears stung my eyes more painfully than ever before. He now would have to face his worst fear—to be alone to confront the real demons within him. He thought I had deceived him, that I had lied to him when I whispered the word *forever*. But I hadn't lied to anyone but myself because I believed that all he needed was my love. Right now, my love was only causing pain.

He had built a separate world, in which only he and I existed. For a while, it had been nice to dream of such a happy place, a mystical Eden for just the two of us. Before long, however, I knew the walls would crumble if he kept relying only on me. Deep down I knew it wasn't healthy for either of us. I simply couldn't hold on to us and this fantasy any longer.

Yesterday, I saw him for the first time in a year. His eyes sparkled, and the light came from within. The darkness is lifting, because he allowed other people into his life, people who helped him in more ways than I ever could have done on my own. Now, he sees the special gifts that he has, and although the painful memories will always remain, he is now beginning to believe in himself. Yesterday, I realized that even perfect love can't protect someone from himself. And, sometimes, the most loving thing you can do for someone is to let him go.

Andrea Barkoukis

Please Sign My Yearbook

The hardest of all is learning to be a well of affection, and not a fountain; to show them we love them not when we feel like it, but when they do.

Nan Fairbother

Sitting in class, I concentrated on the back of Brian's neck. Evil thoughts filled my mind; I was secretly waiting for his head to explode. It didn't, and I was forced to watch my ex-boyfriend laugh and chat with every person in the room while he blatantly ignored me.

After Brian and I broke up, third period became pure torture. While I was still nursing what I considered to be the world's worst broken heart, I was bombarded with the sight of my ex's excessive flirting, as if he were proving to me that he was so obviously over his heartache. During class, Brian would gossip loudly about his weekend, his latest party and his new car.

Maybe Brian was trying to get back at me for breaking off our six-month relationship. Maybe he thought that if he looked happy, it would hurt me more than I had hurt him.

At the end of the relationship, I let him cry on my shoulder but held a strong heart as he begged me not to go. Of course, he covered his pain very well at school, as if our tearful good-bye had never occurred.

Immediately after the breakup, Brian started dating another girl. She was graduating that spring, as if that were a big feat for a junior-year boy. She took him to the prom and announced it right beside me in math class. I, too, had a date for the prom, but it still hurt. My hurt curdled and turned to anger. It felt like he was trying to upset me, trying to rub his happiness in my face. Every time I saw them together, I wanted to scream. It felt like the pain was going to tear me in half, or at least force me to consider tearing her in half.

School was coming to an end, and I eagerly waited for summer vacation, my savior. No more Algebra Two and that gnawing feeling in my stomach each day.

One day in dreaded third period, Brian leaned over to me, and to my surprise, he asked me to sign his yearbook. I must have sat there for a full minute before I got over the shock and said yes.

I thought to myself, *This is my chance.* I could really let him have it! I could tell him that I knew what he was doing, that he was trying to hurt me, and that it wasn't fair. I could tell him that I saw through his act, that he and I both knew it was exactly that, an act. But then it hit me, what good would come of that? Would belittling him make me feel better, or would it just perpetuate the pain that we both needed to recover from?

Instead of writing of the pain I had endured, I listed all of the fun times we had shared. I wrote about the first place we had ever kissed, the gifts he had given me, the lessons I had learned—the ones he had taught me—and the first "I love you" that was whispered between us. It took up one page, and that quickly became two, until my hand was tired of writing. There were still a million more great memories crowding the corners of my mind, and I remembered many more throughout the day. It made me realize the things I learned from him and what great experiences we had shared. I finished by telling him I held no hard feelings, and I hoped he felt the same.

Maybe what I wrote in his yearbook made me look weak, maybe he thought I was pathetic for still holding onto the memories of our relationship. But writing all those things helped me; it helped me heal the wounds that still hurt in my heart. It felt liberating to let go of the grudge; I finally felt free from my anger.

I realized that Brian had taught me one final lesson: forgiveness. Someday, when he is fifty and has his own children, he may stumble upon his high school yearbook, and they will ask who Stacy was. I hope he can look back and say I was someone who really cared about him, loved him, and most importantly, that I was someone who taught him about forgiveness.

Stacy Brakebush

My Knight on His White Horse

I expected to meet my first love in a magical way. Not necessarily "Knight on White Horse" magical, but I had a definite picture in my head—tall, blond, chiseled body, deep voice, designer clothes. He would be romantic, smart and very witty. He would be perfect. One day he did come along, my perfect love, although his perfection wasn't quite there—at first.

He was five years older than I and about five inches shorter. He had a high squeaky voice, considering he was nineteen at the time, and a scrawny little body. He wasn't what you would call "good-looking."

We met at the beach. A mutual friend introduced us. He was annoying and kept cracking jokes and flirting with me. Somehow, he ended up giving my friends and me a ride home that night.

I rolled my eyes as the car pulled up to us. The brakes were shot, the door was broken, and he had to sit on a phone book to actually see over the dashboard. I could not help but laugh at the situation. *How embarrassing,* I thought. But he was far from embarrassed. He kept cracking jokes about his "trusty steed" and had us all laughing to tears. We stopped off at his house on the way home, and I asked him if I could use his bathroom. He stopped, turned and said, "Yes, but . . . those who use my bathroom must give me their phone numbers." He was grinning.

"Whatever. Here." I jotted down my number and then sought out the bathroom.

I guess you could say that was where it all started. We became friends instantly. He would take me out to dinner and to the movies. He even brought me as his date to a Halloween party and stayed by my side the whole night. That Halloween was the night I realized that Chris was more to me than just a friend. We came to the party as "hitch hikers that escaped from prison" and won the prize for most creative costume.

His creativity and silliness was what did it. That's how he won my heart. I was in love with this beautiful friend.

Did I tell him? Oh, no way! I was very proud . . . and very stubborn. I had been hurt many times before meeting Chris, and needless to say, had learned that love confessions are dangerous. But this was different; it felt real. We had been friends for almost a year and knew each other inside out. I knew that he liked me. He told me so all the time. I was confused. I didn't want to ruin the amazing friendship we had.

I hid my feelings for him for another year. It drove me crazy. He gave up on me and got a girlfriend, and I dated off and on; thus, we grew apart. I was never happy with any other guy. I compared every date and hug and voice to his. It hurt inside, and I denied my own true feelings and hid them very well until one day. . . .

He had just broken up with his girlfriend, and I called out of the blue. He asked if I wanted to come over and watch a movie, and I agreed.

"We have some catching up to do," he whispered, his voice giving me chills.

"Yeah, you're right. I've missed ya. . . . You haven't grown have you?" I joked.

"Just come over," he laughed. So I did.

It felt good to be back. I threw my arms around him immediately as I walked through the door. Our eyes met awkwardly, and I pulled away.

We talked about our lives, each other and ourselves. We talked for hours, about everything and anything, until silence interrupted our conversation.

I had always wondered how it would feel to kiss him—soft, sloppy, passionate?

And in that moment I decided that I needed to know. Our eyes met, and I leaned in and kissed him. His lips were soft, the kiss perfect. I was floating in his touch, his arms, his affection. It had been two years of flirting and friendship, and finally we were trapped in the moment, between our own true feelings.

I spilled to him the truth about my feelings. I told him how scared I was that I would lose him as a friend, but that he had become much more than that to me. I told him that I had never cared about someone this way. I told him that he was beautiful and that I was falling in love with him. I even began to cry.

He smiled and kissed me lightly on the cheek. " I love you, too," he whispered. "And I know how you feel. We go perfectly together, Becca."

"I know, Chris." At that moment he was the most beautiful person I had ever seen, every inch, up to his perfect ears. His voice was music, his touch tender. That was when our friendship became more. We were in love.

Months passed and our stability floundered. Love is a roller coaster, and I must admit sometimes all the turns and twists made me sick. But through everything we had an amazing and beautiful relationship. He taught me how to love and admired my passion for life. He instilled confidence in me and supported my individuality.

Love has a tendency to fade. Ours did. We had given each other a lot, including the confidence to grow into our own people, and, ultimately, to grow apart. One day, I just didn't see the love in his eyes any more. His kiss was different. We both felt the slow drift apart, yet neither of us really wanted to admit that our fire was blowing out. We had been together for a year-and-a-half and, secretly, I knew, no longer.

Although our relationship ended, our connection stayed strong. My friends had always warned me never to date your best friend; that you will ruin your friendship and it can never be the same again.

Three years later, he remains one of my best friends. We have changed and grown. I am involved with someone new and wonderful, and so is he. And yet we still remain major priorities in one another's lives.

The fantasy of my magical man has faded, and I no longer search for perfection. I know that it doesn't exist. What I do know is that love is mysterious, beautiful, and, oftentimes, very unexpected.

Rebecca Woolf

The First

Plunge boldly into the thick of life.

Goethe

It ended as abruptly as it began. A brief phone call, then the final good-bye. I hung up the phone and sat silently in a daze for a moment. Then reality sank in, and I began to cry. A friendly breakup of a far-from-perfect relationship, and yet it still hurt. A lot.

It was in the school gym, among all our friends, that he began to weave his magic. It began with a sweet smile and a light brush of his fingers across my arm. A half-hour before the dance ended, he uttered the words I had been dying to hear:

"Want to go to a movie sometime?"

I responded with a calm smile and a confident "yes" that belied the excitement coursing through my body. I felt as though I had won the lottery. My life was now complete. I had a boyfriend.

We walked out to the parking lot together, and with his mother waiting in the car just out of sight, he gazed into my eyes and kissed me on the cheek. Then with a whispered promise to call, he left. It felt so unreal. In one night, we had gone from being mere acquaintances to being the closest of friends. We were a couple.

Soon, we were strolling down the halls hand-in-hand, and I could think of nothing but him. I was nuts about him. I had been eagerly awaiting the experience for what felt like forever—the special bond between first loves that is like no other, the closeness between a couple, and perhaps most of all, my first kiss.

It took four dates before it happened. Up until then, we had held hands and cuddled, sitting close together in the plush seats of a darkened movie theater. The cuddling was just as much fun as kissing turned out to be, if not better. He had this way of rubbing his thumb across my knuckles that gave me butterflies.

Finally, we kissed. I had always wondered what my first kiss would be like. One night his mom dropped me off at my house after a movie, and he walked me to my front door. We stood under the porch light, gazing at each other shyly. Then he slowly came toward me, lowered his head and kissed me. It was over before I even realized it had happened. I wish I could say that fireworks exploded, but they didn't. After all, it was only a two-second meeting of lips. Nonetheless, it was everything I had hoped for. It was sweet and tender and caring, and just the tiniest bit awkward, because it was his first kiss, too.

If only the rest of the relationship had progressed as wonderfully. Sure, we had many good times, but the true meaning of the word "relationship" was missing. He never seemed to notice, but I was miserable for much of the time. It's hard to put a finger on what exactly bothered me. Mostly, it was a whole lot of little things. We used to go to a movie every weekend without fail. That was fun, but I never got to choose what movie we saw. Also, we never did anything *but* go to movies. He didn't like going out to eat or even talking. Sure, we discussed movies and recent releases by our favorite bands, but that's about as deep as our conversations got.

Yet, it still didn't occur to me to break up with him. I don't know if it was him that I was so infatuated with or if I was in love with the fact that I had a "boyfriend." I can't deny the pride and confidence I felt when I walked down the street holding his hand and saw how the other girls eyed me enviously, attracted by his good looks and sweet smile. I don't know why I felt that having a boyfriend was so important or why I somehow used it to judge my self-worth.

Finally, I couldn't take it any longer and I became honest with myself. I wanted the relationship to improve or I wanted to move on. And I told him just that when I called him one Friday night. To my astonishment and disappointment, he responded by saying we'd be better off as friends. I agreed. I didn't say anything; I think I was shocked at how easy it was for him. After promising to stay friends, I hung up and it was over.

After the initial shock wore off, my first feeling was one of relief. I no longer had to wonder what he was thinking all the time or ponder where we stood. Then it hit me: It was over. I cried. And then I got mad at myself for letting him make me cry. I blamed myself for not making it work. I cried some more.

And then one day I woke up and realized that life goes on. I experienced a lot of firsts with him—my first kiss, my first love and even my first heartbreak—and I'm grateful for all of it.

Hannah Brandys

The Love I'll Never Forget

The moment you have in your heart this extraordinary thing called love and feel the depth, the delight, the ecstasy of it, you will discover that the world is transformed.

J. Krishnamurti

My Minnesota hometown is a farming community of eight thousand people, tucked into the northwest corner of the state. Not a lot that is extraordinary passes through. Gretchen was an exception.

Gretchen was an Eickhof, a member of one of the town's wealthiest families. They lived in a sprawling brick place on the banks of the Red Lake River and spent summers at their vacation home on Union Lake, thirty miles away.

But there was nothing snooty about Gretchen. In sixth grade, she broke both legs skiing and for months had to be carried around by her father. After that, she taught herself to walk again. In high school, she tutored students less able than herself and was among the first to befriend new kids at school. Years later, she told me she had also been the "guardian angel" who left cookies and inspirational notes at my locker before my hockey games. She moved through the various elements of high-school society—farm kids, jocks and geeks—dispensing goodwill to all. Gretchen, the Central High Homecoming Queen of 1975, was clearly going places.

I knew her only well enough to exchange greetings when we passed in the halls. I was a good athlete and, in the parlance of the time, kind of cute. But I was insecure, especially around females. Girls were mysterious creatures, more intimidating than fastballs hurled high and tight, which may explain my bewilderment one midsummer night in 1977 when I bumped into Gretchen at a local hangout. I had just finished my freshman year at the University of North Dakota in nearby Grand Forks. Gretchen, whose horizons were much broader, was home from California after her first year at Stanford.

She greeted me happily. I remember the feel of her hand, rough as leather from hours in the waters of Union Lake, as she pulled me toward the dance floor. She was nearly as tall as I, with perfect almond skin, soft features and almost fluorescent white teeth. Honey-blond hair hung in strands past her shoulders. Her sleeveless white shirt glowed in the strobe lights, setting off arms that were brown and strong from swimming, horseback riding and canoeing.

Though not much of a dancer, Gretchen moved to the music enthusiastically, smiling dreamily. After a few dances we stood and talked, yelling to each other over the music. By the time I walked her to her car, Main Street was deserted. The traffic light blinked yellow. We held hands as we walked. When we arrived at her car, she invited me to kiss her. I was glad to oblige.

But where hometown boys were concerned, Gretchen was as elusive as mercury. As passionately as she returned some of my kisses that summer and the next, for her, I was part of the interlude between childhood and the more serious endeavors to come. I, however, was dizzy for her and had the bad habit of saying so. Each time I did, she pulled away from me. These were college summers, not the time for moony eyes and vows of undying devotion.

One night in 1978 when Gretchen and I were together, out of nowhere she spoke the words that guys in my situation dread above all.

"Tim," she said, "I think we should just be friends."

I told her I was tired of her games and was not as much of a fool as she thought. I stormed away. By morning, I had cooled off. I sent her some roses that day, with a note offering an apology and my friendship.

Gretchen and I started dating again about a month later. But this time I had learned my lesson. No more moony eyes. I could be as detached and aloof as the next guy. It worked beautifully, except that after a few weeks Gretchen asked, "What's wrong with you?"

"What do you mean, what's wrong?"

"You're not yourself," she said. "You haven't been for a long time."

"I know," I said, and let her in on my ruse. For the only time I remember, she became angry. Then she proposed a deal.

"You be who you are," she said, "and I won't go anywhere, at least for the rest of the summer."

It was a bargain I quickly accepted. She was as good as her word.

Those weeks seemed golden, a bit unreal. One time as we said good night, I discarded the final wisp of my caution and told Gretchen that I loved her. She only smiled.

I came back from college to see her off to Stanford in mid-September. While Gretchen packed, I absently shot pool at her father's table. When she finished, we took a last walk around her family's horse pasture in the gathering September chill. I thought how dramatically our lives were about to diverge and was saddened. But more than anything, I was thankful for the fine, fun times we had spent over the last two summers.

Gretchen planned to find work in California next summer. For her, the serious part of life beckoned, and I knew what that meant.

"Good-bye," I said as we stood at her front door.

"Don't say 'good-bye,'" she replied. "Say 'see you later.'"

A month later, the last of the autumn leaves were falling, but the sky was a cloudless blue, the air crisp and invigorating. Classes were done for the day.

The telephone rang the second I stepped into my dorm room. I recognized Gretchen's friend Julie's voice on the other end of the line, and my heart soared. Julie was to be married the following month, and maybe Gretchen would be returning home for the wedding after all. But hearing the uncharacteristically quiet scratch of Julie's voice, I knew before she told me that Gretchen was dead.

The previous morning Gretchen had collected one of her birthday presents from a college friend: a ride in a small plane. Shortly after takeoff, the craft lurched out of control and pitched into a marsh. Gretchen and her friend were killed instantly.

"Gretchen's parents wondered if you would be a pallbearer," Julie said.

"I'd be honored," I heard myself reply. The word sounded strange even as it left my mouth. *Honored?* Is that what I felt?

I left my dormitory and walked aimlessly. I am told I sought out a campus priest, but eighteen years later I have no memory of that. *How does a person grieve?* I wondered, unable to cry.

The night after the funeral, I sat with my high-school buddy Joel in his Chevy Vega outside the restaurant where Gretchen's mourning friends planned to congregate.

Seeing him was the beginning of both my pain and my consolation, for as Joel spoke of Gretchen, his voice briefly failed. That tiny catch in my old friend's voice dissolved whatever stood between my sorrow and me. My torrents of grief were unleashed.

The next morning, Joel and I joined a procession from the Eickhofs' lakeside summer house into the nearby woods. Gretchen's sisters took turns carrying a small urn that contained her ashes. It was cool and sunny, and the fallen leaves crackled underfoot.

We came to a lone birch tree, its magnificent white bark standing out among the surrounding maples. Scratched into the trunk were the names of Gretchen, her father and her younger sister, as well as a date many years before.

Someone said a prayer. Gretchen's father placed the urn in the ground below the birch. Above us, wind rustled through newly barren branches.

I was among the last to leave. I emerged from the woods that day into a different world, where memories of first love linger but summers always end.

Tim Madigan

2

FRIENDSHIP

Some people come into our lives and quickly go. Some people stay for a while, leave footprints on our hearts, and we are never, ever the same.

Flavia Weedn

Donna and Claudia

Donna is my sister, and I always thought of her as beautiful. Our father called her his princess. When Donna entered high school, with her long blond hair and incredible blue eyes, she caught the attention of the boys. There were the usual crushes and school dances, phone calls and giggles, and hours of combing and brushing her hair to make it glow. She had eye shadow to match the perfect blue of her eyes. Our parents were protective of us, and my father in particular kept close watch over the boys she dated.

One Saturday in April, three weeks before Donna's sixteenth birthday, a boy called and asked her to go to an amusement park. It was in the next state, about twenty miles away. They would be going with four other friends. Our parents' first answer was a firm no, but Donna eventually wore them down. On her way out the door, they told her to be home by eleven, no later.

It was a great night! The roller coasters were fast, the games were fun and the food was good. Time flew by. Finally one of them realized it was already 10:45 P.M. Being young and slightly afraid of our father, the boy who was driving decided he could make it home in fifteen minutes. It never occurred to any of them to call and ask if they could be late.

Speeding down the highway, the driver noticed the exit too late. He tried to make it anyway. The car ripped out nine metal guardrails and flipped over three times before it came to a stop on its roof. Someone pulled Donna from the car, and she crawled over to check on her friends. There was blood everywhere. As she pulled her hair back from her eyes so she could see better, her hand slipped underneath her scalp.

The blood was coming from her. Practically the entire top of Donna's head had been cut off, held on by just a few inches of scalp.

When the police cruiser arrived to rush Donna to a nearby hospital, an officer sat with her, holding her scalp in place. Donna asked him if she was going to die. He told her he didn't know.

At home, I was watching television when a creepy feeling went through me, and I thought about Donna. A few minutes went by, and the telephone rang. Mom answered it. She made a groaning noise and fell to the floor, calling for my father. They rushed out the door, telling my sister Teri and me that Donna had been in a car accident, and that they had to go to the hospital to get her. Teri and I stayed up for hours waiting for them. We changed the sheets on Donna's bed and waited. Somewhere around four o'clock in the morning, we pulled the sofa bed out and fell asleep together.

Mom and Dad were not prepared for what they saw at the hospital. The doctors had to wait until our parents arrived to stitch up Donna's head. They didn't expect her to survive the night.

At 7:00 A.M., my parents returned home. Teri was still sleeping. Mom went straight to her bedroom and Dad went into the kitchen and sat at the table. He had a white plastic garbage bag between his legs and was opening it up when I sat down at the table with him. I asked him how Donna was and he told me that the doctors didn't think she was going to make it. As I struggled to think about that, he started pulling her clothes out of the bag. They were soaked with blood and blond hair.

Some of the hair had Donna's scalp attached to it. Every piece of clothing she had worn that night was soaked with blood. I can't remember thinking anything. All I did was stare at the clothes. When Teri woke up, I showed them to her. I'm sure it was an awful thing to do, but I was in such shock that it was all I could think of.

At the hospital later that morning, Teri and I had to wait outside for a long time before we could see Donna. It was an old hospital and it smelled old, and Teri and I were afraid of it. Finally we were allowed in to see our sister. Her head was wrapped in white gauze that was stained with blood. Her face was swollen, which I couldn't understand because she had lost so much blood. I thought she would look smaller. She reached up and touched my long brown hair and started to cry.

The next day, I called a neighbor who was a hairdresser and asked her to cut my hair. It's a funny thing—I loved my long brown hair and it curled just right, but I never, ever missed it or wanted it back. All I wanted was for Donna to come home and sleep in the clean sheets that Teri and I had put on her bed.

Donna was in the hospital for two weeks. Many of her friends went to see her, especially Claudia, who was there a lot. Mom and Dad never liked Claudia—maybe because she seemed "fast," maybe because she spoke her mind; I don't really know. They just didn't like her being around.

Donna came home with the entire top half of her head shaved. She had hundreds of stitches, some of which came across her forehead and between her left eye and eyebrow. For a while she wore a gauze cap. Eventually she had our hairdresser neighbor cut the rest of her hair. It had been so soaked and matted with blood that she couldn't get it out. The hairdresser was such a kind person. She found Donna a human hair wig that perfectly matched her hair.

Donna celebrated her sixteenth birthday and went back to school. I don't know where rotten people come from, and I don't know why they exist, but they do. There was a very loud-mouthed, self-centered girl in some of Donna's classes who took great pleasure in tormenting my sister. She would sit behind her and pull slightly on Donna's wig. She'd say very quietly, "Hey, Wiggy, let's see your scars." Then she'd laugh.

Donna never said anything to anybody about her tormentor until the day she finally told Claudia. Claudia was in most of Donna's classes, and from then on kept a close eye on my sister. Whenever that girl got close to Donna, Claudia would try and be there. There was something about Claudia that was intimidating, even to the worst kids in school. No one messed with her. Unfortunately, though, Claudia wasn't always around, and the teasing and name-calling continued.

One Friday night, Claudia called and asked Donna to come spend the night at her house. My parents didn't want Donna to go—not just because they didn't like Claudia, but because they had become so protective of Donna. In the end, they knew they had to let her go, even though they probably spent the whole night worrying.

Claudia had something special waiting for my sister. She knew how awful Donna felt about her hair, so Claudia had shaved off her own beautiful long brown hair. The next day, she took Donna wig shopping for identical blond and brown wigs. When they went to school that Monday, Claudia was ready for the teasers. In a vocabulary not allowed inside school walls, she set them straight so that anyone ready to tease my sister knew they would have to mess with Claudia. It didn't take long for the message to get through.

Donna and Claudia wore their wigs for over a year, until they felt their hair had grown out enough to take them off. Only when Donna was ready did they go to school without them. By then, she had developed a stronger self-confidence and acceptance.

My sister graduated from high school. She is married and has two great kids. Twenty-eight years later, she is still friends with Claudia.

Carol Gallivan

I Need You Now

My friend, I need you now—
Please take me by the hand.
Stand by me in my hour of need,
Take time to understand.

Take my hand, dear friend,
And lead me from this place.
Chase away my doubts and fears,
Wipe the tears from off my face.

Friend, I cannot stand alone.
I need your hand to hold,
The warmth of your gentle touch
In my world that's grown so cold.

Please be a friend to me
And hold me day by day.
Because with your loving hand in mine,
I know we'll find the way.

Becky Tucker

The Tragic Reunion

I almost dropped the phone when I heard the words. "Julia's father died today." After I hung up, I walked to my room in a daze and fumbled with my CD player, hoping that the sound of my favorite songs would provide some comfort.

Although I had known this day was coming, I still felt as if the wind had been knocked out of me. As I sat on my bed, the tears came. My mother came quietly into the room and held me in a gentle embrace.

As I sat cradled in my mother's arms, I thought about last summer. I had gone with Julia and her parents on a trip to an island off the coast of South Carolina. We'd had a great time together, sharing breathtaking sunsets on the beach, eating at posh restaurants and biking along the rugged coastline. Julia's dad had taken it upon himself to fulfill our every desire.

Now I knew that beneath all the laughter and fun, Mr. Yolanda must have been suffering. One night, as Julia and I were getting ready to go out, Mrs. Yolanda came into our room looking upset. She told us that Mr. Yolanda was sick and was not up to coming with us. Julia didn't seem alarmed, and we went out as we had planned without her father.

The next day Mr. Yolanda appeared to be his usual self: soft-spoken, generous and on the go. Since his illness was not mentioned again, I didn't think about it any more for the rest of that wonderful trip.

When school started, my friendship with Julia began to change. I watched as she became caught up in making new friends. She didn't include me in her new plans, and I felt left in the dust. Pretty soon, we were no longer best friends. In fact, we were barely friends at all.

One day, my mother sat me down and told me that Mr. Yolanda had terminal pancreatic cancer. Shocked, my thoughts turned to Julia. At school she seemed a happy-go-lucky teen. Her sunny exterior displayed no sign of any turmoil, but now I knew it had to be present somewhere within her. Not wanting to upset Julia in school, and still feeling separate from her, I didn't say anything to her about her father. But inside, I wanted to run up to her in the hallway, give her a hug, and let her know that I was there and that I cared.

Now I wondered, as I walked nervously into the funeral home, if it was too late. Wakes make me uncomfortable, probably because they make death so real. And the thought of seeing Julia in this setting, knowing what a very private person she was, also made me uneasy. As my friends and I got in line to pay our respects to Mr. Yolanda, I noticed pictures of the Yolandas surrounding the casket. One photograph in particular jumped out at me. It was of Mr. Yolanda and Julia on our vacation in South Carolina.

The photograph triggered an overwhelming sadness in me, and I began to weep. I simply could not understand why God would take a parent away from his child. Julia found me then and seeing me in tears, she too began to cry.

Even though I told her how sorry I was about her father, I realized I could never fully understand what she was going through. What was it like to come home every day to a house where someone you loved was dying, or to head off to school each morning not knowing if your father would be alive when you got home? I couldn't imagine. But I did know how to express support and compassion. It wasn't too late.

Julia apologized for her neglect of our friendship, and we vowed to be friends again. A funeral is a strange place to make up with a friend, but I guess a tragic reunion is better than none at all.

Amy Muscato
Submitted by Olive O'Sullivan

My Fairy Tale

The road to a friend's house is never long.

Danish Proverb

He was the stuff fairy tales are made of—not unrealistically suave, but definitely charming. Tall and handsome, he was a prince by all conventional definitions and had the ability to steal unsuspecting young girls' hearts.

Our first kiss was perfect, and from that moment on, our relationship soared. Some days, he picked me up early for school so that we could eat breakfast together, and other days we sneaked away for snowball fights during study hall. On weekends, I watched him play soccer, and he came to all of my softball games. And then we'd end our week with the ritual of a Saturday night movie at his house. Without fail, we talked on the phone every night until we fell asleep. A few months into our relationship, I had no time for anyone but him. But at the time, I liked it that way. I was perfectly content to be with him every second, because I was, without a doubt, in love.

But sometime during our nine-month walk in the

clouds, the honeymoon stage ended, and our relationship lost its spontaneity and sparkle. Saturday nights spent together became routine, and phone calls and kisses became as natural and expected as breathing.

On one particularly cold June day, Chris broke up with me. He said that he woke up that morning and realized he didn't love me. He said our relationship consisted of nothing but the memories of our past. It was two days before our nine-month anniversary. I felt empty inside, and the thought of being alone was uncomfortable and scary. Moreover, the person on whom I depended to pull me through hard times was the cause of my pain. My heart literally hurt.

Not knowing what else to do, I ran to a familiar place, Ashley's house. It was a place I hadn't visited often in the nine months before this afternoon. I stood at the door, and Ashley, seeing my tears, immediately understood what had happened. Within an hour, my three closest friends, the girls I had once spent so much time with, all arrived at Ashley's house. For the next two days, we camped out at Ashley's and analyzed every aspect of Chris's and my relationship, attempting to pinpoint where it went wrong.

Unable to form any meaningful conclusions, we agreed that we would never understand the male population, and so we moved on to bashing Prince Charming until he was reduced to a creature with the appeal of a toad. It felt good, and I even caught myself laughing for brief moments. Slowly, I began to reclaim my pre-boys, pre-broken-heart days with a little more wisdom and experience than I had before. I realized that life would go on, and I loved and appreciated my girlfriends for that invaluable realization.

Toward the end of our healing party, while we were laughing over ice cream sundaes, Erica looked at me and said, "We've missed you." The truth was, I had really missed them, too. I had unfairly neglected them in the midst of love's wake, and the past two days had shown me just how precious my friends were.

When love had removed its blindfold and all was said and done, I realized that maybe I hadn't had such a fairy-tale boyfriend after all. What I had were fairy-tale friendships. It took a heartbreak to realize the special gift I possessed all along: my girlfriends.

Kathryn Vacca

Kim

Friends are treasures.

Horace Bruns

We both lie sideways on her bed, the screen door slapping open and shut with the California breeze. We thumb through fashion magazines, laughing at the hairstyles and smelling the perfume samples. It seems like any other Sunday between girlfriends; laughter filling the room, a half-eaten carton of cookies between the two of us. This was my Sunday afternoon ritual, the two of us and our magazines, and from the time I was twelve, I lived for these afternoons. She was my friend, but more than that, she was a safe place, an unconditional love, and she was an adult.

I had known Kim most of my life. For the first ten years of my life, Kim wasn't one of the closest adults in my life, but her husband John doted on me and was one of the only "grown-ups" to understand my fearless and abundant energy.

When I was twelve, I moved to Los Angeles to live with

my father. Kim and John also lived nearby, and soon after my move, I began spending time at their home. Kim was fun; she liked to laugh and talk about boys. She listened to me while I talked about my crushes and fights with my family. She spoke to me as an equal, as a friend, not a child.

As I grew older, these visits became more important. I would cry over heartbreaks and whine about the latest rejection. The gap in age between us stayed the same, but the space between us grew closer. I called her with secrets, which she kept, and went to her when I couldn't handle my world for a while.

I think my parents went through periods of jealousy and hurt regarding Kim and our friendship, because they wished they could be the ones to whom I came with my stories. I had reached an age where it was harder to relate to my parents, but I still needed guidance. Kim offered that guidance; she didn't force-feed it.

Soon I was sixteen, and things began to change. I sunk into sadness, and I was slipping away from everyone, including Kim. I was taken to the hospital after swallowing a bottle of pain medication, and there, without question, was Kim. She was two hours away when the call came, and she showed up at the hospital with hair things and, of course, magazines. We didn't talk about the incident, but when she pulled my hair up for me, I saw in her eyes true fear and heartache. She used to say to me, "You wouldn't want to spend so much time with me if I really was your mom." I didn't understand those words until that day when she offered me the feeling of love without obligation. She wasn't my mom; she wasn't obligated to love me, she just did.

After my suicide attempt, things between us, though unspoken, began to change. I stopped spending Sunday afternoons at her house. I called, but not as often. I didn't feel good about myself, so I couldn't feel good about our friendship. I figured I had grown up and that we had just grown apart. Like any normal friendship, it had transformed, and I believed that I no longer needed Kim or the friendship.

The summer before I left for college, I went to say goodbye to Kim. Though we hadn't been as close for the last two years, we both cried when I left. I walked down the walkway from her house, and she called out from the kitchen window, "Call me if you need anything." I knew she meant that.

My first semester was hard. I was far from home, a little lonely, and things began to swing back down for me. With pure instinct, I picked up the phone. It was late. Kim picked up the phone, and I asked, "Were you sleeping?" She replied, "Yes, but it's okay. What's wrong? What do you need?" What I needed was Kim. I needed to hear her voice, and feel that California breeze in her back bedroom. I needed to tell her that our friendship had finally surpassed the age gap.

We talked about once a week after that, every Sunday afternoon. I called with the stress of my finals and with my newest boy problem. When I returned home for the summer, I went to Kim's, and we read magazines and ate cookies. I had become an adult, what she had always been. When I was younger, she had related to me on a level that I needed at that time, and now she relates to me as an equal. She was right; things would have been different if she were my mom. I didn't need another mom. I had one. I needed exactly what she gave: love, unconditional. And because she wanted me in her life, not because she had to have me.

Lia Gay

When Forever Ends

An insincere and evil friend is more to be feared than a wild beast; a wild beast may wound your body, but an evil friend will wound your mind.

Buddha

I look back on it now with only sorrow; the passing of time has worn down the sharp edges of bitterness that plagued me for so long. I switch the bracelet from hand to hand, first yanking at it, then soothingly stroking the well-formed stitches, and admiring the skill and precision of the intricately woven strands. Each tightly pulled knot lends the bracelet a nice shape, but does not destroy its delicate softness. I finger the cheap plastic beads, but I don't think scornfully of the inferior material anymore; I can only cherish the way the beads catch the light, reflecting a deep aquamarine, like the shimmering sea before me. In the imitation crystal surface of each little bead I see myself, I see a precious friendship lost, and I wonder for the thousandth time how it could possibly be that I didn't see it coming.

The sunlight streamed in the French windows of the colonial cottage, an odd location to house ninety middle-schoolers during the daytime hours. I knelt on the rough, maroon carpeting and spun the dial of my combination lock. Clockwise to sixteen, opposite to twenty-four, around and back again to eight. I tossed my American history test into my neat and tidy locker, smiling again in satisfaction at the scarlet "A" scrawled on top. I hastily removed the books that I would need over the weekend and stuffed them into my backpack. As I slammed my locker door shut, I caught a glimpse of the pictures and magazine clippings adorning the inside, and, for a split-second, thought of nothing but the happy times shared with friends and captured for posterity in those photographs. Just then, I noticed a small, white envelope flutter to the ground. Stooping, I picked it up. My name was printed on the front in plain block letters, but the generic envelope and handwriting gave no indication of its author. Consumed with curiosity, I tore it open.

"Dear Molly," it began, "I'm sorry, but we can't be friends anymore."

It went on, but my eyes cut quickly to the bottom, searching for a signature. Katie. Katie wrote it? My best friend wrote me a hate letter? Why in the world . . . ? I took a deep breath and started again from the beginning.

"Look, it's nothing you did, I just don't want to be friends anymore, okay?"

Nothing I did?! Why couldn't we be friends if it's nothing I did?!

The letter continued nebulously, a lot of wishy-washy garbage that skirted around any real issues that should have been addressed (not that I could think of any). Nowhere did she state any reason for writing such a thing to me. We hadn't fought in a long time, not really fought, anyway, just the kind of teasing and bantering that are part of healthy friendship. Out of the blue, my best friend hated me? How could she have put up such a casual veneer if all the while her mind was filled with hatred toward me?

A honk from outside jarred me out of my trance. My ride had arrived. Still contemplating the bizarre and unsettling occurrence, I picked up my bag (which suddenly felt like it was filled with bricks) and, with an even heavier heart, headed outside.

Someone was entering as I was leaving, and I started to brush past until I lifted my eyes from the floor and saw who it was. The crumpled note fell from my dangling palm and tumbled down the gray staircase. The tall, gangly blond started to apologize for running into me, but stopped short when she saw the open confusion and horror that creased my dramatic features. Her mouth opened and closed a few times, but she was lost for words, much like I was at the moment. She knew that I had read it. The anxiety was apparent on her ghostly pale face.

She broke the stare first as her eyes looked to the bottom of the staircase, where her note lay in a wrinkled ball. I heard a cough, and at once realized that we were not alone to do battle. Two piercing orbs behind wire-rim glasses and boy-cut bangs approached when Bev stepped forward, as if to shield Katie from the tongue-lashing she mistakenly thought I was prepared to give.

"Look, Molly, Katie doesn't want to be friends with you anymore, okay? She's my friend now."

If I were good at giving retorts on the spur of the moment, I would have unleashed every bit of antipathy within my petite body towards the controlling witch standing before me. If I had, maybe it would have given my former friend the courage she needed to stand up against her new "leader." However, my mind was unable to process what was happening that quickly, and the hundreds of verbally abusive comments that would flash before me in neon lights five minutes later did me no good. I stood, empty inside, as Bev grabbed Katie's sleeve and pulled her up the stairs. My ex-friend shot me one last helpless look, then straightened her mouth into a grim line and marched up the stairs behind her new friend, leaving her old one lost and powerless at the bottom, left to toy with a simple bracelet of beads and string. I had worn her handiwork from the emergence of our friendship through to its demise at that very moment.

Years later, I fiddle with the very same bracelet as I did on that very afternoon. I ask myself the same questions that tormented me then, and I wonder if fighting back would have saved a friendship that was worth fighting for. Katie was weak; she followed Bev as a sheep follows a herder, without question, without fail. I knew that the two of them had grown dependent on each other over the previous couple of years, widening the swiftly growing chasm between Katie and me, but I never dreamt of such a sudden end to our friendship. It shook me to learn that Bev's jealousy of my relationship with "her" friend would surface so spontaneously and drive her to such cruel and desperate measures. I later learned that she had given Katie an ultimatum: Break off her friendship with me or Bev would stop being friends with her. Bev was clever and conniving; she knew whom Katie would choose. I ask myself for the last time why I didn't see it coming. Then I lift the unwieldy and troublesome burden off my shoulders, and heave it into the ocean in the form of a small, string bracelet. Friendships rise and fall like the tide. I cannot stop the tide; I cannot stop what is beyond my control. We swore to be friends forever, but was it right for us to make that promise?

As the beaded trinket sails through the air, another question for the first time enters my thoughts: *Does she still have the bracelet that I made for her?*

Molly Karlin

Falling Out

Dear Travis,

What's happened to us? I used to feel so close to you, but now it's as if there are miles between us. I have always believed that friends come before everything else—girlfriends and boyfriends—everything. I guess I was wrong. Thanks for the push back to reality. I am sorry that we have had a falling out, but I want you to know that I will still be here when (and if) you need me. I will miss you.

Melissa

No "love you," no "yours sincerely" . . . as I noticed how plain my name looked on the paper all by itself, Travis walked into the hallway where I stood waiting by his locker. I glanced around quickly, looking for a way to escape, but before I could leave without being seen, I heard his all-too-familiar "Hey," as he spotted me.

I put my head down as he approached, hoping that he wouldn't see the pain in my eyes. I handed over the letter, which he took with a small smile. "Thanks, Melissa."

"Can you call me tonight?" I replied, "After you read the letter?" My voice was shaking, and my words were unsure, but if he noticed, he didn't let on. I gave him a quick hug and left the hall, though turning from him was one of the hardest things I've ever done.

An hour later, as I talked with my friend Caitlan on the phone, I explained that I couldn't believe what I had actually given to him. What was he going to think?

"He's your *friend,* Melissa. It's going to be okay," Caitlan reassured me. As I listened to her words, I thought of just how important a friend he was. I had always found it easier to confide in guys, because somehow they seem to judge you a little less, while understanding you a little more. That was definitely what I had with Travis. He could understand me when the rest of the world couldn't. He trusted me, let me grow and listened to what I had to say without judgment—whether it was something he wanted to hear or not.

When I had realized that Travis had a thing for my other best friend Janette, I never thought that his asking her out would affect as many things as it did. Suddenly, it was as if he and I had no chance to talk on the phone or write letters, no freedom to hug or be ourselves. Suddenly Janette, whom I had known since the second grade, didn't trust me enough to be with her new boyfriend. She felt jealous . . . but she didn't realize that I, too, had my own feelings of jealousy. I was jealous of the time she got to spend with Travis, and resentful of the time I could not.

The click of call waiting brought my thoughts back to the present, and I answered the other line knowing that it was Travis.

"Hey, so um . . . yeah, that was the saddest letter I have ever read," he began. "I never knew you felt that way."

"Yeah, well, you weren't exactly around to ask, either," I replied harshly.

"Yeah Missa, I know, I know . . . I am sorry that we haven't had much time together, but all I can say is that it will get better. I mean, it can't get any worse. But we can beat this—you and I will always be friends."

"Trav, everybody says that, but you and I both know that it is not going to happen." My voice trembled, and tears welled up in my eyes, threatening to spill over.

"It's different with us, remember? Nothing can tear us apart. We will be friends forever." I hung up the phone that night feeling a little bit better, yet at the same time, wondering if the promise would last.

Time went on, and nothing seemed to change. We seemed to grow farther and farther apart, and the thought that we would ever be friends again slowly faded. We talked once in a while, usually a polite "hi" in the hallway, but our "friendship," as it was, was making me crazy. The night before winter break, I made the decision to bring closure to the situation. I put everything that reminded me of Travis into a box, and put the box in my closet. There was one thing I could not put away: a stuffed lobster named Allen that I had won on a trip to Las Vegas. It was a trip I had spent with Travis. I knew what I had to do.

I saw him at school the next day, and handed him the stuffed animal.

"What's this?" he asked.

"Allen—you do remember him, don't you?"

"Yeah, but . . . " he started to say.

"It's so he can be with you . . . while I can't." My last few words trickled out, and big tears started rolling down my face as I realized this was the last time I could call him a friend. Travis looked at me, motionless and silent, as if only realizing then that we had grown apart, too far beyond repair.

"Are you sure you want to do this?" he asked me. I nodded my head as more tears streamed down my face. He pulled me into his arms, Allen and all. It was one of those hugs that reassures you that someday everything will be all right. And now, I do not regret what happened between us. It was an experience that will make me stronger and help me grow. I had never paid attention to the saying about how boyfriends and girlfriends will come and go, while your friends will last forever. But now, I see it as the most important advice I had ever been given. One day, I know it will be better. Sometimes I see him with Janette, and before he passes, he always gives me that famous smile. . . .

Melissa Lew

My Best Friend

Mmm. Look at those eyes, crystal-blue with just a touch of green. Those long eyelashes are just reaching for me. I can feel it. Oh, my God! Is he looking over here? No, that's silly. I'm looking at him; therefore, there is no way that he'd be looking at me. I mean, that doesn't happen in my life. Or maybe he actually is! No, no, that's just my imagination playing tricks on me. Well, you never know, crazy things do . . .

"What's up, Katie?"

"Oh, hey," I replied as my best friend, Michelle, abruptly interrupted my ongoing battle of mind versus heart.

"So who have you got your eye on tonight? I see those thoughts circling around in that mind of yours. Maybe tonight you'll actually act upon them!"

"What are you talking about? I don't have any of *those* thoughts in my head, as you like to put it. I'm perfectly content to be by myself right now."

I could feel the obviousness of the lie throughout my entire body as I tried to look Michelle straight in the eyes. I'd never lied to her before, and I'm not exactly sure why I did right then. I couldn't believe that I pulled it off. I mean, that's what best friends are for, to obsess over our crushes with. But something inside me prevented me from telling her about this one. I really liked this guy and, as horrible as this sounds, I didn't want any of my friends to mess it up. Every time I even mention that I think a guy is cute, Michelle goes into full matchmaker mode and won't snap out of it until she feels she has accomplished something. Needless to say, that never happens. She makes my crush into such a big deal that I become completely nervous around the guy, and then he thinks I am a complete idiot. I wasn't about to let that happen this time.

"Well, whatever you say. Let's go talk to Tommy, he's hot!"

What did she say? Tommy?!! How did she know? I didn't even tell her this time. No! Now she's going to become little miss matchmaker again and screw things up. Maybe I'm overreacting. Maybe she just thinks Tommy is cute. No, that's terrible! We can't go after the same guy. Michelle would never be interested in Tommy. He's too short for her. Okay, nothing to worry about.

"Come on, Katie! He's walking away!" Michelle screamed as she forcefully tugged on my cute new suede jacket.

"Okay, okay, I'm comin'."

All right, so now we are approaching him. My right foot just got closer. Now my left, right, left, right. STOP THIS! I'm not in the army! It's okay. I can do this. What is the big deal about talking to a guy anyway? He's just a human like me. Oh, but he's such a beautiful human! Look at that body! I can't do this. I can't do . . .

"Hi, Tommy. How's it goin'?" *Oh, my God, I must have sounded like the biggest nerd!*

"What's up, Katie? Hey, Michelle. You girls are looking good tonight. Having fun?"

His voice is so sexy. And he said I looked good!! But he said girlssss. He can't flirt with both of us. That's not allowed.

"Oh, Tommy, stop it. You're so silly. Ha ha. You're tickling me."

Michelle's giggling was loud enough to interrupt all of the conversations at that party. I couldn't believe how much she was flirting with him. Even worse, he was flirting back! Here is my best friend with the guy of my dreams—even though she doesn't know that—and the guy of my dreams was rejecting me more and more by the second. I couldn't exactly pull Michelle aside and ask her to stop. That would only make things worse. She would either be mad at me for not telling her before or she wouldn't even believe me. The only thing I could do was sit there and be quiet.

The whole drive home from the party I had to listen to Michelle go on and on about how amazing Tommy is. She was completely "in love" with him.

"Did you see the way he was flirting with me? I think he likes me. We were talking for an hour and he didn't seem to be paying attention to anyone else! Aren't you happy for me?"

I had always admired Michelle for the amount of confidence she had when it came to guys. If she wanted one, she went for him. Now she just sounded arrogant, as if any guy would be stupid not to like her. I just clenched my teeth, nodded my head and kept on driving.

After what seemed like the longest car ride in human history, we finally reached Michelle's house. I dropped her off, and the second I heard the door shut I started bawling.

Why was this making me so mad? She is my best friend. I should be happy for her. But I thought this was going to be my turn. I was really going to go for Tommy and make something happen with him. Michelle doesn't like him the way I do. But it's too late to say anything. We always promised each other never to let a guy come between us. I guess this is the tester.

I was awakened the next morning with a phone call, which I thought would be Michelle calling to obsess more about Tommy.

"Hello," I said in that groggy, don't-want-to-answer-it-but-feel-I have-to kind of tone.

"Hi, Katie?" A thick male voice replied through the phone, and I knew in an instant it was Tommy!

Why is he calling me? If this is to ask for Michelle's number, then I'm gonna hang up right now. No, I have to be mature about this. I should be nice. Yeah, right, man, I don't have to be nice to anybody.

"Katie, are you there?"

"Yeah, yeah, I'm here."

"Well, how are you?"

He wants to know how I am! I'll tell him how I am! I'm a depressed teenage girl who thought she had a chance with a guy who she thought had some class. But now she finds out that this guy is in love with her best friend when he has no clue what he'd be missing by going out with her. I've been bawling and tossing all night as if I was trying to quit an addiction, and hearing his voice right now drives me even crazier because it reminds me how much I still like him.

"Oh, I'm fine, just catching up on some sleep." It's amazing how the lie seemed to shoot right out of my mouth.

"I'm sorry if I woke you. I was just calling . . . well . . . I feel kind of weird doing this . . ."

Just get it out already! I'll give you her number!

"Okay, here goes. Do you want to see a movie or something tonight? You probably think I'm really weird since we haven't even spoken that much. But you seemed really cool, and I thought I would take a chance. If you really don't want to it's okay, I'll understand. I just thought . . ."

Oh, my God! Oh, my God! What's happening here? He's asking me *out! What happened to Michelle? This can't be right.*

But it is. It is! It is! It is! I have to say something now. Breathe. Calm. Act like a sane person.

"That sounds great, Tommy. Which movie were you thinking?"

Which movie?! Why did I say that? It doesn't matter which movie we see!

"I don't know. Why don't I pick you up at seven and we'll go and see which ones are playing?"

He sounds so calm. I wonder if I sound that calm.

"Okay, great, I'll see you at seven. Bye."

"Bye."

I am going on a date with TOMMY!!! I can't believe this. This is amazing, it's incredible, it's . . . terrible! What about Michelle? She's going to kill me. I have to call her.

"Michelle, I really need to talk to you." My voice was as shaky as my body, she had to know something was up.

"What's wrong? Are you okay?" She was worried about me. Great, I'm about to hurt my best friend.

"Yeah, I'm fine. I just wanted to tell you that Tommy called me. He wanted . . ."

"He wanted my phone number, huh? I knew it!"

"Well, not exactly. He seemed kind of, well, I don't know . . . he asked me to go see a movie tonight." The words came out slower than imaginable. I thought I was about to be attacked by Michelle's raging hormones any second now. "Before you get mad, I want to explain myself, and you have to believe me."

I was completely honest with Michelle. I explained how I liked Tommy for a long time and apologized profusely for not telling her sooner. I told her about her matchmaker disease and how I had cried the whole night before. I recited my conversation with Tommy word for word and poured out a million more apologies. The weight had been lifted off my shoulders, but I felt I had just passed it on to her. The long period of silence that followed assured me that Michelle was not going to accept my apology that quickly.

After not being able to take the silence any more, I broke in and asked, "Are you all right? What are you thinking? Do you hate me? Do you want me to break my date? What? At least give me an idea of how you feel."

The heavy breathing on the other side of the phone was about to become a whimper when I heard the *click*. She didn't even say a word, just hung up. I called her back fifty times that day only to hear an answering machine that demanded that I never call her again. I have never felt so torn before in my life. The first time that something exciting actually happens to me, it has to break up the only solid relationship that I have in my life. Michelle and I always thought we were above this type of situation. Our friendship was too strong to let a boy break it up. We refused to be like those other cliques of girls that back-stabbed each other all the time.

I called Tommy and explained the whole situation. He felt terrible and agreed that we could cancel our date for the night. He was disappointed but he understood. Every day for the following three weeks, I felt like I was in some never-ending chase. I would track Michelle down whenever I could and try to convince her to talk to me. I would fail each time. She would either snicker some rude comment or just shoot me down or she wouldn't say anything at all. I never realized she had the ability to be so cruel. After the countless number of rejections, I slowly began to give up. I couldn't keep chasing after something that she seemed to have given up on a long time ago. It was too frustrating and disappointing.

Tommy was great throughout the whole ordeal. We continued to see each other and became extremely close. I could safely say he was my best friend. As for Michelle, her hostility toward me slowly began to wear down but we still weren't friends. We had one of those say-hi-to-each-other-in-the-hallway relationships. The pain of losing her friendship never diminished either. I would find myself suddenly crying sometimes when I would think of what happened to our relationship. I wondered if she ever even missed me.

About a week ago, eight months after everything had happened, I built up the courage to ask Michelle if she wanted to go out to lunch with me. To my ultimate surprise, she agreed. We spent most of the lunch having little chit-chat conversations about the things happening in our lives. The whole time I wanted to scream at her about how much I missed her. I wanted to go back to my house, change into our pajamas, and gossip about every little detail about every little thing that could possibly be gossiped about! I wanted to laugh with her and feel comfortable around her. I wanted to curl up and eat five scoops of Häagen-Dazs coffee chip ice cream while we watched our favorite movies that we've both seen 50 million times. Most of all, I wanted the security of knowing that I had my best friend back.

The meaningless chit-chat continued until I reached Michelle's house to drop her off. The last time I had dropped Michelle off I had wanted to strangle her for obsessing over Tommy so much. Now all I wanted to do was hug her so tight so that she could never leave me again. Fortunately, I didn't have to. As I pulled the car over to the curb, Michelle looked at me with her welcoming warm eyes and said the four words that brought my whole eight months of misery to an end, "I've really missed you!"

Tears began to fall down my face but no words would come out. I looked into her eyes, leaned forward and gave my best friend a big hug.

Lisa Rothbard

My Star

My head plopped down right in the middle of my open calculus book.

Maybe the information will just work its way into my brain through osmosis. I was beginning to think that was my only hope for learning this material. I felt like I was on a different planet. *How could this seem so foreign to me?* Of all the classes that I had taken so far in college, I could not make this one work. I couldn't even lay out a logical study plan. *What now?* I pondered, with my head down on my desk in the middle of class.

When I lifted my head off the page, unbeknownst to me, a Post-it Note had stuck to my bangs. There was a pretty picture. I turned to face the guy next to me; he laughed and reached over to pull the note off my bangs in hopes of retrieving some of my dignity.

That was the beginning of a great friendship. The guy who was willing to pull a sticky note off my hair would soon become my calculus savior. I didn't know it at the time, but Matt Starr was the literal "star" of the class. I was convinced he could teach it. And, as luck would have it, he was willing to help me.

He lived in an apartment just off campus, and I would

go over there for tutoring. In exchange for his help, I cleaned his apartment and brought over bribe treats. Cookies, snacks, even dinner sometimes. He was so smart and would get so involved in the material. He would say, "Don't you realize that this is the stuff that the universe is made of?" Not *my* universe. I told him that my universe was made up of child development and psychology classes and an occasional shopping mall, not equations like this. He would just laugh and persevere. He was convinced that he could get me to understand this material, and in a way he was right. He was so crystal clear in his understanding that I began to see it through his eyes.

Matt and I started spending more time together. We would take long walks, go to movies—when he wasn't forcing me to study. I helped him put together a very hip wardrobe, and he taught me how to change the oil in my car—something every girl should know. When I brought home a B in calculus, we celebrated for three days.

Throughout college we stayed as close as a guy and a girl who are friends can be. We dated, only briefly, but the chemistry we shared was more like that of a brother and sister. We did, however, help each other through our other various and odd relationships; and when it looked hopeless, like neither one of us would ever find a mate, we took the next logical step—we got a puppy. Having rescued it from the pound, we called this little shepherd mix Tucker. We had been spending so much time together that when I moved out of my dorm, Tucker, Matt and I became roommates.

The day he came home and told me he was sick, it was raining. It rained that entire week, almost as if the world was mirroring our tears. Matt had AIDS.

Two weeks later, he was in the hospital with pneumocystis. The hows and the whys didn't matter when we were both spending every moment trying to get him better. Between taking final exams, figuring out medications, visiting healers and making Matt drink wheatgrass juice, I was exhausted—but he was getting better.

Matt and I decided that we were going to make the time either one of us had left on this planet count. By the time we arrived at our senior year, I had lived life more fully than I had in all my twenty previous years. When we graduated, we all proudly wore our caps and gowns, Tucker included. Two months later, Matt went home to Minneapolis to live with his family.

Life continued; we e-mailed each other voraciously. I sent him tons of JPEG images of Tucker and his antics, and we went back and forth recounting stories of our lives.

Matt lived only two years more. When I got the news that he had been taken to the hospital, I flew out to be with him. By then, he had fallen into a coma from which he would never awaken. At the funeral, I artfully arranged a yellow Post-it Note in my hair and put one of Tucker's favorite chew toys in the casket.

One night, about a year after Matt's funeral, Tucker and I were driving in the hills of Mulholland. Suddenly, I smelled something so very familiar to me, and yet I couldn't place it. It was a lovely cologne-like fragrance. Then Tucker began acting peculiar.

"What's the matter, boy, did you smell it, too? What is that smell? I just can't place it."

Stopped at a red light, I looked up at the night sky and Tucker barked. What I saw next amazed me. It was a shooting star. A star! Of course, Matt Starr! It was his cologne I smelled.

"Is our friend trying to say hello and tell us he's okay?" Tucker started wagging his tail furiously. Whether it was a sign or not, I felt the warmest and most secure feeling I've felt while thinking about Matt since his death. The giant gaping void that was created when he left was suddenly filled with that warm love the two of us always shared. He wasn't gone, he was right here with me, as he always would be.

Suddenly and quite clearly, I understood how it all fit together. The universe, my friend and his beloved calculus.

Zan Gaudioso

Have a Seat upon a Cloud

Have a seat upon a cloud and make yourself at home
You are now inside my dreams, inside a book, inside a poem.

Where anything can happen if you only make it real
Plunge into my waters if you're not afraid to feel.

Take off your shoes and close your eyes, relax upon my sand
Join me in my land of dreams, reach out and take my hand.

Let me share my dreams with you until you find your own
I'll take you there if you believe, take mine out on loan.

Where birds are words so gracefully they glide across the sky
Leave behind your worries, here the rules do not apply.

Pick my flowers if you like and plant a seed or two
Paint the sky in polka dots if you do not like it blue.

Climb my trees, face your fears; erase them one by one
See the world from up above and don't stop at the sun.

When the world starts raining down and the sun is out of sight
Let your dreams control your mind and help you through the night.

There's a place inside my dreams for all who care to roam
So have a seat upon a cloud and make yourself at home.

Danielle Rosenblatt

Tinfoil and a Hair Ribbon

Not a letter, not a card, and not even a call.
How could Jane have forgotten, when they'd been through it all?
Teardrops and heartache, they'd shared many things,
Crushes on boys, their hopes and their dreams.

Haircuts and makeup and CDs and clothes
Secrets and habits, they even shared those.
So where could she be, didn't she care?
Why didn't Jane come, why wasn't she there?

Through the second grade, third grade, fourth grade, too,
The fifth, sixth and seventh, their friendship grew.
Always and forever, they vowed till the end
To faithfully be there, as the other's best friend.

And they always had been, even when Jane moved away.
But for whatever reason, she wasn't there on that day.
And Allie felt sad as she circled the crowd
As her graduation party grew increasingly loud.

And then she heard it, a loud knock on the door
As she quickly hurried across the bustling floor.
Weaving through family and friends without care
Hoping and praying, when she opened the door, that Jane would be there.

But there on the stoop was a deliveryman instead
In his hand was a package, addressed to Allie, he read.
She reached for the package and brought it inside
And as she tore open the cover, she started to cry.

For the package was wrapped in tinfoil, with a hair ribbon tied with great care
And a million memories came flooding back, as Allie stood tearfully there.
For Jane hadn't forgotten, and as a smile crossed her face
Allie's memories took her back to another place.

Many years prior when she and Jane were so young
When they joined the local Brownie troop all in great fun.
And Allie was so excited about the Christmas party her troop was to have
That she never noticed that Jane didn't seem quite as glad.

On the day of the party, everyone brought an unmarked gift, and numbers were drawn
And with anxious eyes, Allie and Jane both looked on.
At the table piled high with presents galore
Wrapped in beautiful paper and ribbons bought from the store.

But one particular gift seemed out of place and well hidden
For it was wrapped in tinfoil and tied with a worn-out hair ribbon.

"What kind of person would give a gift that's so lame?"
The girl who received it cried out in blame.

Tears stung Jane's eyes as the girl carried on
Complaining quite loudly how much she'd been wronged.
As her accusing eyes searched, looking at each girl all around
Jane shifted nervously and stared at the ground.

For inside the package was Jane's favorite bear
And the ribbon on the package, Jane had worn in her hair.
And because Jane lived with her grandma, and money was tight
She gave away her most treasured thing, because she felt it was right.

And just when Jane felt the presence of tears
She heard her friend Allie saying quite clear.
"I'll trade you," she said, as she offered her gift
Of nail polish and jewelry, all glamour and glitz.

"I've always loved bears, and that one is especially neat"
As she grabbed the bear from the girl and returned to her seat.
And it was then on that night, they each knew for all time
They'd found a true friend, a one-of-a-kind.

For Allie knew what it meant for Jane to give up that bear
And she knew how special the ribbon was that Jane once wore in her hair.
For Jane's mommy and daddy died when she was just five
And the bear and the ribbon helped to keep their memory alive.

For Jane's daddy had lovingly given his daughter that bear
And Jane's mommy had crocheted the ribbon to put in Jane's hair.
And so as the girls walked side by side together alone
Allie handed the bear and the ribbon back to Jane before they got home.

And no words had to be said, as they both started to cry
And then they each headed to their houses, waving good-bye.
Tears streaked down Allie's face, as she stared again at that old bear
And the crocheted ribbon Jane once wore in her hair.

And then with trembling hands, she retrieved from the box a handwritten note
And read over and over the words Jane had wrote.
"I'm sorry I couldn't be there, Allie, but Grandma is ill
Yet I wanted you to know that I think of you still
As my very best friend whom I always will love.

"And so with my bear and my ribbon, I send you a hug.
I should have called sooner, but I didn't want to dampen your day.
And I knew if I told you about Grandma, you would have hurried my way.
And I wanted your party to be all you deserve.
I'm still your best friend, Allie, you have my word."

Always and forever, they vowed till the end
To faithfully be there, as the other's best friend.
And as Allie held the ribbon and hugged that old bear
She knew Jane was the one friend who always would care.

And then Allie decided her best friend should not be alone
As she went to her bedroom and reached for the phone.

Cheryl Costello-Forshey

Saying Good-Bye

Today I said good-bye to my best friend—the one person I have been able to count on for so many years. She has been my companion through low self-esteem, hard tests and bad prom dates. She's someone who could finish my sentences, who never failed to understand me, yet whom I could talk to for hours on end. My friend when friends seemed scarce and life too hard. Who'd laugh with me at jokes no one else understood. Though it took me a while to realize that a best friend is more than a title or an old habit, she was always there.

High school flew by so quickly that I hardly knew what I always had in front of me until it was getting ready to end. Our last year together was spent with late-night outings to 7-Eleven and the playground or to the river. Exploring our small town convinced me that we could discover something for ourselves. The realization that her home had become another home to me, her family an extension of my own. College applications, tears of frustration and anger, AP Exams and SATs, and, hardest of all, sitting there in my cap and gown with my classmates, listening to her speech. My best friend: intelligent, president of the Student Council, funny, beautiful, amazing. She's someone I'm honored to lean over and whisper about to a classmate: "She's my best friend."

A friend who didn't have to ask, "Are we going out Friday night?" but instead, "So, what are we doing Friday?" Attached at the hip through disloyal people, bad dates, long nights spent studying. And now, because we are "old enough," we must head our separate ways—her on one side of the country, me on the other. Tears and discussion, excitement and fear for weeks beforehand. Last movies, dinners—the last everything. All this pain, and always putting the good-bye off until the last moment. Funny how, at the last moment, as I drove to her home this morning and hugged her for the last time for four months, the tears fell only for a few minutes. Because I've realized that it's not good-bye forever, just until again. We'll always have e-mail and phone calls, and Christmas, spring and summer breaks. When you have a once-in-a-lifetime friend, you're always together, no matter how much distance is between you. Real love stretches and bends; it does not see state lines.

Or maybe the reason the tears dried up and the sobs stopped wracking my body as I drove away from her house, seeing her wave until I was out of sight, is because I've realized how amazingly lucky I am to have someone who is so hard to say good-bye to.

Kathryn Litzenberger

I Hope

I hope you surf the waves in from the ocean,
big and small.
I hope you watch the sunset,
from a mountain straight and tall.

I hope you sing a song to all the angels,
loud and clear.
I hope you'll always try new things,
never giving in to fear.

I hope you fall in love,
with one who makes your world go 'round.
I hope that if you fall out,
your feet stay on the ground.

I hope that you can understand,
that true love waits for you.
That you may have to wait awhile,
but when it comes it will be true.

I hope you feel the sand,
hot on your toes on summer's day.
I hope you learn that sandals,
help to keep the pain away.

I hope you find a rainbow,
and realize it was worth the rain.
I hope that through your journey,
you'll learn to balance smiles with pain.

I hope that you will realize,
life isn't always on your side.
I hope you know when hope is lost,
in me you can confide.

I hope that your glowing smile,
brings someone out of gloom.
I hope you taste your life,
with more than just a spoon.

I hope that when you're lost,
you are also one to find.
And I hope that your hand,
never grows too big for mine.

I hope you watch the stars shoot by,
upon a grassy hill.
I hope you know I love you,
always have and always will.

Laura O'Neill

Losing My Best Friend

In a friend you find a second self.

Isabelle Norton

Tears streamed down my face as I hugged Kristen tightly. I whispered good-bye and got into the van to travel back home to Tennessee, which meant I would be leaving my best friend in the whole world hundreds of miles away at her new home in Texas. I didn't know how I would ever be able to deal with this terrible loss. As I left I clutched my favorite pillow close to me, wondering what my life would be like without Kristen in it. Trying to stop the pain I shut my eyes and let all the memories of joy I had shared with her slowly flow into my thoughts. Pictures of smiling faces and the sound of laughter played out in my head.

For six years we had shared every detail of our lives, big or small, with each other. We constantly helped each other deal with all the pain, suffering and joy that comes with the new experiences you face as a teenager. I depended on her for so many things, and she was unceasingly there for me. She always listened closely to my problems with a nonjudgmental ear and helped me solve them. When I desperately needed someone to laugh at my jokes and give me encouragement to follow my dreams, her words always reassured me. When I needed someone to help me understand why I cried because my heart was breaking, she simply cried with me. I shared every secret with her, causing me sometimes to wonder if she knew more about me than I did about myself. Being around Kristen helped me to learn who I was and who I wanted to be.

As I felt another teardrop roll slowly down my face, I was hit with the horrible memory of the night Kristen called me with the bad news.

"What? You have to move? Your dad is being transferred to Texas?" These questions tumbled out of my mouth. I felt myself panicking as my mind began to race, searching for some explanation that would help all of this make sense. Please, please let this be some cruel joke. I wanted to scream, but it was true. Kristen would be leaving in just a few months. I was devastated. This was one problem that we couldn't resolve. There was nothing either of us could do to change what was going to happen.

The memories of Kristen's farewell party flashed before me. Balloons, presents, food and friends filled the room. Kristen was opening her presents. As she opened mine, a photo album filled with pictures, I stood up to read her a poem I had written.

Remember Me Always

So many memories we've made together
As the years have slowly passed.
Tears may have been cried
But our laughter drowned them all out.
Sharing my deepest-most secrets

'Til one in the morning at your house.
Talking forever about things
Until our words just ran out.

But now you must leave,
And I stay behind.
Who will I call
When I just need to talk?
Who will you lean on
When your problems weigh you down?
Who will laugh at my jokes?
Who will make you smile?

I can't tell you the answers
To the questions I have.
But I want you to know
I will always love you as my friend.
And when your heart is troubled,
I want you to think of me.
Remember the times of joy
We have shared
And maybe it will make you smile.
And since you can't take me with you,
Take the memories we have made
And cherish them
As I always will.

I quickly pushed that memory aside, not wanting to relive the emotions written on everyone's faces as I read aloud. More images zipped through my head.

It was the week I traveled with her and her family to Texas. I remember sitting on Kristen's kitchen floor of her bare house waiting for the movers to finish packing some of the last belongings and feeling extremely lost. Once we arrived in Texas we stayed at a hotel for a few days while they moved into their new house. Kristen unpacked her keepsakes, placing everything down with care and asking me if it looked all right. No, of course it didn't. She wasn't supposed to be here and neither were any of her possessions. But I simply told her that it all looked fine. For the rest of the week, we went swimming and to the mall trying to make new memories that we could reminisce about later. We stayed up every night until the early morning hours just talking. Then the day came when I had to go back home. I wasn't going to relive that morning with all the tears and good-byes. I popped open my eyes, snapping myself back into reality.

That dreadful week happened almost two years ago, but the memories of it are as vivid as if it happened yesterday. Kristen and I call each other all the time and write each other every detail about our lives. Sometimes when I talk to her on the phone, I forget she's hundreds of miles away. She's still as large a part of my life as she was before and vice versa. Our friendship is so strong that it can face anything. I am very lucky. I've found my soul sister, and I am able to share my life with her. The distance just doesn't matter.

Amanda Russell

My Friend Andrea

Those who do not know how to weep with their whole heart don't know how to laugh either.

Golda Meir

I felt tears well up in my eyes as I heard my best friend's name called and watched her walk across the stage to receive her high-school diploma. She shook hands with the school-board president, had her tassel turned by the superintendent, and finally received her diploma from our principal. She stopped briefly to face the audience while they took pictures and applauded her. She was an honor student and first in her class. I felt a sense of pride and smiled to myself as flashback after flashback of our childhood paraded through my mind.

I remembered the winter that we decided to become bobsledders. We packed snow on the front steps of my house and let it set up overnight so we could sled down the icy strip on orange saucers at breathtaking speeds to the street that separated our houses. I relived the excitement of singing into our baking spoons about "rocking the town inside out" while sliding across the kitchen floor in our socked feet. One summer we both had Nickelodeon Moon Shoes. We would bounce all over Andrea's front yard and make music videos—without a video camera.

I had to suppress a laugh as I thought of the time that we lit a bonfire in our clubhouse that was located under my front steps. It was a normal summer day, and I was just hanging out in our clubhouse. As I looked around, I decided that we had too much garbage lying around and needed to dispose of it. Andrea came over in a flash and was more than willing to join the fun. We filled an ice-cream pail with water in case something should happen, then out came the matches. We put the garbage in a pile and lit it up. It got a little out of hand and started climbing the wall. Fortunately, we had the bucket of water and put it out before anything of importance caught on fire. Yep, we got in trouble for that little episode. The front entryway of my house smelled like a chimney, and when my parents caught a whiff they herded us in for a lecture.

We took a stab at writing songs and hosting our own talk shows. We dealt with important issues like what kind of shoes we were wearing and what our moms were making for supper on that particular night. We also addressed the fact that Mr. Freeze Popsicles were part of a balanced diet and should be included in one of the major food groups. Our friendship was full of slumber parties and now somewhat embarrassing escapades.

As she sat back down in her seat, one last memory came to mind. This one, however, was not quite a happy one. Even though Andrea is only two weeks older than me, she is a grade ahead. I was born two days after the cut-off to be part of her class. When Andrea started her freshman year in high school, we drifted apart. She made new friends, and we both got involved in our own activities and interests. Even though it bothered me a great deal, I kept it to myself. She didn't seem heartbroken, so I acted like I wasn't either.

For two-and-a-half long years we went about our lives separately. Our friendship dwindled to a nod in the hallway at school or maybe a "hello" on rare occasions. I wanted to talk to her so badly. I would go to the phone to call her, but would hang up before the call went through. I was afraid that she wouldn't want to talk to me. The truth was, she wanted to call me, too, but would hang up for the exact same reason. We found out later that even though the other hadn't known it, we were both hurting and longing for the friendship we used to have.

I don't even know how it happened. I guess we finally realized that we had had too good of a friendship to ignore each other any longer. The months ahead held a lot of catching up. We found out that we were experiencing many of the same things and that we understood each other like no one else. We began what we later called cocoa talks. Even when the weather was warm, we would spend the evening sitting on Andrea' s front steps, drinking hot cocoa with marshmallows and talking about everything that was going on in our lives. We laughed, and we cried. Sometimes we laughed so hard it made us cry. No matter what, we always left feeling better, feeling understood. It's been a bumpy road, but I wouldn't change any of it. In the nine years that she has lived across the street from me, we have formed an unbreakable bond of friendship that we both know is hard to come by. We are always asking each other how we got to be so lucky as to have our best friend living right across the street.

This next year holds uncertainty for both of us. Andrea will be starting college in the fall, and I will be left to survive my senior year alone. But one thing remains certain: Andrea and I have a friendship that will never graduate.

Laura Loken

3

LOVE

Kindness in words creates confidence.
Kindness in thinking creates profoundness.
Kindness in giving creates love.

Lao-tzu

The Secret of Happiness

If you would be loved, love and be lovable.

Benjamin Franklin

There is a wonderful fable about a young orphan girl who had no family and no one to love her. One day, feeling exceptionally sad and lonely, she was walking through a meadow when she noticed a small butterfly caught unmercifully in a thornbush. The more the butterfly struggled to free itself, the deeper the thorns cut into its fragile body. The young orphan girl carefully released the butterfly from its captivity. Instead of flying away, the little butterfly changed into a beautiful fairy. The young girl rubbed her eyes in disbelief.

"For your wonderful kindness," the good fairy said to the girl, "I will grant you any wish you would like."

The little girl thought for a moment and then replied, "I want to be happy!"

The fairy said, "Very well," and leaned toward her and whispered in her ear. Then the good fairy vanished.

As the little girl grew up, there was no one in the land

as happy as she. Everyone asked her the secret of her happiness. She would only smile and answer, "The secret of my happiness is that I listened to a good fairy when I was a little girl."

When she was very old and on her deathbed, the neighbors all rallied around her, afraid that her fabulous secret of happiness would die with her. "Tell us, please," they begged. "Tell us what the good fairy said."

The lovely old woman simply smiled and said, "She told me that everyone, no matter how secure they seemed, no matter how old or young, how rich or poor, had need of me."

The Speaker's Sourcebook

Smile

She smiled at a sorrowful stranger.
The smile seemed to make him feel better.
He remembered past kindnesses of a friend
and wrote him a thank-you letter.
The friend was so pleased with the thank-you
that he left a large tip after lunch.
The waitress, surprised by the size of the tip,
bet the whole thing on a hunch.
The next day she picked up her winnings,
and gave part to a man on the street.
The man on the street was grateful;
for two days he'd had nothing to eat.
After he finished his dinner,
he left for his small dingy room.
(He didn't know at that moment
that he might be facing his doom.)
On the way he picked up a shivering puppy
and took him home to get warm.
The puppy was very grateful
to be in out of the storm.
That night the house caught on fire.

The puppy barked the alarm.
He barked 'til he woke the whole household
and saved everybody from harm.
One of the boys that he rescued
grew up to be President.
All this because of a simple smile
that hadn't cost a cent.

Barbara Hauck

Mrs. Link

I was eighteen, about to start college and broke. To make some money, I plodded down a quiet street of older homes, selling books door-to-door. As I approached one gate, a tall, handsome woman in her eighties came to the gate in her bath robe. "There you are darling! I've been waiting for you! God told me you'd be coming today." Mrs. Link needed help around her yard and house, and, apparently, I was the one for the job. Who was I to argue with God?

The next day I worked for six hours, harder than I had ever worked before. Mrs. Link showed me how to plant bulbs, what flowers and weeds to pull up, and where to haul the wilted plants. I finished off the day by mowing the lawn with a mower that looked like an antique. When I had finished, Mrs. Link complimented me on my work and looked under the mower at the blade. "Looks like you hit a stone. I'll get the file." I soon learned why everything Mrs. Link owned looked like an antique, but worked like brand-new. For six hours of work she gave me a check for three dollars. It was 1978. God's funny sometimes, isn't he?

The next week I cleaned Mrs. Link's house. She showed

me exactly how to vacuum her antique Persian rug with her antique-looking vacuum. As I dusted her beautiful treasures, she told me where she had acquired them while she traveled the world. For lunch she sautéed fresh vegetables from her garden. We shared a delicious meal and a lovely day.

Some weeks I got to be a chauffeur. The last gift to Mrs. Link from Mr. Link was a glorious new car. By the time I met Mrs. Link, the car was thirty years old, but still glorious. Mrs. Link was never able to have children, but her sister, nieces and nephews lived nearby. Her neighbors also were fond of her, and she was active in civic affairs.

A year and a half passed since I met Mrs. Link. School, work and church were taking up more of my time, and I saw Mrs. Link less and less. I found another girl to help her around the house.

Valentine's Day was coming, and being very undemonstrative and very broke, I was compiling a very short list of my valentines. Mom glanced at my list and said, "You need to get Mrs. Link a valentine."

I incredulously asked, "Why? Mrs. Link has a lot of family, friends and neighbors. She's active in the community. I don't even spend a lot of time with her anymore. Why would Mrs. Link want a valentine from me?"

Mom was unimpressed. "Get Mrs. Link a valentine," she insisted.

On Valentine's Day I self-consciously presented Mrs. Link a small bouquet, which she graciously accepted.

A couple of months later, I visited Mrs. Link again. Centered on her mantle, in her living room full of beautiful things, stood my wilted and faded Valentine's Day bouquet—the only valentine Mrs. Link received that year.

Susan Daniels Adams

A Gift for Two

You never know what happiness a simple act of kindness will bring about.

Bree Abel

It was a beautiful day for sightseeing around downtown Portland. We were a bunch of counselors on our day off, away from the campers, just out for some fun. The weather was perfect for a picnic, so when lunch time came, we set our sights on a small park in town. Since we all had different cravings, we decided to split up, get what each of us wanted, and meet back on the grass in a few minutes.

When my friend Robby headed for a hot dog stand, I decided to keep her company. We watched the vendor put together the perfect hot dog, just the way Robby wanted it. But when she took out her money to pay him, the man surprised us.

"It looks a little on the cool side," he said, "so never mind paying me. This will be my freebie of the day."

We said our thanks, joined our friends in the park, and dug into our food. But as we talked and ate, I was distracted by a man sitting alone nearby, looking at us. I could tell that he hadn't showered for days. Another homeless person, I thought, like all the others you see in cities. I didn't pay much more attention than that.

We finished eating and decided to head off for more sightseeing. But when Robby and I went to the garbage can to throw away my lunch bag, I heard a strong voice ask, "There isn't any food in that bag, is there?"

It was the man who had been watching us. I didn't know what to say. "No, I ate it already."

"Oh," was his only answer, with no shame in his voice at all. He was obviously hungry, couldn't bear to see anything thrown away, and was used to asking this question.

I felt bad for the man, but I didn't know what I could do. That's when Robby said, "I'll be right back. Please wait for me a minute," and ran off. I watched curiously as she went across to the hot dog stand. Then I realized what she was doing. She bought a hot dog, crossed back to the trash can, and gave the hungry man the food.

When she came back to us, Robby said simply, "I was just passing on the kindness that someone gave to me."

That day I learned how generosity can go farther than the person you give to. By giving, you teach others how to give also.

Andrea Hensley

Kids Who Are Different

Here's to kids who are different,
Kids who don't always get As,
Kids who have ears
Twice the size of their peers,
And noses that go on for days.

Here's to the kids who are different,
Kids they call crazy or dumb,
Kids who don't fit,
With the guts and the grit,
Who dance to a different drum.

Here's to the kids who are different,
Kids with a mischievous streak.
For when they have grown,
As history has shown,
It's their difference that makes them unique.

Digby Wolfe
Submitted by Vania Macias

McDonald's

Most of my friends are what society would call "punks." We are the teenagers who hang out at the coffee shops or the movies for lack of anything better to do. But being punks doesn't mean much.

One evening, after a day of not doing much, we were sitting in McDonald's when a guy in our group whom I had just met that day walked in. Brian was the typical punk teenager, dressed in black with the dyed hair. Right before he stepped inside, he yelled something outside to a man walking down the street. I just hoped he wasn't trying to start trouble. He sat down and a minute later, a burly homeless man stuck his head in and looked at Brian.

"Did you say something to me?" the man demanded, and I thought I saw a mean glint in his eyes. I shrank back, thinking that if Brian had tried to pick a fight, this was the wrong guy to do it with. I had seen too many people and places kick teenagers like us out for pulling stuff.

While the rest of us were looking for a place to back into, Brian got up and walked up to him. "Yeah . . . would you like something to eat?"

The relief was almost audible, and the man smiled and walked in.

After a large meal of hamburgers, fries and dessert, the man left, and even the staff waved good-bye to him. When we asked Brian about it, he explained how he had money that he didn't need and the man had none, so it was only right.

Shelly Miller

A Valentine for Laura

Ann, a friend of mine, disliked Valentine's Day as a girl. She was plain—not ugly, but not beautiful. Valentine's Day is not kind to plain girls. It wasn't so bad in elementary school, when the obligatory thirty valentines arrived: one from each classmate. She overlooked the fact that her cards were not oversized like those of the popular girls, and did not contain the love notes like those of the pretty girls. But later, in middle school, the valentine exchange was no longer mandatory. Just when the yearning for romance budded, when the desire for admiration and flirtation became imperative, and a valentine was needed most, no card arrived. Not for Ann. Not for plain girls anywhere. Only for the pretty and the popular. At such a time, stories of ugly ducklings that will one day turn into beautiful swans do not assuage the hurt and rejection.

As fate would have it (and often does), in subsequent years Ann did become pretty and turned many a boy's head. As she received more attention and flirtations, she came to feel—and therefore to be—very beautiful. But even years later, grown and with a family of her own, she did not forget those long-ago days of rejection and dejection.

Today, Ann's family includes two boys in middle school. For a dollar, their Student Council will deliver a Valentine's Day carnation. Ann gives a dollar to each of her boys to buy flowers for their girlfriends. Then she adds another dollar apiece with this instruction: "Pick another girl, one who is nice, but plain—someone who probably won't get a flower. Send her a flower anonymously. That way she will know that someone cares, and she will feel special."

Ann has done this for several years, spreading Valentine's Day a little beyond her own world.

One year, Laura, who was plain to behold but beautiful to know, received one of these gifts. Ann's son reported that Laura was so happy and surprised, she cried. All day long, she carried the flower on her books and chattered with the other girls about who her admirer could be. As Ann heard the account, she too had to dry her eyes—for she remembered.

Don Caskey

My Friend Charley

As an insecure and scared freshman in college, my first year was filled with many new and strange experiences. I quickly learned the difficult lesson that things aren't always what they seem and love can be found in the most unexpected places.

My first introduction to the "real world" began at Camp Virginia Jaycee, a camp for people who are mentally retarded or handicapped. Twice a year, my college offered a volunteer opportunity to students who wished to donate a weekend of their time. At the last minute and after much deliberation, I made a decision that would soon change my life. I volunteered for camp.

I had no idea what to expect, and it was the complete and utter unknown that scared me the most. As the campers slowly arrived, the noises and sounds of the unfamiliar filled the air. I looked around the room at faces that expressed no clue just how different they really were.

Each student volunteer was assigned one camper for the weekend. As a counselor, I was expected to help "my" camper eat, bathe and walk. I was expected to be his friend.

My camper's name was Charley. He was forty years old, with a severe case of autism and no visible means of communication. I was scared. My hands shook with fear as I tried to introduce myself. His attention roamed everywhere except to me. He seemed completely uninterested in anything I had to say. We stood outside waiting to get into our cabin, when suddenly he went to the bathroom, right in front of everyone. I discovered that he was just as scared as I was; we just had very different ways of showing it.

Charley couldn't speak, but he could eat and walk. That night I showed him how to take a shower. As I stood in front of the shower and told him what to do, he did everything I said. I guess he did understand me, in some strange new way. By the next night when it was time for Charley to take his shower, he laughed and smiled like a young schoolboy. I proudly tucked him in that night, but as I started to walk away from his cot, he grabbed my arm. He placed my hand on his head wanting only comfort. It was so overwhelming that this complete stranger could need me to love him. For that instant, Charley made the world seem so simple.

As the weekend came to a close and the time to leave approached, Charley reached out to hold my hand. We were two scared human beings experiencing something so new that it was frightening. I forgot about facades and fake smiles, and instead felt a genuine love for another human being from the depths of my soul.

Robin Hyatt

Losing an Enemy

If your enemy is hungry, feed him; if he is thirsty, give him something to drink.

Romans 12:20

Last year, my brothers were enrolled in Pioneer Clubs, a weekly kids program at our church. Daniel was nine, and Timothy was seven. My sister, my dad and I were all teachers at the same church program. At one point during the year, my brothers began to complain that a boy named John was picking on them.

John, an eleven-year-old foster boy, was in my dad's class. He was the type of kid who always seemed to be in trouble. Worse, he didn't consider that it was his behavior that was the problem, but instead decided my dad was picking on him. He often took it out on my brothers by knocking off their hats, calling them names, kicking them and running away. Even I received the occasional rude remark from John. We all thought he was a real pain.

When my mom heard about the problem, she came home from town a few days later with a bag of wrapped butterscotch candies.

"These are for John," she told Daniel and Timothy.

"For *who?*"

"For John." Mom went on to explain how an enemy could be conquered by kindness.

It was hard for any of us to imagine being kind to John; he was so annoying. But the next week the boys went to Pioneer Clubs with butterscotch candies in their pockets—one for themselves and one for John.

As I was heading to my class, I overheard Timothy saying, "Here John, this is for you." When we got home, I asked Timothy what John's response had been.

Timothy shrugged. "He just looked surprised, then he said thank you and ate it."

The next week when John came running over, Tim held on to his hat and braced himself for an attack. But John didn't touch him. He only asked, "Hey, Tim, do you have any more candy?"

"Yep." A relieved Timothy reached into his pocket and handed John a candy. After that, John found him every week and asked for a candy, and most times Timothy remembered to bring them—one for himself, and one for John.

Meanwhile, I "conquered my enemy" in another way. One time as I passed John in the hall, I saw a sneer come over his face. He started to open his mouth, but I said, "Hi, John!" and gave him a big smile before he had a chance to speak.

Surprised, he shut his mouth, and I walked on. From then on, whenever I saw him I would greet him with a smile and say, "Hi, John!" before he had a chance to say anything rude. Instead, he started to simply return the greeting.

It's been a while since John picked on my brothers, and he's not rude to me anymore, either. Even my dad is impressed with the change in him. He's a nicer John now than he was a year ago—I guess because someone finally gave him a chance.

He wasn't the only one to change. My whole family learned what it meant to love an enemy. What's strange is that in the process, we lost that enemy—he was "conquered" by love.

Love: It never fails.

Patty Anne Sluys

Forgive

Forgive the sun who didn't shine
The sky had asked her in to dine

Forgive the stars that heard your wish
The moon prepared their favorite dish

Forgive the rain for its attack
The clouds have tears they can't hold back

Don't hate the birds 'cause they are free
Don't envy all the things they see

Don't block the wind, but hear its cry
Or else that wind may pass you by

Forgive the storm it means no harm
Could not resist to show its charm

Forgive the earth that never turns
Don't hate the sun, because too much burns

Life intends to not cause pain
The flowers bloom from all the rain

The storm will come and it will pass
The sun that shines, it grows the grass

The wind it cannot help but cry
The stars at night light up the sky

Forgive the world in which we live
We'll all find peace if we forgive

Danielle Rosenblatt

Someday When I'm Older

I am only seven and a lot of things are confusing to me. Grown-ups tell me that someday I'll understand, but I wish that "someday" were now. Life is really complicated. I always have to say "please," be nice, clean up—and sometimes I just don't want to. Then there is something grown-ups call death. I know it's not a good thing, but I don't know quite what it is. I think I am supposed to understand, but no one wants to help me; maybe someday when I'm older.

* * * *

I don't usually wait with Grace for her bus before school in the morning, but today we are sitting on the steps together. Christmas is just two weeks away, and there is fresh snow outside from last night. I can't wait until recess so I can go out and play in it. The bus has just stopped outside our house. Grace is eleven and she doesn't like to hug me too often, but this morning, she hugs me good-bye. I don't know why.

In art class today, I drew a picture for Grace's teacher: baby Jesus in the manger with an angel above him. But now school is over, and I don't know where my picture is. I never gave it to her. One of the teachers tells me that she has to drive me home. She says that Grace was in an accident. I wonder if she'll have to wear a cast in the Christmas pictures.

Now I'm walking into my house. Mommy's crying. She never cries, even when I'm really, really bad. Two policemen are in our living room. No one is telling me why they are there. All the grown-ups are talking, but I can't understand what they are saying; maybe someday I will. Daddy is the only one who says anything to me.

"You have to go to Mrs. Riffs's house for awhile." I like Mrs. Riffs, but I really want to stay with Mommy and Daddy. No one is listening to me, so I will just keep that inside. Mommy is really sad. I think Grace has more than a broken arm. All I can do is pat Mommy on the shoulder and whisper like she does when I'm sad.

"Grace is going to be okay," I say. I'm not quite sure though. No one will tell me how bad things are, and seeing Mommy crying scares me most of all. But Grace *has* to be okay. I already made her Christmas present, and we are supposed to make snow angels together on the front lawn.

Mommy and Daddy are always telling people that I have a short "tensions pan." I think that means I don't like to watch movies that are too long. Tonight seems to be taking a lot longer than the longest movie I have ever seen. It is past my bedtime, and I just want to go home. I think I hear a car in the driveway. Mommy and Daddy are coming inside now. Daddy wants to talk to me, but I don't want to hear what he is going to say.

"Grace has gone up to heaven."

I'm crying now. I don't really want to, but Mommy is, and I think it's the right thing to do. I am so confused. Mommy and Daddy told me that heaven is where we go when we die, but Grace can't be dead. I want to ask questions, but I know I'm supposed to just be sad now. This is really complicated. I want someone to explain, but as usual, I'm too young to understand anyway. I feel bad for not feeling like crying, so I am trying my best.

It is past Christmas now, but I still have a lot of questions. I try to keep them inside because I don't want Mommy to cry again. Sometimes they tell me more about "the accident": Grace was waiting for the bus after school with some other kids. A car was driving too fast on the icy road, went out of control and hit her. They tell me she didn't feel any pain. That's good, because I don't want Grace to be hurting.

I am trying very hard to understand death. I read the books that people give me about Joe and what happened when his dog died. I still feel too young to get it. I feel sad and angry and frustrated. I love Grace, and I miss playing with her. Mommy is crying less now. I think it's okay to ask her a question.

"Mommy, why did it have to be Grace that was hit? Why couldn't it have been someone else who was standing there?" Mommy has started crying again and I wish I didn't ask her the question, but now she is smiling and hugging me. She says, "Because then another family would have to go through all the pain and sadness that we feel." I am not sure why she said that, but it's not the time for any more questions.

Now it is a few weeks later. Mommy and Daddy tell me that the man who hit Grace found out that he killed her, so he killed himself. I think I am old enough to understand what this means.

"That's good, right, Mom? Now he has paid for what he did." Mommy speaks very quietly when she answers. She tells me, "No, it's not good. Now his family has to go through everything that we felt. They shouldn't have to do that."

* * * *

I am sixteen now and I know a lot more than I did then. I know that seven years is a short time to learn about forgiveness. Back then, I didn't quite understand why Mom didn't want the man to be punished, but I trusted that she was right. Now Mom's words echo in my heart as clearly as they did when I first heard them nine years ago. Since that time, there have been so many instances when I have found it difficult, almost impossible to forgive someone. Then I hear Mom again. I realize that if Mom could forgive the man who killed her daughter, surely I can forgive my best friend for forgetting our Saturday afternoon plans.

It took me a long time to understand exactly what that horrific day and my sister's death meant. I have gradually accepted that I will not see Grace for a long time, but I know I will see her again in heaven. I also know that Grace is happy and that she is still with me. With time, my wounds have healed. I have learned that it's okay to be sad, and it's also okay not to be sad. As I have learned more about life, I have also come to understand death better. More important than all this, though, I will never forget Mom's lesson of the ultimate forgiveness.

Andrea Gonsalves

Dear Child—A Sister's Message

Today I look into your tender young face, you're all of eleven years old, and I shudder at that thought. Perhaps I am trying to relive my adolescence through you and I recall how tough that age was for me. It was about the time Mom and Dad divorced, the year I had my first real crush and the beginning of junior high—three hard-hitting blows to a confused, awkward kid. That is possibly why I want to write a letter that could somehow condense all my experiences and all my sufferings in one neat page, for you to look at and say, "my mistakes—never!" You see, my experiences weren't unusual or extraordinary, but at the time they took place I felt as if the world would sooner swallow me whole, than allow me to overcome it with some sense of self intact.

So, somehow, I want to call upon that girl I once was and ask her to help me find the words that will give you the armor, that will make all the cruel insults you will surely encounter simply roll off your back. I want to find the potion that will make you see how extraordinary you are so that when that first heartbreak comes along, although you may doubt the love of others, you will never once doubt the love you hold for yourself. I want to make you aware of the beauty that is woman, so that you will always be proud and bold, never flinching in the eye of a man, or most likely a boy, who will try with all his might to convince you that you have a lesser place in the world. I want to show you how to adore this temple in which you house your mind and soul, always respect it and treat it as the jewel that is you. Remember, dear child, that whomever you allow near this temple, this possession that is solely yours, is completely your choice. No amount of convincing or begging could ever change that. Your heart—the treasure box that holds dreams and secret wishes—don't allow it to become a house for fear. Fear will consume you; it will beckon you to keep from shining, to step down for the light on the horizon. Don't hesitate, not even for a moment, because in that moment you may be draining the life of your spirit. Instead, walk with firm, steady steps into the glare of failure and humiliation, two of your greatest foes—believe me, they are no match.

Friends will test your best judgment. You will ask yourself if you chose wisely, or perhaps you will not choose carefully enough and in desperation of walking alone, you will allow yourself to be surrounded by meaningless acquaintances, who have little interest in your true self. These friendships could at times prove to be soul-killing and exhausting, and, although this may seem out of touch right now, I want you to know that at times there is more dignity in marching alone. Loneliness is what you will feel if you build your friendships on longings of being mirrored by visions of your self.

There will always be those that are different from you, in aspects ranging from ethnic background to physical challenges. I wonder, "will she be gracious and kind, an angel cloaked in a child's disguise, or will she be cruel and sharp with a tongue solely shaped to stab at the heart?" Who will you be, sister? Will those around you regard you as boring and snotty for not wanting to partake in the spirit-bashing of those unaccepted souls? Or will you be leader of such tragic slander? Although you may be cast out for any goodness you exhibit, will you have the commanding strength to remain true to what you've been taught? True to yourself?

Dear child, I know this is huge and unsettling, and perhaps too much to digest at this place and time, but will you tuck this away in a safe, unrelenting place so that its presence will always peer into your conscience? Perhaps you will have a question someday and you will remember these words, my words, which today seem unfitting, uncompromising. I don't think I've covered every possible adolescent terror that you will be struck with, but I can't possibly anticipate all the life that will come your way. What I can say is that you will survive, but not without scars in the most unimaginable place—your heart. Wear them like a badge of courage once you have survived this battle referred to as "growing up." You will be all the wiser, dear child—I know I am.

Danette Julene Gomez

Finger Paints and Crayons

With chalk in hand she wrote her name across a board once bare
And then she sat behind her desk without a single care
And for fifteen minutes, she did not make a sound
Until the final student, had finally settled down
Then she stood before them, and told them all her name
And then politely asked, each student to do the same
Then without hesitation, she took papers from a sack
And placed them in two piles, one white, the other black
And deliberately quite slowly, with a slight, mischievous smile
She began handing out the papers, up and down each aisle
And once each student had a piece; she continued within their sights
To gather two piles of crayons, one black, the other white
And then she took a painting, from behind her walnut desk
Then placed a painter's smock, overtop her navy dress

And to no one in particular, she spoke in peaceful tones
"I've been working on this painting, for years in my own home."
She stood staring at the painting, its brilliant colors mixed as one
Upon a vast horizon, the presence of a sun
It indeed was not a Rembrandt, a Picasso, or Michelangelo to say the least
But it nonetheless was beautiful; its presence spoke of peace
And no doubt that lovely painting, had taken so much time
For every color known to man, seemed to intertwine
And so it came with wonder, what they witnessed with surprise
The act that took them all off guard, done right before their eyes
With finger paints now gathered, and opened on her desk
She smeared the colors upon her hands, in an entangled awful mess
And then as though she'd lost her mind, she smeared her hands across
The painting once so beautiful . . . now a total loss
It did not make a bit of sense, they did not understand
As they sat and watched their teacher, wipe the paints from off her hands
And then she took the crayons, and went up and down the rows
And handed to each student, the colors that she chose
"Now," she told her students, "I want you to create
A picture filled with beauty, devoid of any hate."
Mouths dropped open widely; mumbles filled the room
And students looked to one another, as unasked questions seemed to loom

For the students with white paper, were given crayons
the same shade
And the students with black crayons, had been given a
raven-colored page
And how could one create splendor, with no colors to
mix and match
The students were quite certain, their teacher had left
out most the facts
"Teacher," a student's voice was heard, "I'm not so sure
I can"
Staring at the white crayon, and white paper in her hand
Silence overtook the room; it eerily crept about
Causing the teacher's gentle voice, to erupt into a shout
"You each share the same problem, you each possess
the power to resolve
But only the students with open minds, will have the
ability to solve."
Minutes ticked away, class was nearing to an end
And not one single student, knew quite how to begin
And when the bell rang out, and they hurried to their feet
Their teacher told them commandingly, to return back
to their seat
"Before you leave this classroom, I think you each
should know
For this assignment you receive a failing grade, for you
have no work to show
And tomorrow and the next day, your assignment shall
be the same
And those who fail my class, will have only themselves
to blame."
The next day and the following, students weren't quite
sure what to do
Until at last, a solution, began to surface through
When one student with his crayon, and paper both in
black

Turned to the student behind him and asked, "May I borrow that?"
The student hesitated, but then gave up his crayon made of white
And ultimately the assignment, no longer seemed a plight
For students all throughout the class, switched crayons up and down the aisles
And certain that they'd found the solution, their faces lit with smiles
And just as every student began to draw, across an empty page
The teacher whom they'd all began, to see as certainly quite strange
Collected all the pages and crayons, without a single mark
And then spoke aloud, "Thank you, for bringing hope into my heart
You see, I wanted you to realize, that in order to create
A picture filled with beauty, devoid of any hate
You needed first to recognize, that a problem did exist
And that a practical solution, could be found within your midst
And that racism is a problem, each of us must face
Working all as one, before it's much too late
And with open eyes and open hearts, we must see the person, not the color of their skin
And come to the understanding, that racism has to end
For together we are family, we cry tears, we all feel pain
And though we may not look the part, that's exactly what we do
For crayons are just colors, that's all our skin is, too."

Students looked about the room, a variety of colors on their skin
As the point she was trying to make, began to settle in
The looks upon their faces, readily explained
That they each were trying to contemplate: that indeed they were the same
A nervous shuffling of papers, and coughs throughout the room
Portraying the vital image, that fighting over crayons was a stupid thing to do
It was then each student realized, the purpose of crayons and papers the same shade
Was to prove they each needed the other color, to help fill their empty page

Silence seized the moment, as one student raised his open hand
And then spoke in hesitation, "I just don't understand . . .
Why you took your painting, the one you seemed to enjoy so very much
Gathered up your finger paints, to destroy it in a touch."

Sadness filled her face, as a tear trailed upon her cheek
And in slow and heartfelt words, she began to speak
"To show you each that colors can be beautiful, but they also can destroy
Everything we love and work for, everything we each enjoy
And the destruction of something that I loved, was to make a point to you
That racism destroys the beauty in us all,
And that fighting over colors, is a destructive thing to do."

Cheryl Costello-Forshey

4

ACTS OF KINDNESS

You give but little when you give your possessions. It is when you give of yourself that you truly give.

Lao-tzu

The Stranger Within

After the verb "to love," "to help" is the most beautiful verb in the world.

Bertha von Suttner

It was one of those sweltering, hot days in the middle of July when all you can do is dream of the cold winter days that you hated only months earlier. One of those sultry days when you either yearn for a swim in a pool or crave a cool drink. In my case, all my friends who had pools I could invite myself into were away on vacation, and the public pools were out of the question unless I could learn to enjoy suffocating myself in chlorine with hundreds of other delirious people. Instead, I decided to go to the neighborhood café where they sold my favorite dessert, frozen yogurt. Since my parents hadn't given me a car for my sixteenth birthday, the only option I had was to walk.

Dragging a friend along, we headed for the ice-cream shop, almost passing out from the burning heat of the angry sun on the way. As we trudged along, my friend continuously grumbled about the heat and why she had so foolishly decided to come with me on this hair-brained quest for frozen yogurt. I just shrugged, perspiration dotting my forehead, mumbling.

"We're almost there. Just think of cool air conditioning and the sweet taste of frozen yogurt on your tongue. It'll be worth the walk," I assured her.

I had to admit to myself that the café was quite a distance from our house. I was beginning to get extremely thirsty, and my head was reeling from the smoggy air.

When we were about a block away from the café, I noticed her for the first time. She was old, somewhere in her mid-seventies I guessed. She had this awful arch in her burly shoulders as if she couldn't hold the heavy weight of her large chest. Her curly hair was frizzy from the heat and dyed a horrible greenish-yellow, which was clashing dreadfully with her neon pink shirt. She was struggling, pushing a squeaking grocery cart full of what appeared to be beauty-salon items.

Besides all her extraordinarily gaudy clothing, her most dominant feature was the deep frown she wore. At first, I thought it was from the harrowing heat, but with each step toward us her scowl increased, creating a more disturbing picture of a very unhappy soul. It seemed as though she hated the very air she breathed, reminding me of the cantankerous lady who used to live on our street, the one my friends and I called The Witch.

I glanced at my friend to see if she had noticed her. I could tell she had, for she was wearing the usual disgusted face she wore when she disliked something and somehow felt superior to it. My friend was the type of person who was very conscious of what others might think of her. She wanted to remain flawless to the world so, when she was presented with someone who was different in any way, she became arrogant and condescending.

As we drew closer to the lady pushing the grocery cart,

my friend directed us as far away as she could, until we were nearly walking on the road. I began to observe the many others that were passing by. They, too, were avoiding her at all cost as if she were a leper or a criminal of some kind.

The lady stared blankly ahead, her wobbling knees hitting the sides of the cart. Somehow, I felt ashamed at my reaction, but that didn't stop me from hurrying by. Just as we made it past her, I heard this horrible sound from behind me and quickly turned around to see what it was.

The lady's cart had been knocked over and her soap, perfume and shampoos were scattered across the pavement. Shocked, I looked at the lady's hunched back trembling as she slowly bent with great care to begin collecting her items.

I gulped. Many things were running through my head. I looked at my friend inquiringly. "What should we do?" I asked quietly.

"What should we do? We shouldn't do anything!" my friend said, rolling her eyes heavenward.

"Yeah, I know, but it looks like she needs help," I responded softly as the lady began feebly assembling a couple of perfume bottles into her lap.

"Well, I'm sure she's okay. Someone else will help her. Besides, we didn't knock her cart over . . . ," my friend said with cold logic and then started to walk ahead. I stood there for a minute thinking. Something was tugging at the strings of my heart and, all of a sudden, I felt great compassion for this pitiful lady. At that very moment, I knew what I had to do.

"Are you coming?" my friend called over her shoulder impatiently.

"No, I'm going to help her," I said with determination as I began to head back toward the lady.

"What? Amy . . ." my friend groaned through clenched

teeth, giving me that look that said, *Don't test me, and don't expect me to follow you.*

I didn't pay attention to my friend as I cautiously knelt down beside the lady who was now furiously attempting to set her cart upright once more. I could feel the inquiring, skeptical eyes of the passersby. I knew they were thinking I was crazy for helping her or, worse, that I had clumsily knocked over her cart and therefore was assisting her out of duty.

"Here, let me help you," I said gently, as I began to position the cart upright.

The lady slowly glanced up, her large eyes filled with such fear, sadness and pain that I was frightened by her stare. I gulped and then, hesitantly, began putting the items back into her cart.

"Go away," she grumbled, throwing a tube of cream into her cart. "I don't need your help."

Shocked, I backed away from her seething stare and looked up at my friend who was haughtily standing by, glaring with her arms folded smugly against her chest. I sighed.

"No, I want to help you," I continued, putting three more shampoo bottles into the cart. The lady peered at me as though I was crazy. Maybe I was, but I knew that I was supposed to help her. She didn't stop me this time so I helped her put away the rest of her items. I was stunned by how many people walked by and hopped over certain disarrayed items in their paths, not even offering a sympathetic word or glance. What astounded me even more was when a cute guy whom I had liked for as long as I could remember was one of the uncaring, selfish people who strolled by. I was embarrassed by his reaction when he first saw me in a humiliating situation and then disgusted by his self-centered attitude.

When the last item was put back into the cart, I slowly

rose to my feet, flinching as the lady awkwardly stood as well. I supposed she would walk by without looking at me, but then I realized I was guilty of misjudging her character.

I waited as she straightened her bent head, sniffled and slowly peered up at me. Her large dejected eyes were filled with a wonder I couldn't express in words. As an innocent tear dribbled down her ashen cheek, I was sure I could see a hint of a smile.

"Thank you," she whispered in a hushed tone. My throat tightened and tears threatened to fall down my cheeks.

"You're welcome," I murmured, offering a smile.

And you know what? She smiled then and a beautiful peacefulness washed over her once-stern countenance. I grinned widely as she cordially nodded her head and continued down the street, slowly creeping out of my life as quickly as she had appeared. Yet I knew that her smile and gratefulness would always be imprinted upon my life and heart.

When I finally had my frozen yogurt and my friend was still complaining about the embarrassment I had caused her, I felt gratitude well up within me. At that very moment, I didn't care anymore what other people thought. I was going to do the right thing, even if it meant losing or embarrassing my friends. I smiled to myself because even though I had helped that lady in such a small way, she had helped me more by showing me how I could be different in the world and how good that could feel.

Amy Hilborn

One Single Rose

It's not how much we give, but how much love we put into giving.

Mother Teresa

It was Valentine's Day, my freshman year of high school. I was so young, the romantic type, and I longed for a boyfriend or secret admirer. I walked the halls seeing couples holding hands, girls with huge smiles on their faces, and dozens of roses being delivered to "that special someone." All I wanted was a rose. A single rose to brighten up my Valentine's Day. But I was picky. I didn't want the rose from my parents, my sister or even my best friend. I wanted it from a secret admirer.

Valentine's Day at school was over, and I had no rose to hang in my locker like I had hoped. I came home a little sad and hoped next year's Valentine's Day would be better. I sat in my room dreaming about next year's romantic Valentine's Day when the doorbell rang. There at the front door was a deliveryman bringing one single rose to my house. Surely this rose wasn't for me. I didn't have such luck. I closed the front door with the rose in my hand and gave it to my mother. "Open the card!" she insisted when I told her it must be for her. I unsealed the envelope as my hands were shaking. Why were my hands shaking? I knew it wasn't for me. I slowly lifted the card and read what it said:

To Amanda

From someone who cares

I must have read it twenty times in a matter of seconds, praying my eyes weren't playing tricks on me. But they weren't. The rose was for me. I must have been happy for about five minutes, until I started calling the obvious people and accusing them of sending me a rose and playing a joke on my hopelessly romantic heart. No one knew who sent it to me. My friends, family and relatives were as surprised to hear I got a rose from a secret someone as much as I was. I was on cloud nine for weeks. Every time in high school that I felt down, I would think about my freshman year's Valentine's Day and a smile would appear.

Senior year rolled around and the dreaded February fourteenth was once again upon us. This year I received at least six carnations (a carnation-selling fundraiser was held at school that year), all from my best friends. I walked around with a big smile on my face, holding my flowers. Even though they were just from friends, they made me happy.

The end of the day was drawing to a close, and I had two classes left to show off my flowers. I walked into my French class and noticed one of my closest French class friends looking upset. I had grown to know my French classmates pretty well, since I had spent three of my high-school years with the same people in one class. We'd turned into a little French family. Well, my friend saw me walk in with my six flowers and lowered her head with tears in her eyes. She hadn't received a single flower, not even from her best friend.

We talked a few minutes before class, and some very familiar words came out of her mouth. "All I wanted was one single rose." My heart ached as I heard those words. The familiar sense of loneliness I had felt as a freshman, she was feeling now. I wanted to do something. It was too late to purchase carnations and I couldn't get her anything on a break because school was almost over. Finally, I figured it out. My freshman year. The single rose. That was it; that was what I had to do.

I told my mom about my plan and asked her if we could try to find a rose after our Valentine's dinner out. She remembered having seen a bucket of roses at a local drug store, so we rushed over and purchased the last good-looking rose and a small card. In order to preserve my identity, my mom wrote what I dictated to her in the card:

To Kristen
From someone who cares

We drove to her house trying to be discreet. I ran up to the front door, put the rose in her mailbox, rang the doorbell, ran back to the car and drove away. All the feelings of happiness I had felt my freshman year had all come flooding back. I just kept thinking that I was going to make someone feel as special as I had three years earlier.

The next day in school Kristen came up to me and gave me a hug with tears in her eyes. She had realized it was me by the handwriting. I guess my mom and I are more alike than I thought. She cried and said it was the nicest thing anyone had done for her in a while.

I never did figure out who it was who sent me that rose. But I did figure something else out. It didn't matter if it was a guy who secretly loved me, my mom trying to make me feel loved or an acquaintance who knew what I needed. What matters was that it was from someone who cared about me and who went out of their way to brighten up my day.

Amanda Bertrand

The Graduation Dance

A kind and compassionate act is often its own reward.

William John Bennett

I watched as my son walked purposefully toward the car with a look on his face that I knew so well. He was bursting to tell me some news about the eighth-grade graduation dance he'd just attended. As I waited in the parking lot with the windows open on that warm summer night, I had to smile. Adam had always been the type of kid to come home from school spurting out exciting or unhappy experiences about his day before the screen door had even slammed behind him.

"I did the best thing I ever did in my whole life tonight," he blurted out as soon as he put one foot in the car. The smile on his face spread from earlobe to earlobe. Pretty strong words for a person who's only been in existence for fourteen years.

The story spilled out of him like a hole in a bag of coffee beans.

"I was standing with Justin, Mark, Kristen and Britney,"

he began. "It was noisy and dark and everyone was dancing and laughing. Then Britney pointed out a girl to me who was standing off into a darkened corner, kind of crying to herself.

"She told me, 'Go dance with her, Adam.'

"I told her she was crazy. First of all, I didn't even know the girl. I mean, I've seen her around, but I didn't know her name or anything. It's not like I'm friends with her or anything.

"But then Britney started bugging me. She told me how I have a responsibility to people because I was voted Most Popular. She said I should be a role model, and that I had the chance to do something special by dancing with this girl. She said we're here to make a difference in other people's lives, and if I danced with this girl, I'd make a difference."

"Did you dance with her?" I asked him.

"No, Mom. I told Britney she was really crazy, because she didn't even know why the girl was crying. That's when she said something that really made me think. She said, 'You know why she's crying, Adam. We both do. Look at her. It's her eighth-grade graduation dance, and she's standing alone in a corner. She's a little overweight, and she's in a room full of teenagers who only care about what kind of clothes they're wearing and what their hair looks like. Think about it. How long did you spend trying to decide what you were going to wear tonight? Well, she did the same thing. Only no one is noticing, and no one cares. Here's your chance to prove you deserve to be voted Most Popular.'"

"So did you then?" I asked.

"No," he said. "I told Britney she was right, but that everybody would laugh at me if I danced with her. So I told Britney I didn't want to look weird and I wouldn't do it."

"What happened?" I asked.

"Well, Britney wouldn't stop bugging me. She told me that if people laughed at me because I danced with an unpopular girl, then they weren't people I needed to care about. Then she asked me if I saw any guy dancing with her, would I laugh? Or would I secretly have a lot of respect for that person?

"I knew she was right. But it was still hard to go over and ask her to dance. What if I walked all the way across the room in front of everyone and she turned me down? But Britney said, 'She won't turn you down, but even if she does, you'll get over it. I promise you, if you dance with her, she'll remember you for the rest of her life. This is your chance to make a difference.'

"So I went over to the girl and asked what her name was. Then I asked if she wanted to dance. She said yes and as we walked out to the dance floor, the music changed to a slow dance. I felt my face turn all red, but it was dark and I didn't think anyone noticed. I thought everyone was looking at me, but no one laughed or anything and we danced the whole dance.

"The weird thing is that Britney was right. It was three minutes out of my life, but it felt so good. And for the rest of the night, a lot of the guys danced with her and with anyone else they saw who hadn't danced yet. It was like the greatest eighth-grade graduation dance, because no one got left out. I really learned something tonight, Mom."

So did I, Adam, so did I.

Linda Chiara

Mary

I met my friend Mary when I was fifteen years old. Our friendship was different than most. Mary was ninety-three years old when I met her. Almost a century separated us.

Mary's family lived far away, and they considered sending her to a nursing home so she could receive proper care. She, however, desperately wanted to stay in her own little home. My best friend's mother was visiting Mary one day and suggested that someone come into her house to take care of her. Mary asked her if she knew anybody who would be interested and my friend's mother told her I might be. I had been looking for a little extra cash.

A couple of days later, my mom and I went over to Mary's to get acquainted. I got the job and we shook hands. After that I came to her house every evening at 6:00 P.M.

Our nightly ritual consisted of:

Her telling me about her day.

Me telling her about mine.

Her telling me what she wanted fixed for dinner (every detail).

Me fixing dinner.

Me serving her dinner, filling up her water glass and getting her pills.

Watching *Wheel of Fortune.*

Then, watching *My Three Sons* or *Leave It to Beaver* (I think I've seen every episode by now).

Me washing the dishes.

Me sometimes taking out the garbage or washing clothes.

Me shaking her hand (it became our little ritual) and leaving.

This filled up a couple of hours each night. I already had a busy schedule, so my mom would help out and take care of Mary some evenings.

Going to Mary's gave me some relief from the pressure-filled world of adolescence. Just being with her gave me a mental rest from my busy life. Also, she was a kindred spirit. She never got angry at me when I boiled the potato instead of baked it, or when I (constantly) set off the fire alarm due to baking challenges. She would tell me stories, and of course she had many. She talked to me about her late husband and her children growing up on their old farm. She knew about everything. Well, she had ninety-three years of experience. She showed me pictures and told me what it used to be like when she was a teenager in the early 1900s. I told her about the changing world and what it was like for me to be a teenager.

About a year and a half later she got sick and had to go to the hospital for a couple of days. The next thing I knew, she had died. It was a shock. Many people in my life have died, but Mary had become such an everyday part of my life. At her funeral, Mary's daughter thanked all of us who had made it possible for her to stay in her home for the last year of her life. I was thankful that I could be a helping hand. But when I thought about it more, I realized that Mary had helped *me.* She taught me lessons that school could never teach, and her house was a sanctuary for me during some hard times.

I slipped inside the house to say my good-byes. First, to her family, and then to her. The living room was completely empty, but it still had that indescribable smell. I could picture her in her armchair, smiling. I whispered my good-bye.

Mary was my friend. She didn't care if my hair was messy or if my clothes were not name-brand. I could even go to her house in my PJs. I could be me. And that's the greatest gift a friend can give.

Jodi Rudin

May I Help You?

Something that has always puzzled me all my life is why, when I am in special need of help, the good deed is usually done by somebody on whom I have no claim.

William Feather

We stood in the street and cried. Not great, heaving sobs, but the slow, sweaty tears of desperation. We were eighteen and crying, alone on a sidewalk only hours after arriving in Honduras, Central America. We were there to join a development project called Project Bayan as volunteers, but apparently we had the wrong number for the project headquarters because we were unable to make contact.

The massive humidity was piggybacked by an intense heat that parched our throats. Where would we find purified water in the steaming jungles of Honduras? Our vocal chords were strangled by an inability to speak Spanish. It was all we could do to stand in the street and cry.

To our left was a jumble of automotive confusion, and to our right was an open-air bakery. We didn't notice the table of Spanish speakers commenting on our obvious plight until a man approached us.

"Hello," he said, in perfect English.

Our tear-streaked faces stared at this unexpected friendliness.

"My name is Henry Wilkins," he continued. "I don't like to see people crying in my country. May I help you?"

It was three simple sentences. But it was all we needed. We poured out our dilemma. We were lost; we were exhausted; we were hungry; and we were thirsty. We didn't know what was safe to eat or drink, and we didn't know how to get in touch with people who seemed to exist on the other side of an inaccessible language barrier. Neither one of us, accustomed to the security of family and friends, had ever felt so alone.

And somehow, Henry Wilkins, a man who'd grown up oppressed because of the color of his skin, poverty-stricken because of the state of his country's economy, and without stability because of the corruption of his government, took us to the supermarket and found us food. Then he took us to the café and found us water. Henry Wilkins took us to the phone and found our friends. And Henry Wilkins did this because he didn't like to see people crying in his country.

I have been home from Honduras for over two years now, but I still think often of Henry Wilkins. I remain convinced that Henry Wilkins was an angel. I also remain convinced that Henry Wilkins taught me one of the most valuable lessons of friendship I learned during my entire, life-changing stay in Honduras. It was three simple sentences that are etched into my heart and that I intend to keep with me the rest of my life: "My name is Bobbi Smith. I don't like to see people crying in my country. May I help you?"

Bobbi Smith

5

FAMILY

Other things may change us, but we start and end with family.

Anthony Brandt

My Big Brother

First say to yourself what you would be; and then do what you have to do.

Epictetus

I never thought that the absence of smelly socks and loud music would make my heart ache. But my brother is off at college, and at age fourteen, I miss him terribly. We share a rare kind of closeness for siblings, but then, my brother is a rare kind of guy. Of course he's smart and kind, plus my friends say he is gorgeous and all that. But it's more how he handles things, how he treats his friends and his family, how he cares about people that makes me so proud. That's the stuff that I aspire to be. If it's okay with you, I would like to show you what I mean. . . .

He applied to fourteen colleges. He was accepted to all but one, the one he wanted, Brown University. So he opted for his second choice, and off he went to a fine though uneventful first year. When he came home for summer vacation, he informed us that he had come up with a plan. He was going to do whatever it took to get into Brown. Would we support him?

His plan was to move to Rhode Island near Brown, find a job, and do whatever he could to become known in the area. He'd work his heart out, he said, and do the very best at everything. Someone, he was sure, would notice. This was a big deal for my parents because it meant agreeing to a year without college, a scary thing for them. But they trusted him and encouraged him to do whatever he thought it would take to achieve his dream.

It wasn't long before he was hired to produce the plays at—yes, you guessed it—Brown. Now was his chance to shine, and shine he did. No task was too big or too small. He put every bit of himself into the job. He met teachers and administrators, talked to everyone about his dream and never hesitated to tell them what he was after.

And sure enough, at the end of the year, when he reapplied to Brown, he was accepted.

We were all really happy, but for me the happiness went very deep. I had learned an important lesson—a lesson no one could have taught me with words, a lesson I had to see with my own eyes. If I work hard for what I want, if I keep trying after I've been turned away, my dreams also can come true. This is a gift I still hold in my heart. Because of my brother, I trust life.

Recently, I flew to Rhode Island all by myself to visit him, and I had a blast hanging out for a week in an apartment without parents. The night before I left, we were talking about all kinds of stuff like boyfriends, girlfriends, peer pressure and school. At one point, my brother looked me right in the eye and said he loved me. He told me to remember to never do anything that I feel isn't right, no matter what, and never to forget that I can always trust my heart.

I cried all the way home, knowing that my brother and

I will always be close, and realizing how lucky I am to have him. Something was different: I didn't feel like a little girl anymore. Part of me had grown up on this trip, and for the first time I thought about the important job that I had waiting for me at home. You see, I have a ten-year-old little sister. It looks as though I've got my work cut out for me. But you know, I had a great teacher.

Lisa Gumenick

The Champ

He had a featherweight build, but what this fifteen-year-old lacked in strength and speed, he made up for in attitude. Jason never missed a practice, even though he rarely got playing time, and then only in the fourth quarter when our team outdistanced the opponent by at least three touchdowns. Even so, number thirty-seven never so much as frowned, let alone complained, and always put forth his best effort—even if it amounted to very little.

One day he didn't come to practice. When he didn't show up on the second day, as his concerned coach, I telephoned his home to check on him. The out-of-town relative I spoke with informed me that Jason's father had passed away and the family was making funeral arrangements.

Two weeks later, my faithful number thirty-seven was again in the lineup, ready for practice. Only three days of practice remained before our next game. This was an important game because it was against our most fierce opponent and late in the season, and we only had a one-game lead over them. This was a critical game at a pivotal point in the season.

When the big day rolled around, my top players were ready to bolt onto the field. All the familiar faces were there but one—Jason. But suddenly, Jason appeared at my side and with a totally uncharacteristic look and manner said, "I'm going to be a starter today. I'm ready now." He left no room for refusal or argument. When the game began, he was in position on the field. The regular starter whom he replaced sat awestruck on the bench.

Jason played like a first-stringer that day. He was in every respect equal if not better than the best player on the team. He ran fast, found every open hole in the line, and jumped up after every tackle as if he had never been hit. By the third quarter he had run for three touchdowns. As a grand finale, as if to remove even the slightest doubt in anyone's mind, he scored another touchdown in the last seconds of the fourth quarter.

As he ran off the field with his teammates, Jason received a volley of body slaps and body slams against the backdrop of thunderous applause from the crowd. Despite all the adulation, Jason managed to maintain his characteristic humble, low-key manner. Puzzled by Jason's sudden transformation, I approached him and said, "Jason, you played an extraordinary game today. By the second touchdown, I had to wipe my eyes and pinch myself. But by the time the clock ran out in the fourth quarter, my curiosity got the best of me. What happened to you?"

Jason, hesitating at first, said, "Well, Coach Williams, as you know, my father recently died. When my dad was alive he was blind, so he couldn't see me play. But now that he has gone to heaven, this is the first time he has been able to see me play. I wanted to make him proud."

As told by Nailah Malik, the "Vela Storyteller"

I Love You, Dad

If God can work through me, he can work through anyone.

St. Francis of Assisi

I met a man who came to Tampa for his father's funeral. Father and son hadn't seen each other in years. In fact, according to the son, his father had left when he was a boy, and they had had little contact until about a year ago, when his father had sent him a birthday card with a note saying he'd like to see his son again.

After discussing a trip to Florida with his wife and children and consulting his busy schedule at his office, the son tentatively set a date to visit his father two months later. He would drive his family down when school was out for vacation. He scribbled a note and with mixed emotions, dropped it in the mail.

He heard back immediately. Written on lined paper torn from a spiral notebook, such as a schoolboy would use, were words of excitement penned in a barely legible scrawl. Misspelled words, poor grammar and incorrect punctuation bounced off the page. The man was embarrassed for his father. He thought twice about the upcoming visit.

It just so happened that the man's daughter made the cheerleading squad at her school and had to go to a camp conducted for cheering techniques. Coincidentally, it started the week after school was out. The trip to Florida would have to be postponed.

His father said he understood, but the son didn't hear from him again for some time. A note here or there, an occasional call. They didn't say much—muttered sentences, comments about "your mother," a couple of clouded stories about the man's childhood—but it was enough to put together a few of the missing pieces.

In November the son received a call from his father's neighbor. His father had been taken to the hospital with heart problems. The son spoke with the charge nurse, who assured him his father was doing well following a heart attack. The doctor could provide details.

His father said, "I'm fine. You don't have to make a trip out here. The doctor says there was minor damage, and I can go home day after tomorrow."

He called his father every few days after that. They chatted and laughed and talked about getting together "soon." He sent money for Christmas. His father sent small gifts for his children and a pen and pencil set for his son. It was a cheap set, probably purchased at a discount pharmacy or variety-type store, and the kids tossed their tokens from Grandpa aside without much notice. But his wife received a precious music box made of crystal. Overwhelmed, she expressed her gratitude to the old man when they called him on Christmas Day. "It was my mother's," the old man explained. "I wanted you to have it."

The man's wife told her husband that they should have invited the old man for the holidays. As an excuse for not having done so, she added, "But it probably would be too cold for him here, anyway."

In February, the man decided to visit his father. As luck would have it, however, his boss's wife had to have an operation, and the man had to fill in and work a few extra hours. He called his father to tell him he'd probably get to Florida in March or April.

I met the man on Friday. He had finally come to Tampa. He was here to bury his father.

He was waiting when I arrived to open the door that morning. He sat in the chapel next to his father's body, which had been dressed in a handsome, new, navy blue pinstriped suit and laid out in a dark blue metal casket. "Going Home" was scripted inside the lid.

I offered the man a glass of water. He cried. I put my arm around his shoulder and he collapsed in my arms, sobbing. "I should have come sooner. He shouldn't have had to die alone." We sat together until late afternoon. He asked if I had something else to do that day. I told him no.

I didn't choose the act, but I knew it was kind. No one else came to honor the life of the man's father, not even the neighbor he spoke of. It cost nothing but a few hours of my time. I told him I was a student, that I wanted to be a professional golfer, and that my parents owned the funeral home. He was an attorney and lived in Denver. He plays golf whenever he can. He told me about his father.

That night, I asked my dad to play golf with me the next day. And before I went to bed, I told him, "I love you, Dad."

Nick Curry III

Role Reversal

It was a Friday night, and I had just returned from climbing one of the Red Rocks of Sedona. The night was chilly, the moon was high and I was looking forward to crawling into my warm bed. My faculty adviser, Bunny, approached me as I walked through the arches to my dorm room. She took me to her home where she told me that my mother had been in a terrible car crash and had been taken to the intensive care unit of a nearby hospital in critical condition.

When I got to the hospital my grandmother pulled me aside and said whatever I did, I mustn't cry in front of my mother.

A nurse unlocked the door that led down a wide hallway with machines all around. A strong smell of medicine brought a nauseous feeling to my already turning stomach. My mother's room was right next to the nurses' station. As I turned into the room, I saw her lying on her side, with her tiny back to me and a fluffed pillow between her bandaged legs. She struggled to turn around but couldn't. I slowly crept to the other side of the bed and said "hi" in a calm voice, stifling my urge to cry out.

The cadaverous condition of her body stunned me. Her

swollen face looked like it had been inflated and kicked around like a soccer ball, her eyes had huge dark bruised rings around them, and she had tubes down her throat and in her arms.

Gently holding my mother's cold swollen hands, I tried to keep my composure. She kept looking at me and rolling her eyes into the back of her head as she pounded her hand against the bed. She was trying to tell me how much pain she was in. I turned my face away from her, trying to hide the tears that were rolling down my face. Eventually I had to leave her for a moment because I couldn't hold my anguish in any longer. That was when it struck me that I really might lose my mother.

I kept her company all day long; in time the doctors took the respirator out of her throat for a short while. She was able to whisper a few words, but I didn't know what to say in return. I felt like screaming but knew I mustn't. I went home and cried myself to sleep.

From that night on, my life completely changed. Up to that point, I'd had the luxury of just being a kid, having to deal with only the exaggerated melodramas of teenage life. My concept of crisis was now forever altered. As my mother struggled first to stay alive and then to relearn to walk, my sense of priorities in life changed drastically. My mother needed me. The trials and tribulations of my daily life at school, which had seemed so important before, now appeared insignificant. My mother and I had faced death together, and life took on new meaning for both of us.

After a week of clinging to life in intensive care, my mother's condition improved enough to be taken off the respirator and moved to a regular hospital room. She was finally out of danger but, because her legs had been crushed, there was doubt that she would be able to walk again. I was just grateful that she was alive. I visited my mother in the hospital as often as I could for the next two months. Finally, a sort-of hospital suite was set up in our family room, and to my relief and joy, she was allowed to come home.

My mother's return home was a blessing for us all, but it meant some unaccustomed responsibilities for me. She had a visiting nurse, but much of the time I took care of her. I would feed her, bathe her, and when she was eventually able to use a toilet, would help her to the bathroom. It struck me that I was pretty much playing the role of mother to my own mother. It wasn't always much fun, but it felt good to be there when my mother really needed me. The difficult part for me was trying to always be upbeat, and to keep my mother's spirits up when she became frustrated with the pain and her inability to do simple things for herself. I always had a smile on my face when, really, I was suppressing tears in my heart.

My mother's reliance on me changed our relationship. In the past, we had more than our share of the strains of mother-daughter relationships. The accident threw us into a relationship of interdependence. To get my mother back, I had to help her regain her strength and ability to resume an independent life. She had to learn to accept my help as well as the fact that I was no longer a child. We have become the closest of friends. We genuinely listen to one another, and truly enjoy each other's company.

It has been over two years since my mother's crash. Although it was devastating to see my mother go through the physical pain and emotions that she still continues to experience, I have grown more in that time than in all the years before. Being a mother figure to my own mother taught me a lot about parenthood: the worries, the protectiveness and, most of all, the sweetness of unconditional devotion and love.

Adi Amar

My Most Memorable Christmas

The fall of 1978, our daughter Carol, age thirteen, was thrown from a motorcycle on which she had been a passenger. She sailed eighty-nine feet through the air and landed in a ditch, where she almost died. My wife and I were on a mission in Korea when we got the news that the doctors were in the process of amputating her left leg.

Our flight home took twenty-two hours. I suppose I did more crying on that flight than I ever have in my entire life. When my wife and I arrived at our daughter's side, unable to think of adequate words of comfort, surprisingly enough, Carol began the conversation.

"Dad," she said, "I think God has a special ministry for my life to help people who have been hurt as I have." She saw possibilities—positive ones—in tragedy! What a lift those words gave me. But we were just beginning what would prove to be a long, exhausting battle.

Carol's femur had broken in four places and plunged through the thigh bone into the ditch of an Iowa farm, next to a slaughterhouse. There it picked up a form of bacteria that had previously been resistant to any known antibiotics.

In November, Carol went back into the hospital for surgery that would, hopefully, release muscles in her knee that might make her leg more usable. The doctor was delighted when he opened her thigh and knee and discovered no pus pockets. But the hidden bacteria, which until that time had remained dormant, erupted like a prairie fire when exposed to the open air. Three days after surgery, she was the sickest little girl I've ever seen.

Each passing day, the bacteria multiplied with increasing impatience. Carol's fever soared to 104 degrees and lingered there day after day, night after night. Her leg continued to swell and the infection raged out of control.

About that time, we were blessed with a minor miracle. With no knowledge of my daughter's need, the Federal Drug Administration released, for the first time, an antibiotic that was declared significantly effective against the specific strain of bacteria that Carol contracted while lying in that Iowa ditch. She was the first human being in Children's Hospital, Orange County, California, to receive it. In a matter of hours after the first dosage, her temperature went down. Each successive culture reading showed fewer and fewer bacteria. Finally, about three weeks before Christmas, a culture came back that showed no bacteria growth.

Lying in her hospital bed with the intravenous tubes still in her hands, Carol asked the visiting doctor, who was standing in for her own surgeon, when she would be released. "Will I be home for Christmas, Doctor?" she asked.

"I don't know," he replied cautiously.

"Will I be able to get my new prosthesis?" she asked.

"Well," the doctor cautioned, "I don't believe you can get it yet."

But when her own doctor returned, he checked her over. That same day Carol called me at my office. "Daddy, I have good news," she announced.

"What is it?" I asked.

"Doctor Masters is an angel," she exclaimed. "He said I can come home for Christmas!"

On December 16, a Saturday night, Carol was released from the hospital. I was told to stay home and await a surprise. My wife went to pick her up. I saw the lights of the car as it rolled up the driveway, and I ran to the front door. My wife barred my way and said, "Bob, you have to go back in and wait. Carol wants you to wait by the Christmas tree."

So I waited nervously by the Christmas tree, counting the seemingly interminable seconds. Then I heard the front door open and the squeak of rubber on the wooden floor. I knew the sound came from the rubber tips of Carol's crutches. She stepped into the open door, ten feet away from my seat by the Christmas tree. She had gone straight from the hospital to the beauty parlor, where her hair stylist gave her a beautiful permanent. There she stood with lovely curls framing her face. Then I looked down and saw two shoes, two ankles, two legs and a beautiful girl.

She had come home and, because of it, made that Christmas my most memorable.

Reverend Robert Schuller

There Is an Oz

They arrive exactly at 8:00 A.M. to take her home, but she has been ready since before seven. She has taken a shower—not an easy task lying down on a shower stretcher. She isn't allowed to sit up yet without her body brace, but regardless, here she is, clean and freshly scrubbed and ever so anxious to go home. It has been two-and-a-half months since she has seen her home—two-and-a-half months since the car accident. It doesn't matter that she is going home in a wheelchair or that her legs don't work. All she knows is that she is going home, and home will make everything okay. Even Dorothy says so: "Oh, Auntie Em, there's no place like home!" It's her favorite movie.

As they put her in the car, she thinks now of how much her father reminds her of the scarecrow in *The Wizard of Oz.* Like the scarecrow, he is built in pieces of many different things—strength, courage and love. Especially love.

He isn't an elegant man. Her father is tall and lanky and has dirt under his fingernails from working outside. He is strictly blue collar—a laborer. He never went to college, didn't even go to high school. By the world's standards he isn't "educated." An awful lot like the scarecrow—but she knows differently. He doesn't speak much, but when he does, she knows it is worth remembering. Even worth writing down. But she never has to write down anything that her father says because she knows she'll never forget.

It is hard for her to sit comfortably while wearing the body brace and so she sits, stiff and unnatural, staring out the window. Her face is tense and tired and older somehow, much older than her seventeen years. She doesn't even remember the world of a seventeen-year-old girl—it's as if that world never was. And she thinks she knows what Dorothy must have meant when she said, "Oh, Toto, I don't think we're in Kansas anymore." It is more than an issue of geography, she is quite certain.

They pull out onto the road to begin their journey and approach the stop sign at the corner. The stop sign is just a formality; no one ever stops here. Today, however, is different. As he goes to coast through the intersection, she is instantly alert, the face alive and the eyes flashing. She grips the sides of the seat. "Stop! That's a stop sign! You could get us killed! Don't you know that?" And then, more quietly and with even more intensity, "You don't know what it's like—you have never been there." He looks at her and says nothing. The scarecrow and Dorothy journey onward.

As they continue to drive, her mind is constantly at work. She still hasn't loosened her grip on the seat. She thinks of the eyes, the eyes that once belonged to her—big, brown, soulful eyes that would sparkle with laughter at the slightest thought of happiness. Only the happiness is gone now and she doesn't know where she left it or how to get it back. She only knows that it is gone and, in its absence, the sparkle has gone as well.

The eyes are not the same. They no longer reflect the soul of the person because that person no longer exists. The eyes now are deep and cold and empty—pools of color that have been filled with something reaching far beyond the happiness that once was there. Like the yellow brick road it stretches endlessly, maddeningly, winding through valleys and woodlands, obscuring her vision until she has somehow lost sight of the Emerald City.

She lightly touches the tiny gold bracelet that she wears. It was a present from her mother and father, and she refuses to remove it from her wrist. It is engraved with her name on the side that is visible to others, but as in everything there are two sides, and only she knows the other is there. It is a single word engraved on the side of the bracelet that touches her skin and touches her heart: "Hope." One small word that says so much about her life and what is now missing from it. She vaguely remembers hope—what it felt like to hope for a college basketball scholarship or maybe a chance to dance professionally. Only now, she's not sure she remembers hope as it was then—a driving force, a fundamental part of her life. Now, hope is something that haunts her.

The dreams come nightly. Dreams of turning cartwheels in the yard or hitting a tennis ball against a brick wall. But there is one, the most vivid and recurring, and the most haunting of all. . . . There is a lake and trees, a soft breeze and a perfect sky. It is a scene so beautiful it is almost beyond imagining. And in the midst of it all, she is walking. She has never felt more at peace.

But then she awakens and remembers. And remembering, she knows. She instinctively fingers the bracelet, the word. And the fear is almost overwhelming—the fear of not knowing how to hope.

She thinks of her father's God and how she now feels that God abandoned her. All at once, a single tear makes a trail down her thin, drawn face. Then another and another, and she is crying. "Oh Daddy, they say I'll never walk again! They're the best and they say I'll never walk. Daddy, what will I do?"

He looks at her now and he stops the car. This is the man

who has been with her down every road, every trail and every path—so very like the scarecrow. And he speaks. "I know that they can put you back together. They can put steel rods in your back and sew you up. But look around you. Not one of your doctors can make a blade of grass."

Suddenly she knows. He has taught her the most valuable lesson in her life and in all her journey: that she is never alone. There is an Oz; there is a wizard; there is a God. And there . . . is . . . hope. She releases her grip on the seat, looks out the window and smiles. And in that instant she loves her father more than she has ever loved him before.

Terri Cecil

The Perfect Family

Divorce. That's a word I dreaded more than any other word in the English dictionary.

All my life, I thought I had the perfect family. Perfect parents, two great sisters and a younger brother. We all got along well. But during the last several years, my parents had started to fight more and more.

My dad came home less and less, working more hours than ever in Vermont. And now here we all were, sitting in the television room as a family, with my parents saying they had an announcement to make. I began to cringe.

There it was: that nightmare word, the one that made me sick to my stomach. They were, they announced, getting a divorce. The big D word. My sisters and brother and I gaped at each other. How many times had I asked my mom and dad: "Are you getting a divorce?" How many times had they assured me that would never happen and given me hugs and kisses?

"This is some sort of April Fool's joke, right?" I said.

My mom's eyes welled with tears and she held me in her arms.

"No, Marc, I'm sorry," she whispered.

I felt betrayed. How could they do this to us? Most of all, I wanted to know what we had done wrong. What had *I* done wrong?

My mother could see the dread in my eyes, the fear, the hurt and the pain. It all welled within my belly and I felt sick. She promised she would take care of me, of us. All of us.

But how could I believe her now? My family had collapsed before my eyes. We were splintered. Shattered. There would be no more perfect family. And of course, things would get worse rather than better. They'd get a lot worse.

My mom told me that we would have to leave our home. The home I'd lived in all my life.

I felt like I was losing everything. My family. My home. My dad. The good news: My mother would have custody of all of us and my father wouldn't dispute it.

We moved into a tiny home with my mom's parents. At first, I wasn't very happy. The house was small. We were all squished in together. Sometimes I felt there wasn't enough room to breathe. There was one thing, however: We loved each other. My grandparents, Mom, sisters, brother and visiting aunts and uncles tried to do everything to fill the house with warmth and caring. My grandparents paid special attention to all us kids. I'd never felt so close to them in my life.

They asked me about school and were actually interested. They asked me about my friends, my grades. We sat at the kitchen table and talked often. They could never replace my father, but they spread their warmth to all of us.

Still, I carried a lot of guilt. I couldn't understand what bad thing happened to split up my parents. At times, I agonized over it, lying in bed, wondering in a cloud-like state what possibly could have been the reason that my parents quit loving each other. Was it something I had done?

And then more unexpected news: We learned my father was gay.

I was sure as word got around that the other kids would laugh and make fun of me. Some did. But, there were a lot of kids, however, who didn't say a word. They still hung around me and could care less what my dad did. They liked me before and they liked me still. I had learned who my real friends were, and the ones I lost were not the kind of people I wanted in my life anyway.

I also learned that I was really loved by my family. They supported me. They cared about me. My grandparents adored me. Eventually, we were able to move out from their home and get a condominium. I started junior high school and started doing well.

I have since learned to redefine that funny concept I had about a perfect family.

Maybe a perfect family really means a lot of love and a lot of support. Maybe it really means giving, sharing and caring. Maybe I still have a perfect family after all.

Marc St. Pierre

Ghost Mother

Six months before my thirteenth birthday, my parents gave my brother and me "the talk." The one about their loving us, but not each other and how much happier everyone would be if they separated. Yet, my parents rewrote the ending: "We think it would be best if you lived with your father." My mother was the one who said this, running her red nails through my hair. That moment has stayed in the center of my stomach since then, like a jagged stone rolling around.

Mothers are supposed to be that one person who represents home, who somehow makes everything okay when your world is shaking. A mother should be there for you no matter how many times you change your Halloween costume, how messy your room gets or what happens to her marriage. But mine saw motherhood as an optional endeavor, something she could easily discard like a sweater that no longer fit.

She quickly settled into her own life and her new apartment. Having married at twenty-one, this was the first time she was on her own. Her decorating business was growing, and she was more interested in catering to her clients than to two kids and a husband of fifteen years.

A few weeks after she moved out, she called on a Friday night. "Tomorrow, let's have lunch and then go shopping. Okay?" she asked. I was so excited that I could hardly answer. That night I dreamed of riding beside my mom in the car. Saturday, I woke early, put on my favorite overalls and finished my homework in case she wanted to spend Sunday together, too. My friend Jennifer called. "Aren't you coming to the movies?" she asked. "Everyone's going."

"My mom and I have stuff to do. Shopping or something," I said, forcing my tone to be matter-of-fact. But morning turned into afternoon, and she didn't call. I spent the day by the phone pretending to read, playing solitaire and braiding my hair. I wouldn't eat anything because I thought at any minute she'd be there and want to take me out for lunch. And I didn't want my mom to have to eat alone. But she didn't call until after six o'clock. "Sorry, honey, I was working all day and not near a phone," she said quickly. "And now I'm so tired, I just need to take a nap. You understand, don't you?" No Mom, I didn't understand.

This same scenario happened many weekends for several years after she left. The rare times I did see her, she'd rent me four-hour movies like *Tess* and leave me alone to watch them. Or I'd go on her errands or to her office, never really with her, more like a balloon trailing after her. I'd sit alone at a desk in her office eating Chinese food out of a paper carton while she worked or talked on the phone. But I never complained or stopped going. How could I when this was all I had of her?

Almost a year after she moved out, the clothes she didn't want remained in her walk-in closet. My father said he was too busy to pack them, but I think that—just as I did—he hoped it meant she wasn't gone for good. I used to sit in that closet, breathing in the lingering smell of her Ralph Lauren perfume. I'd wrap myself in her ivory cashmere cardigan and run my fingers along the beaded surface of a pink bag, remembering when she'd carried it with a chiffon dress. She had looked just like a princess. I'd rock the bag gently, feeling sorry for it that she had left it behind, too.

Living with my father and brother in their masculine world of boxer shorts and hockey games wasn't easy. Just when I should have been stepping out of my tomboy stage of wearing my brother's worn Levi's and button-downs and starting to become a young woman, I was screaming at the basketball players on TV and munching on Doritos. Each of my friends watched her mother apply eyeliner and blush and practiced with her makeup while she was out. The only makeup I knew about was the black smudges under football players' eyes.

Growing up without my mother, I always had to carry myself to each new stage of life or get left behind. I wore the same clothes that my friends did, bought my first bra by myself and started shaving my legs when they did. But to me I was just following clumsily behind them, self-conscious that my motherlessness was showing. When I got my period, I huddled in my pink bathroom, feeling like a little girl at this sign of being a woman. Having to say, "I got my period, Dad," was mortifying. But the truth was, I felt more comfortable telling him than my mother. When she called the following week, she said, "Dad told me what happened, but he took care of it." This was a statement, not a question.

My mother became like a distant relative whom I saw several times a year, who sent a birthday card if she remembered and to whom I was stiffly polite and didn't curse in front of. The word "mom" was foreign to me. She never asked about my friends or school or seemed to notice that I was struggling to grow up without her. Each time I said good-bye, I knew it would be months before I saw her again.

Why didn't my mother want me? I wondered. Teachers and friends' parents always wore a look of pity when my father picked me up from parties, came alone to plays and parent-conference day and talked to them to arrange car pools. Hating their pity, I'd mix the few minutes my mother did give me with my imagination. Then I'd casually talk about her at lunch or at friends' houses so they wouldn't see that all I had was a ghost mother who touched my life only in memories.

Although it was tough at first, my father tried to do everything he could to fill the gaps my mother left. He put my brother and me first, at times sacrificing his own happiness for ours. Despite losing his wife and marriage, my father wore a smile on his face. After all, he was the person we looked toward to tell us everything was going to be okay, so we couldn't see him sad. He had no spouse to pick up where he left off or to help him with daily issues and unexpected situations. He took us to the doctor, listened to our problems and helped us with homework. He was there with treats when my friends slept over and told the kind of dumb fatherly jokes that made us laugh and roll our eyes. He was always at all my school plays and softball games. He never missed a gymnastics meet or recital. Most fathers never took off work to come to even one of these things; my father was at all of them. Most of all, he was always conscious of my disappointments and tried to make a bad situation better. After a while, all the people who pitied me noticed my father's intense interest in my well-being and realized, as I did, that though my life was different, there was nothing wrong with it or me. In time, I adjusted to this. And though I never stopped wishing my mother were a more central part of my life, I saw the fact that she wasn't; she was just a part of who I am.

In recent years, I have become closer with her. I accept her for who she is, regardless of the fact that she wasn't always the mother I wanted her to be. As I have gotten older, I can look at what she did from a different perspective. And I think I've reached this point because my father taught me to be understanding of and sensitive to others. I've realized it's okay not to have a storybook home with a mom, dad, two kids and a dog. Who said that is the definition of family? My home may have been unique, but it had in it the same love and loyalty as other families.

Michele Bender

Dear Diary . . .

The greatest happiness of life is the conviction that we are loved—loved for ourselves or rather, loved in spite of ourselves.

Victor Hugo

Dear Diary,

Drip. Drip. Drip. For three hours I've waited in this train station and for three hours I've heard the faint splash of water fall from an old water fountain onto the cold, hardwood floor. The wood is old and worn but somehow doesn't allow any of the water drops to seep through. Funny, how something . . . Suddenly a horn whistles from a departing train, interrupting my thoughts and allowing them to come crashing back to reality.

I glance at my watch and realize I've missed my train, and the next one isn't going to leave this town for the next four hours. What am I going to do now? It's a quarter past midnight, and I'm cold and hungry. I have a meeting with the admissions officer in a college at 8:00 A.M., and by the look of things, I'm not going to make it on time. What a way to make a first impression, huh?

I begin to feel the tears burn the back of my eyes, and soon they are dancing upon my cheek. I am here alone. There isn't a familiar face around to comfort me. My mother was supposed to be here with me, to say one final good-bye before I enter adulthood. But with the many fights and unkept promises we've shared I didn't expect her to want to come here with me. Maybe I shouldn't have left the house this evening without saying I'm sorry. Sorry for the many disagreements and disappointments. Sorry for my hurtful words and actions. But we've passed the point where "sorry" heals things and makes them better again. Still, what I wouldn't give to have her here with me. Maybe she's right. Maybe I'm not the know-it-all mature adult I think I am. Maybe I am still just a scared kid who needs the protection of a mother's love.

It's almost 4:00 now, and the morning sun should be rising soon. I am able to grab a cup of coffee and change my clothes during the wait. I figure if I catch a 7:00 bus in Boston I can still make my appointment. . . .

Until next time,
Me

Putting away my journal I reach into my bag to get out my ticket, but instead a plain white envelope emerges in my hand. I don't need to read the name on the front to know who it's from. She wants us to have a better relationship and put the past behind us. Have a fresh start. My mother even admitted she was sorry for all the arguments we've had over the course of the years. The note also said she would be waiting for me at the train station in Boston and we would walk into college together. Enclosed was an upgraded ticket and a "P.S." telling me to look in the bottom of my bag. There I would find money for a bite to eat and a sweater in case I got cold in the station. As I make my way to the train I pass the broken water fountain, which no longer drips, and I realize, for the first time in this life, I'm about to see a woman for who she truly is. My mother.

Liz Correale

A Birthday Gift

She lived a life of solitude.
She lived a life in vain.
She lived a life in which there was
A strong, ongoing pain.

She had no friends on which to lean
And cry her problems to.
She had no friends to give her love
And hope and kindness, too.

She thought about it day and night;
She lay upon her bed.
Her mind made up, she grabbed a gun
And put it to her head.

Just then a ring came from the phone.
She pulled the gun away.
Her mom was on the other end
And wanted just to say,

"Happy Birthday, my dear girl.
Today is just for you.
I care for you with all my heart,
I hope you know that's true."

These words ran through her mind so much.
The gun was down for good.
She changed her mind about her life
And then she changed her mood.

She thought about this special day
And what her mom had said.
The gift her mom gave her that day
Was the gift of life, *again.*

Thad Langenberg

My Real Father

I came across a quotation the other day: "He who raises a child is to be called its father, not the man who only gave it birth." How true this is! I only wish I had realized it sooner, for my failure to do so caused every person in my family a lot of unnecessary grief, including me.

My mom married the man I knew as Dad when I was four years old, and even then I felt this animosity toward him that was incredible, especially for a child so young. My dad tried so hard to be a good father to me, and I responded with spite and anger. He showered me with love, and I spit in his eye. Oh, he legally adopted me, and I called him Dad, but in my heart, I was a fatherless child. This incredible anger only grew when we moved from Ohio, where I had relatives on every street corner, to South Dakota, where I knew nobody. When I reflect now on my terrible behavior, I feel such shame. Just because he loved my mother, he was stuck with a little brat whose every move was calculated to bring him grief. But he didn't give up on me as a lesser man might have.

The strange thing is, I had come to love this man, but I didn't know how to stop my hateful behavior. I can only be glad that eventually, I grew out of it.

When people find out I'm adopted, their first question is always, "Who's your real father? Do you know him?" My answer is, "Yes, I know him. I live with him."

My dad is the man who refused to spank me, even though I deserved it. He's fed me and clothed me and loved me for thirteen years. He's there when I cry, and when I feel sick. Dad can always fix it with something out of his magical medicine collection. He worries about me if I'm out late. He bought me my first car, my first prom dress. He's the one who is proud of me when I get a good report card or win an honor or just handle a difficult situation in a mature way. He's my father, my dad and my daddy in every way except the one that doesn't count.

And as soon as my daddy gets home, I'm going to tell him, for the first time, how much I love him and how much I appreciate that he didn't give up on me . . . even when I had given up on myself.

Anonymous

Angel

I just sit here, watching the funny looking bird through the window. It is washing itself in the driveway, which is full of rain from last night's shower. I think, *What if I were a bird? Where would I go? What would I do?* Of course, I know that is not possible, especially now. I'm just sitting here, watching my life pass by, second by second, minute by minute. I know I should do something productive, like homework, but I just feel like it's my job to watch the funny looking bird. Then the bird flies away, and I turn on the TV and watch a show about buffalo.

School's almost out, but I'm not there. I have to be sick, stuck inside with the flu, stuck inside underneath this blanket.

It's such a beautiful day outside, and I feel so sick. I feel like I am falling up (which just isn't possible, but I still feel like it). My head is spinning, almost as if I am in a daze. My brain starts pounding, like someone is hitting my skull with a hammer. The sun is shining, which doesn't help; it just makes it worse. I hide under the covers. This is the one time I feel like the sun is a bad thing.

Now my stomach starts to ache, so I move from the

couch to my room to lie on my bed. Even though my brain hurts, I start to think. I let my imagination go.

I think about how much easier it is to tap your foot to a country song than to a rock song. I think about how long a day seems when you're bored, but when you do something fun the time flies by. I think about how they make us go to school for seven hours, then expect us to do three hours of homework every night and endure a big test in science or history the next day.

I start to dream, daydream that is, even more. I wander even further into my imagination. Somehow the thought of an angel comes into my head. *What do they look like? Do they have golden wings? Do they live in the moment, rather than the past or the future? Are they light?*

For some reason I can't stop wondering about them. *Can a human being become an angel after life?* My friends tell me no, but I think my grandpa is my grandma's guardian angel. I take out a piece of paper and start drawing what I think an angel looks like. In the finished drawing, the angel has golden hair as rich as the sun and gold wings that stretch from her body so that she can touch everyone's heart. She is wearing a smile and a pure white robe. A golden halo of stars floats atop her head.

The drawing makes me smile, and I feel a little better. *Tomorrow will be a better day,* I think. At that, I fall asleep.

"Anyone home?" greets me as I awaken.

"Hi, Mom," I reply.

"How are you feeling?" she asks.

"Better."

She insists on making me some chicken noodle soup anyway. Moms sure know how to make me feel better when I'm sick. Seems like she would take my sickness away from me in a second and give it to herself if she could. That's what moms are for, always there for you. Mothers hate to see their children suffer, even if it's just a little flu bug.

I don't need to know what an angel looks like, I think, *I already know.* An angel is a mom, my Mom. Her smile is that light that fills the room when it's dark. And her thoughtfulness touches my heart. My mom is an angel, watching over me. Thanks, Mom.

Nathen Cantwell

My Little Brother

A sibling may be the sole keeper of one's core identity, the only person with the keys to one's unfettered, more fundamental self.

Marian Sandmaier

It was a stormy Saturday afternoon when my mother took my five-year-old brother, Christopher, and me to a new enormous toy store she had read about in the newspaper. "So many toys," the advertisement had shouted in full and flashy color, "that we had to get a huge warehouse to fit them all!" Christopher and I couldn't have been more excited. We ran across the parking lot, through the cold and biting rain, as fast as our little legs could carry us. We left our mother outside to battle with the frustrating umbrella, which never worked when she wanted it to.

"Christine! I'm going to find the Lego section! There's a new pirate ship I want, and I have four dollars! Maybe I can buy it!" Christopher exclaimed and ran off excitedly. I only half heard him. I took a right turn and, to my wide-eyed delight, found myself in the midst of Barbie World.

I was studying a mini mink coat and doing some

simple math in my head when suddenly an earthshaking clap of thunder roared from the storm outside. I jumped at the noise, dropping the accessory to the floor. The warehouse lights flickered once and died, covering the stuffed animals, matchbox cars and board games in a blanket of black. Thunder continued to shake the sky and whips of lightning illuminated the store for seconds at a time, casting frightening shadows that played tricks on my mind.

Oh no, I thought, as my stomach twisted and turned inside of me. *Where's Christopher?* I ran up and down the aisles through the darkness, panic filling my small chest and making it difficult to breathe. I knocked into displays of candy and tripped over toys, all the while frantically calling my brother's name. I needed to know he was all right, but I could barely see. Tears of frustration and fear trickled down my face, but I continued to run. I found Christopher in the Lego aisle. He was standing alone, perfectly still, clutching tightly to the pirate ship set. I threw my arms around him and hugged him until he couldn't breathe. Then, I took his hand in mine and we went to find our mother.

Years later, on a beautiful Tuesday morning, I was leaving my computer class on my way to sociology. As I drove, the radio filled my ears with horrendous news: A hijacked plane had crashed into the Pentagon and two other planes had crashed into the World Trade Center. Fires, destruction and chaos echoed across the east coast from Washington to New York City. My first thought was of Christopher.

My brother had joined the Air Force just a year earlier, and he was stationed in Washington. I had grown used to seeing him for a few days every five months or getting 2:00 A.M. telephone calls just to let me know he was alive and well. But as the Towers collapsed and newscasters began to cry, I was overcome with the need to see Christopher, to hug him and make certain he was all right. I pulled over to the nearest pay phone and frantically dialed my grandmother's number. Christopher would call her to let the family know what was happening. The operator asked me to hold; it seemed as if everyone in the nation was on the telephone, trying to get through to loved ones. I felt the familiar panic steal my breath as I waited for a connection. Finally, I heard my grandmother's voice.

"He's fine. He's okay. They might have to move him out. He might be called to help somewhere in some way, but he's fine, Christine. He called and told us he was fine."

I spoke with my grandmother for a few more minutes. Boston was evacuating its tallest buildings. Schools were closing. Some workers were being sent home. All airplanes were grounded. The sky was silent and crystal clear. As I hung up the phone, I began to cry from relief. It was silly of me to worry about Christopher, I scolded myself. He was an adult. He stood 6'2" while I, his big sister, never hit 5'5". He could fit both of my hands into one of his. Christopher could take care of himself. But I realized at that moment that there is still a piece of my heart that will always run to try to protect him, no matter how big he may be or where in the world he is located. That same piece will always remember the five-year-old boy standing in the dark toy store with the pirate ship clutched to his chest, saying, "I knew if I just waited here, Christine, you would find me."

Christine Walsh

My Sister, My Enemy, My Friend

If your sister is in a tearing hurry to go out and cannot catch your eye, she's wearing your best sweater.

Pam Brown

It is eerily ironic that two people who share the same genetic makeup can be so drastically different while sustaining such a mutual dislike of one another. Sure, we have the same plain, straight brown hair, freckled noses and bright blue eyes. However, apart from that, it seems we are two complete and total opposites, two sparring discordant mortals absurdly sharing the same mother and father. Until a few years ago, I thought there existed only one phrase to adequately describe the situation of my sister and me: dumb luck. Now that we've both grown a little, I realize we are much more alike than anyone ever knew, and our relationship has transformed into a bond deeper than any I'll ever know.

I guess it's just the way we were raised. We were always very competitive. She was successful at everything she attempted, and I was always five years behind, hopelessly trying to catch up. I resented her for her excessive achievements: the way she always won the science fairs, the way she always received such glowing report cards, the way she always exhibited such poise and self-control in her sophisticated, mature demeanor. Wildness and obnoxiousness were my claims to fame, and my sister bitterly despised my annoying quest to be the constant center of attention. Growing up, we had more than our share of fights. She would give me bruises, then buy my silence with a Barbie doll. At night, I would sneak in and steal her stuffed animals. For thirteen years, we were literally enemies next door, every day providing a new and devious battle in our quest to conquer one another.

As I became a teenager, the gulf between us grew, and that tumultuous year that she was a high-school senior and I had just entered the seventh grade became the most arduous trial I'm sure my parents have ever endured. She was afflicted with near-adult conceit and I was tortured by post-child insecurity. Between the two of us, enough screaming and hair-pulling occurred to scar anyone for life. We both strived for the attention of our parents yet we both pushed it away, competing in a sport where neither of us knew the rules or even where the finish line was. To keep the peace, we became mutes in each other's presence. Acknowledging the tension but savoring the silence, we tried to avoid each other altogether and became absorbed in other activities to stay away from home. We were like two warring armies building a wall to temporarily stave off battle.

I don't really know exactly what happened that caused us to come together. There isn't one particular incident or event that sparked our reconciliation, just a process that slowly unfolded as she developed a life away at college and I developed my own life in high school. Maybe it was that we both matured, or that we finally reached a point where five years didn't make such a big difference in our ages. I'm not really sure, nor do I care. Ironically, now she's the only one with whom I share all my secrets, all my insecurities and all my most fervent dreams. She laughs at my unwavering, silly, boy infatuations, and helped me cry over my first broken heart. We've spent many a night discussing life, expectations, our parents and even God. It turns out that although our actions are incredibly different, our thoughts are remarkably the same. We are both afraid of failure. We are both afraid to be alone.

My sister is neither the enemy nor simply just another human being. She is a woman, a loyal companion and ultimately a part of me. She knows my life better than any other person in this world, and she has accepted me, weaknesses and all. Sometimes we laugh at the way we used to act and reminisce about the evil pranks we used to play on each other. There is an intangible bond that binds us together. Unfortunately, we didn't discover it until we lived apart. We are two souls sharing the same heart and forever holding hands.

Allison Thorp

Always There for Me

She takes my hand and leads me along paths I would not have dared explore alone.

Maya V. Patel

I look around my room, and I see hundreds of faces. All over my walls are pictures of smiling moments, dramatic moments, teasing and playful moments. They scream with character or whisper of adventure or mischief. They each have their own personality, but in many of them there is the same person standing right next to me, many times holding me up. She is my identical twin sister, Sarah.

Sarah and I have never been apart for more than forty-eight hours. From the moment we were born, she has been the bigger one, the stronger one, the one most likely to take the brunt of a conflict and shield me from pain. We have gone through every aspect of our lives together, but sometimes that doesn't make life all peaches and rose-buds.

Two years ago, Sarah and I started to board a plane for our cross-country trip to California. I thought my heart was going to pound right through my chest. I could hear the blood rushing through my veins as I saw my parents' faces get swallowed up in the hustle and bustle of the terminal. As we sat in our seats, it felt like adrenaline alone was going to propel me right off the runway. Just then, I felt a warm pressure on my hand. Sarah was holding it firmly while gazing out the window.

"Just grab my hand, Kelley," she said reassuringly. "It'll be okay." And I believed her. I knew she would never lie to me. I knew that, after it all, she would be there for me.

We've gone through even rougher times together. I was there right beside her last summer when her boyfriend of fourteen months broke things off so abruptly that neither she nor I had known it was coming. I watched her sob on the weather-beaten picnic table in the backyard and knew I couldn't just stand there. I could hear her cries between birdcalls and mosquitoes buzzing as I ventured out onto the grass. Coming along beside her, I felt my heart tear as I saw her red, swollen eyes and clenched fists. I pulled out a wad of Kleenex and offered it to her.

We didn't say anything for a while. I just sat beside her on the picnic table and listened to her raspy breathing. Nobody else knows her breathing. They haven't listened to seventeen years of it at night, while she's reading or watching a movie. Every breath she takes is a sign of the most profound and special friendship I've got. Having a sister as a friend has meant the world to me, but having a soul mate who knows every nuance of my spirit has allowed me to survive, to live and to be happy. She's there for me, and I have tried to be there for her, too. I think my sister says it best in the heart-shaped stained-glass sun catcher she gave me years ago. It says simply: "Chance made us sisters; hearts made us friends."

Kelley Youmans

The Bigger Man

Although I am the younger brother, I have always felt like my brother's keeper. Even now that Brian is seventeen and I am sixteen, I still watch out for him because, though chronologically I lag behind, my parents have encouraged me to take the nurturing role.

You are probably thinking that my brother is either mentally or physically handicapped—he is neither. I'm not sure if his "nature" was born or created. My mom has treated him like fine china ever since his birth. Maybe it's because there were problems with his delivery. She often recounts how the umbilical cord became wrapped around poor Brian's neck, and how he could have strangled on it had the doctor not rescued him with a Caesarean delivery. Although Brian went full-term, his tiny size reflected his future fragility within the family.

After Brian's birth, my mom grew more religious. She made all sorts of deals with God to watch over her tiny infant in exchange for her spiritual devotion. A year later, I was born. I was the quintessential bouncing baby boy. From the way my mom describes it, I practically walked home from the hospital and was eating solid food by the time I was a month old—probably raw steaks.

My mom saw my larger size and strong constitution as a sign from God that I was to be a kind of guardian angel for my older brother, Brian. It was not at all strange to see me reminding Brian to tie his shoes, or asking the waiter for another glass of water for him. No one ever thought our reverse relationship was odd, since by the age of five I was a head taller than him anyway.

I could never leave the house without my mom telling me to drag Brian along. He was smaller and fit in better, size-wise, among my group of friends. But defending and protecting him became tiresome. And then there were those luscious desserts my mom would bring home to fatten up poor little Brian. I would watch him longingly while he delicately sipped at chocolate milkshakes and critically picked at the strawberry cheesecakes I would have gladly scarfed down if given half the chance. And when my hand, through no power of my own, would drift toward a tempting slice, my mom would reprimand me, saying, "That's for Brian. You don't need that."

And so, though I loved my older brother, I began to resent him as well.

One day our school sponsored a pumpkin-carving contest. First prize was one-hundred dollars, and I knew just how I would spend it. There was a brand-new Sega game—Dungeons and Dragons—that I was dying to own. Realizing that my birthday and Christmas were nowhere in sight, I decided that the first-place stash definitely had to land in my pocket.

I ran out to the market and picked out the nicest pumpkin I could find. Then I set out to draw on the most gruesome face. In my third-grade mind, I had created a Pumpkin Freddy Krueger, of sorts. Now all I had to do was carve the face. That's when it dawned on me. With my big clumsy mitts I'd surely screw it up. I thought of Brian's smaller delicate hands and knew he was the man for the job.

I pleaded with Brian to carve the pumpkin, but wise fourth-grade businessman that he was, he asked for a cut.

"How does eighty-twenty grab you, Bri?"

"You mean eighty for you and only twenty for me? Forget it. It's either fifty-fifty or nothing."

Quickly doing the math in my head, I figured out that even if I split the first prize fifty-fifty, I'd still have enough cash for the game—and I knew this pumpkin had to win the grand prize. It was just so awesome. So, I gave in to Brian's demands.

With skillful hands Brian carved the blood-slashed face, and then we sat back to admire our handiwork. Together, we had created the goriest Halloween pumpkin ever, which I was sure nobody could deny.

Then the unexpected happened: We came in second. Unfortunately, second prize was only fifty dollars, and I needed every penny of that to buy the game. The day of the awards ceremony, the principal handed over the money to me because Brian was home sick with some fragile kid's illness like a cold or something equally pathetic.

God, I thought to myself, *if he really wanted to win, he would have been here today. And I need the whole check to pay for the game.* I was able to justify stealing the cash from under poor Brian's runny nose. With hardly a thought, I ran over to my friend Glenn's house and his mom drove us out to the mall to buy the game. I felt no guilt that night as Glenn and I pounded away on our controllers having the time of our lives.

That night when I got home, I found Brian lying on the couch watching TV.

"Did we win?" he asked.

I tried not to flinch as I stared down at his cheesecake-eating, milkshake-sipping face, and I answered, "No."

I hid the game over at Glenn's and never told anyone in

my family about it. I thought it was pretty pathetic anyway that Brian never found out. What a dork.

As Brian got older, he began to loosen up a little and Mom did, too. He actually had a growth spurt, and though I'm still a head taller than him, he's wider from side to side now—guess those milkshakes finally caught up with him.

With Brian's hearty physique and persistent begging, Mom even gave in to allowing him to attend college away from home. I played my usual role in helping him pack, although I had mixed emotions about seeing him go. I'd miss having the geek around.

As I rifled through one of his desk drawers, a photo of our gruesome pumpkin dropped to the floor. We both laughed as we looked at the ridiculous face we'd thought was so frightening. Then Brian said, "And we actually thought that squash was going to make us rich. We didn't even win third prize."

A kind of guilt rose up in my throat, and I felt a confession of sorts was needed.

"Brian, uh . . . hate to admit this, but we kinda did win. In fact, we kinda won second place."

"Huh? Is that so?" he said scratching his head. Brian rustled through his desk drawer again and pulled out another photo of our pumpkin with a blue satin second-prize ribbon flanked across its bloodstained face.

"I took this the day after the contest, Worm Brains. What did you think, I didn't know? I was the photographer for the school newsletter, Einstein."

"What? You actually knew and didn't say anything? Why?"

Brian looked down at his half-packed suitcase, and then up at me. "Don't you think I knew how Mom always forced you to watch out for me, and don't you think it made me feel really small? I'm supposed to be the bigger brother, Numb Nuts."

Actually, I'd never thought about how Brian might feel; it just always felt like I was the one being put out. Everyone always seemed to care more about Brian. Everyone needed to protect poor, pathetic Brian—I was just the big, dumb bodyguard for hire.

"I wanted, just once, to do the same for you," Brain said, interrupting my thoughts. "Just once, I wanted to be the bigger man."

"It always looked to me like it would be way better being smaller," I confessed. "I wanted to be the one who everyone wanted to take care of."

"You're such a jerk," Brian said, shaking his head. "Do you know how lousy it feels when everyone thinks you're so lame you can't even take care of yourself? It sucks!"

We sat silently on Brian's bed, just staring at one another. As dense as we were, something finally sunk in. How pathetic. We'd each lived our lives secretly wishing to be the other.

"I'm sorry, Bri," I mumbled.

"For what? About that pumpkin? Forget it."

And then another uncomfortable silence lay upon us. I wanted to tell Brian how much I loved him and how cool I thought he was. But I felt really dumb saying it out loud. Then Brian kneeled over, scooped up his football and threw it at my head. I lunged for him and pounded him in the gut. This was the way we communicated our understanding.

C. S. Dweck

6

LEARNING AND LESSONS

I am always ready to learn, but I do not always like being taught.

Winston Churchill

Challenge Days

Shared joy is double joy.
Shared sorrow is half sorrow.

Swedish Proverb

My name is Tony. I always looked out for myself because I thought no one else would, and I thought it would always be that way. That changed the day I got out of class for something called Challenge Day.

The people running it had big hopes of helping us join together and making us leaders. I just wanted to get out of class. I figured that after signing in I would sneak out.

In the school gym, I found myself sitting in a big circle, face to face with a hundred students that no one could have paid me to spend the day with. I was keeping up my front, my cool, but I was kind of nervous. I'm used to either sitting hidden in the back of a classroom waiting for a break, or skipping school and hanging with the guys. I wasn't used to not knowing what was going to happen.

I made fun of how a bunch of kids were dressed and of a girl who was fat. Some of the girls had worn pajamas and brought stuffed animals. Pretty stupid, I thought.

The day started with each of us standing up and saying our names into a microphone "loud and proud." A bunch of kids were really shy, but since I rap sometimes, I acted really cool when it was my turn. No one knew there was a lump in my throat. You see, I'm from a tough neighborhood, and showing your weakness only makes you a target. I was a target when I was real young, both for my brothers and for the people who called themselves my friends. We sure didn't know how to be friends, though. Fighting and putting each other down were a normal way of life.

Anyway, we started playing these games I thought were really childish. I hung back a little with my buddies, acting cool and not wanting to play like a little kid. After a couple of games, though, it didn't seem like anyone else was hanging back, and they were all having a good time. I thought, "Why not me?" I have to admit that I was playing a little rough, but it beat sitting on the edge.

What happened next was almost unbelievable. Carl, one of the only guys who is more feared and respected than me at school, was helping one of the leaders demonstrate how to give hugs. Everyone was laughing at first, but it was getting harder and harder to put anyone down that day. The leaders kept teaching us to open our hearts and minds, to share our true feelings and to give put-ups instead of put-downs. It wasn't what I was used to.

Then we did an exercise called "the power shuffle." Before the game started, the leaders talked about oppression. "Yeah," I thought, "like they really know what it's like to be oppressed. Here I am, a young Latino growing up in a white society. I get harassed and pushed around every day by store owners, teachers and all these adults who think I'm a gangster just because of the color of my skin. Yeah, I act hard, but what am I supposed to do when I have to watch my friends drop from drive-bys?"

The leaders said we had to be silent, to make it safe for everyone. They called out broad categories and asked us to cross over the line if we fit into the category. I was still snickering in my buddy's ear as the first few were called out.

But the leaders meant it about being quiet. One of the adults softly put his hand on me and said, "You'll want them to respect you; please respect them."

Category after category was called out. In silence, group after group, people crossed the line. Then a topic was called that I fit into, and I figured I would be the only one who experienced this kind of pain. "Cross the line if you've ever been hit, beaten or abused, in any way." I walked heavy in my shoes. Looking straight down as I walked, I turned around, having a hard time not laughing to cover what was going on inside me.

But as I looked up, half the group was walking with me. We stood together in silence, looked into each other's eyes, and for the first time in my life, I felt like I wasn't alone.

One by one we dropped our masks. I saw that these people, whom I had judged before, were in reality very much like me. Like me, they, too, knew how it felt to be hurt.

I walked back across the line. My friend tried to joke with me but it didn't seem right any more. Another topic was called, one where all the women and girls crossed. I had never seen before how much men and boys disrespect and hurt women. I became more uncomfortable as I noticed tears appearing in many of my friends' eyes.

We crossed the line next for having lost someone close to us in gang violence. So many of us crossed that line. It just wasn't right! I started feeling really angry inside, and tears were coming to my eyes. The leaders kept saying, "When the tears are on the outside, the inside is healing," and, "It takes a strong man to cry."

I had to make the choice of whether or not to have the courage to show my tears. I was still scared of being called names, but the tears came out. I cried, and with my tears I proved that I was a strong man.

Before we left that day, each of us stood up and shared our experiences. I stood up, again not sure if I should fight the tears or not. The leader encouraged me to look out at the group and ask if it was okay for a man to cry. So I did.

Then each person stood up in front of their chairs to show they respected me for showing my tears. Amazed, I started talking. I said I was sorry to a few of those people I had judged and pushed around in the halls because I thought they had it so much better than me. With tears in their eyes, they came up to me, one by one, and gave me a hug. Now I know what it is really like to share love with someone. I hope I can do this with my dad some day.

Here was a day I thought I was cutting from school, but instead I found myself telling the people I hurt that I was sorry, and people were saying the same thing to me. It was like we were all one family and we never knew it until that day. It wasn't magic—we just looked at each other in a different light.

Now it is up to us. Do we look through these eyes for just one day, or do we have the courage to remember that most people are just like us, and help others learn that it is safe to be themselves?

As told to Andrew Tertes

The Bat

The best part about running, for me, is the finish. The moment when, flushed and out of breath, I reach my destination: my backyard. Ironically, I have run full circle, ending up where I began. Yet, I have also taken a positive step forward in my life, determined and acted out by no one other than myself. My decision, my action.

As I sit and wait for my breathing to slow and the rush to subside, I wish upon a star. "Star light, star bright . . ." A bat flits across my path of vision and my eyes follow it. Without any warning, the bat suddenly swerves and changes direction. It has changed its path forever.

And now, having been interrupted, my wish seems futile and absurd. I am filled with a rushing understanding of the part I play in my own life.

I am not just a bystander. My life is not to be controlled by the stars, but by me, and me alone. Like the bat, I am free to choose my own path, however haphazard and illogical it might appear to be.

Bryony Blackwood

Lessons in Baseball

There are always two choices, two paths to take. One is easy. And its only reward is that it's easy.

Unknown

As an eleven-year-old, I was addicted to baseball. I listened to baseball games on the radio. I watched them on TV. The books I read were about baseball. I took baseball cards to church in hopes of trading with other baseball card junkies. My fantasies? All about baseball.

I played baseball whenever and wherever I could. I played organized or sandlot. I played catch with my brother, with my father, with friends. If all else failed, I bounced a rubber ball off the porch stairs, imagining all kinds of wonderful things happening to me and my team.

It was with this attitude that I entered the 1956 Little League season. I was a shortstop. Not good, not bad. Just addicted.

Gordon was not addicted. Nor was he good. He moved into our neighborhood that year and signed up to play baseball. The kindest way of describing Gordon's baseball skills is to say that he didn't have any. He couldn't catch. He couldn't hit. He couldn't throw. He couldn't run.

In fact, Gordon was afraid of the ball.

I was relieved when the final selections were made and Gordon was assigned to another team. Everyone had to play at least half of each game, and I couldn't see Gordon improving my team's chances in any way. Too bad for the other team.

After two weeks of practice, Gordon dropped out. My friends on his team laughed when they told me how their coach directed two of the team's better players to walk Gordon into the woods and have a chat with him. "Get lost" was the message that was delivered, and "get lost" was the one that was heard.

Gordon got lost.

That scenario violated my eleven-year-old sense of justice, so I did what any indignant shortstop would do. I tattled. I told my coach the whole story. I shared the episode in full detail, figuring my coach would complain to the League office and have Gordon returned to his original team. Justice and my team's chances of winning would both be served.

I was wrong. My coach decided that Gordon needed to be on a team that wanted him—one that treated him with respect, one that gave everyone a fair chance to contribute according to their own ability.

Gordon became my team member.

I wish I could say Gordon got the big hit in the big game with two outs in the final inning, but it didn't happen. I don't think Gordon even hit a foul ball the entire season. Baseballs hit in his direction (right field) went over him, by him, through him, or off him.

It wasn't that Gordon didn't get help. The coach gave him extra batting practice and worked with him on his fielding, all without much improvement.

I'm not sure if Gordon learned anything from my coach that year. I know I did. I learned to bunt without tipping off my intention. I learned to tag up on a fly if there were less than two outs. I learned to make a smoother pivot around second base on a double play.

I learned a lot from my coach that summer, but my most important lessons weren't about baseball. They were about character and integrity. I learned that everyone has worth, whether they can hit .300 or .030. I learned that we all have value, whether we can stop the ball or have to turn and chase it. I learned that doing what is right, fair and honorable is more important than winning or losing.

It felt good to be on that team that year. I'm grateful that man was my coach. I was proud to be his shortstop and his son.

Chick Moorman

Terri Jackson

On the first day of sixth grade, I sat in my quiet homeroom class and observed all the people who I would eventually befriend and possibly graduate with. I glanced around the room and noticed that the majority of the middle-class kids were dressed in their nicest first-day outfits. My glance stopped on a shy-looking girl in the back of the room. She wore a stained, yellow plaid shirt with a pair of frayed jeans that had obviously had several owners before her. Her hair was unusually short and unwashed. She wore dress shoes that were once white, and frilly pink socks that had lost their frill with too many wearings. I caught myself thinking, "That's disgusting. Doesn't she know what a bathtub is?" As I looked around, I figured others were probably thinking the same thing.

The teacher began checking the attendance, each person casually lifting his or her hand as names were called in turn.

"Terri Jackson?" the teacher asked, following the roll with her finger. Silence. "Um, Terri Jackson?"

Finally we heard a meek answer from the back of the room, followed by the sound of ripping cloth. We all shifted in our seats to see what had happened.

"Scary Terri ripped the armpit of her shirt!" one boy joked.

"Eww, I bet it's a hundred years old!" another girl commented. One comment after another brought a roar of laughter.

I was probably laughing the loudest. Sadly, making Terri feel insecure made me feel secure and confident. It was a good break from the awkward silence and uncomfortable first-day jitters.

Terri Jackson was the joke of the whole sixth grade that year. If we had nothing to talk about, Terri's trip through the lunchroom was an entertaining conversation starter. Her grandma-looking dress, missing front tooth and stained gym clothes kept us mocking and imitating her for hours.

At my twelfth birthday party, ten giggly, gossipy girls were playing Truth or Dare, a favorite party game. We had just finished a Terri Jackson discussion. It was my turn at the game.

"Umm . . . Sydney! Truth or Dare?" one of my friends asked.

"How about a dare? Bring it on. I'll do anything." Oh, if only I'd known what she was about to say.

"Okay, I dare you to invite Terri Jackson over to your house next Friday for two whole hours!"

"Two whole hours?! Please ask something else, *please*!" I begged. "How could anybody do that?" But my question was drowned out by a sea of giggly girls slapping their hands over their mouths and rolling on the floor, trying to contain their laughter.

The next day, I cautiously walked up to Terri as if her body odor was going to make me fall over dead. My friends huddled and watched from a corner to see if I would follow through with the brave dare.

I managed to choke out, "Hey Scary—I mean Terri—you want to come over for two hours Friday?" I didn't see her face light up because I had turned to my friends and made a gagging expression. When I was satisfied with their laughter of approval, I turned back to Terri. Terri's face was buried in her filthy hands; she was crying. I couldn't stand it. Half of me felt the strongest compassion for her, but the other half wanted to slap her for making me look so cruel and heartless. That was exactly what I was being.

"What's got you all upset? All I did was invite you over," I whispered, trying not to show my concern.

She looked up and watched my eyes for what seemed like forever. "Really?" That was all she could say. Her seldom-heard voice almost startled me.

"I guess so, if you're up to it." My voice sounded surprisingly sincere. I'd never seen her flash her toothless smile so brightly. The rest of the day I had a good feeling, and I was not dreading the two-hour visit as I had before. I was almost looking forward to it.

Friday rolled around quickly. My time with Terri passed by in a flash as the two hours slipped into four hours, and I found myself actually enjoying her company. We chatted about her family and her battles with poverty. We discovered that we both played violin, and my favorite part of the afternoon occurred when she played the violin for me. I was amazed by how beautifully she played.

I would love to tell you that Terri and I became best friends and that from then on I ignored all my other friends' comments. But that's not how it happened. While I no longer participated in the Terri bashings and even tried to defend her at times, I didn't want to lose everyone else's acceptance just to gain Terri's.

Terri disappeared after the sixth grade. No one is sure what happened to her. We think that she may have transferred to a different school because of how cruelly the kids treated her. I still think about her sometimes and wonder what she's doing. I guess all I can do is hope that she is being accepted and loved wherever she is.

I realize now how insecure and weak I was during that sixth-grade year. I participated in the cruel, heartless Terri-bashing sessions because they seemed kind of funny in a distorted way. But they were only funny because they falsely boosted my own self-confidence; I felt bigger by making someone else feel smaller. I know now that true confidence is not proven by destroying another's self-esteem, but rather, by having the strength to stand up for the Terri Jacksons of the world.

Sydney Fox

My Most Embarrassing Moment

[AUTHOR'S NOTE TO HER MOM AND DAD: *I'm sorry you have to find out about this at the same time all of America does. I never told anyone.*]

Honor student, tennis team player, Spanish Club president. Sunday school teacher assistant, Swing Choir piano accompanist. Although these publicly recognized accomplishments of my teenage years went on to influence my life in many ways, there was one particular group activity I participated in that had an even greater impact on me: Mustard Gang Member.

The fall of 1977 found me enrolled as a freshman in the school system I had attended since kindergarten. My student file over the last ten years could be summed up with positive comments such as "consistently above average," "enjoys extracurricular activities" and "cooperates with teachers and fellow classmates." No suspensions. No detentions. Basically, a model student. However, within a total time period of approximately one hour, this trademark behavior would fly right out the window (at the speed of sound).

Three of my lifelong girlfriends—who would fall under a fairly close ditto description of that above—caught up to me after school on a Friday afternoon. One of them had just received her driver's license and was going cruising in a nearby town to celebrate. She asked if I would like to come along. (Rhetorical question.) The final bell was sounding as we piled into an older model Dodge Charger on its last leg of life. Regardless of its condition, it had a full tank of gas and the ability to get us from Point A to Point B.

Within minutes of leaving the school parking lot, we were on the open highway. As I look back now, that highway was pretty significant. It not only separated two towns, it separated those of us in the car from the people who knew us and the people who didn't. We became daring.

When the novelty of just driving around wore off, someone suggested it might be fun to squirt mustard on parked cars as we drove past them. *(Author's sensible reaction twenty years later: WHAT?!)* A unanimous agreement must have followed, because all four of us stood beside each other in the checkout line where the bottle of mustard was ultimately purchased.

Loading back into the car, each of our faces looked as though we couldn't believe what we were doing. We couldn't. Four kids, four clean records. *Lost time was about to be made up for.*

We decided that the person sitting by the passenger's side window would be the Designated Squirter, while the others in the car would be responsible for choosing the target ahead. Since I was cowardly, trying to hide in a corner of the backseat, I thought this sounded swell. Feeling my guilt would be somewhat lessened if I didn't actually *touch* the mustard bottle, I thought. I was off the hook. A nervous sigh of relief was escaping me until the words "and we'll pull over every other block and switch seats so it will be fair." Hook re-inserted.

The "talk" in the car proved to be more productive than the "action" as the first and second girls took their turn in the passenger seat, both chickening out at the last second, squealing, "I can't!" Before I knew it, the car had stalled and it was me who was climbing in beside the driver. Sliding my sweaty palms up and down the bottle's sides, the target was being pointed out to me, loudly and with demanding encouragement. The attack was to be launched on a little red Volkswagen up ahead, fast approaching. "Do it! Do it! Do it!" my friends chanted. . . . *And I almost did.* But, as was the case with the girls before, feathers grew from within me and we soon sped past the car, leaving it as solid red as it had been when first spotted.

Since the driver couldn't take a respective turn as the shooter, we headed for home, the mischief supposedly ended. Just when we were nearing the highway, we passed two girls jogging, their hands moving up and down in front of them. Still looking for trouble, we interpreted their innocent actions. "Hey! They just gave us the finger!" And of course, if we had been needlessly insulted, they certainly would have to pay. Simple as that.

Within seconds, they were jogging into a Kmart parking lot. . . . And we were right behind them. Jumping out of the car, we ran toward our unsuspecting prey yelling, "Get 'em!" We did. Well, *I* did. After all, there was only one bottle, and it was my turn. Silently, they just stood there.

My hearing must have been the last of my senses to fail, for the car door did not slam shut behind me without the words from one of these mustard-covered strangers ringing in my ears: "That wasn't very funny, Rochelle." Clear words. Echoing words. Rochelle. Rochelle. Rochelle. Not only had I just left two people covered with mustard back in a parking lot, but at least one of them wasn't a stranger.

Although no one in the car physically recognized either victim, there was no doubt among any of us that the voice that just spoke was a familiar one. But whose? The longest minute of my life followed until I figured it out: *Miss Greatens, MY TYPING TEACHER!*

Miss Greatens, fresh out of college, was committed to making a strong professional impression on the business class students she taught. Her hair was always gathered on top of her head, large glasses covered her eyes and crisp business suits were her chosen attire. And yet outside of her work environment, she suddenly changed. Drastically. Her hair looked as though it grew a foot or so (since just this afternoon), she shrank a solid two inches (heels removed), contact lenses replaced glasses and her business suit was traded in for a sweatsuit. She no longer looked like Miss Greatens; she looked more like . . . well, *us!*

Situation assessment: WE HAD A PROBLEM. The Dodge Charger immediately went chasing back to the parking lot, but the joggers were nowhere in sight. Plan B was implemented. A telephone booth directory could provide her home address. Success. She lived right across from Kmart in an apartment complex.

Little did we know that Miss Greatens was doing some of her own phone referencing while we were trying to find her. First she called the school principal at home, then she called my parents. *(My life, as I knew it, was about to end.)* However, she hung up after the first two rings before anyone answered either call. She had decided to speak to us first.

And here we were.

Miss Greatens answered the door graciously, standing before us with mustard-stained clothes and tear-stained cheeks, wanting to hear what possible explanation warranted her pain. There was none. Absolutely none. What we had done was uncalled for. Our consciences made that perfectly clear as we poured out a flood of genuine remorse and tears to equal her own.

Then something extraordinary happened: *She forgave us.* Fully. Right there on the spot. She could have spoken to all of our parents about what happened, but didn't. She could have contacted school officials and sought stern reprimands for each of us, but didn't. And she could have held the incident over our heads for a very long time and reminded us of what we had done at will, but didn't.

Will we ever do anything like that again? NO WAY. You see, that is the power of forgiveness.

Rochelle M. Pennington

Firmer Ground

I'd had a crush on him for as long as I could remember. His sandy blond hair was to his shoulders. His eyes were brown, his skin pale. He was quiet, mild-mannered. Most of all, I was drawn to his smile—when I could coax it out of him. I was in junior high. He was in high school.

He was my friend's brother and, for some reason, I believed he was taboo. Maybe because I knew instinctively my friend would be angry if I ever started to see him. Or maybe I knew the age gap of three years would not sit well with my parents. Or maybe, more than anything, I was terrified he'd reject me.

So I kept my feelings as quiet as a cat hiding from a pack of dogs. But every time I saw him at my friend Tina's house, my heart beat hard and I could barely breathe. When I saw him walking up the street alone, I'd rush over to him and glow in his warmth. He'd wave, smile a weak hello and ask me how I was doing.

He was an artist and a good one, and the day he gave me a pen drawing of a seagull soaring through the sky, I was in my glory. I saw it as a symbol, a sign perhaps, of affection shown by an older boy who felt it wise to keep his love for me inside. Of course, it was more likely that he just felt sorry for such a gangly kid.

It didn't matter. I cherished his artwork and truly believed that he would be a great artist someday. If only I had such talent, I'd moan. He'd always tell me that I probably did have a lot of talent. I just hadn't found it yet.

Somewhere as we were growing older and suffering the pangs of adolescence, Mike lost his ground. I'm not sure if he knew where to put his feet anymore. His family life was a disaster: a mentally ill mother, a father with a wicked second wife (at least that's how the children saw her) and a new baby who took all the interest away from three other kids.

Whenever I walked by his home, there was always a man—often a different man—parked in a car across the street from Mike's house. It happened so often that I began to wonder what was going on. I began to ask questions of my friends. I learned that my sweet, reserved Mike had turned into a high school drug dealer. Not the small kind of drug dealer. He was a big fish and according to my friends, he was in trouble. Someone was closing in on him—the police or the creeps who got him involved in the first place.

I knew that a lot of kids dabbled in drugs—mostly marijuana. But no one, and I mean no one, took the risk of dealing. The odds of getting hurt or busted were far too great in this middle-class neighborhood. I often wondered what led Mike there. Did he hate his parents? Did he feel lost? Did he want payback time for his dad remarrying and leaving his mom? Who knows what went on in his brain. I just wished he had talked to me because I really cared about him. The problem was that he didn't care. And I was too afraid to go to Mike and confront him about whether he was selling drugs.

When the knock on the door came, I looked out the

balcony of my house and saw one of my neighbors standing there. "I thought you and your family should know I found Mike in the canyon this morning. My sons and I were walking there and I saw Mike bowing as though he were praying. It didn't look too good."

Our neighbor had held his young boys back as he investigated. Mike was dead. He had hung himself from a tree, and had died in a kneeling position on the ground, his head slumped forward. The news pounded my face as if a block of cement had struck. I thought I would pass out, but instead, I was sobbing. Within the hour, I raced up to Mike's to see how Tina was.

She was sitting on her bed, just staring out at empty space. I would learn later that she was in shock. In a dull voice, she explained that she and her older brother, Gary, had known that Mike was dealing drugs. After Mike's body was discovered, Gary went into Mike's room and cleaned out Mike's top drawer before the police came. There, tucked underneath a few shirts, was every drug imaginable: LSD, cocaine, pot and an abundance of colorful pills. Soon after, Tina ran away. It took us hours to find her.

My parents tried to explain why Mike died. But they couldn't. They didn't even know he was a dealer. They didn't know the ugly things we kids faced going to school every day. It was a trying time not only because Mike died, but because I was shocked to peel away the layers and find a Mike I had never known. Or maybe he was that kind, sweet boy who let his difficult life suck him into a world of deceit, fast bucks and danger.

To this day, I always wonder if he really killed himself or if some other drug dealers helped him along the way. It was just too odd that he had supposedly hung himself from a thin tree limb but was kneeling, his weight supported by the earth.

I will never know the answer. But I do know this: He

was a good artist. I kept that drawing he gave me for years after, always looking at it with wonder and admiration, wishing I could sketch that way.

I also know that along the way Mike lost his ground, but he gave me a lot to think about, and what I thought about gave me strength. My family moved to the East Coast my first year of high school. My new friends were just beginning to experiment with drugs, and there was tremendous peer pressure for me to go along.

But by now, I felt old and weary when it came to drugs. Been there, done that, seen what they can do. I decided I wanted the chance to know what I was going to be in the future. Mike had given me some firm ground to stand on.

Diana L. Chapman

What I Wish I'd Known Sooner

For the past year or two, I have devoted a section of my home page on the Internet to a list entitled "What I Wish I'd Known Sooner." Since I am seventeen, there are a lot of stupid things I do that make me wish I had already known not to do them! Anyone can add to this list—I have received additions from all over the world, by people of all ages. I often add to it myself (after the fact)!

Some are lighthearted, some are serious, all are very true. Here are a few of the gems:

- Don't drink grape juice while wearing a white shirt and driving to school.
- Don't let your life wait for other people.
- Dropping a cellular phone into a bathtub of water kinda kills the phone.
- Your mother will find out if you dye your hair purple.
- You haven't really lived until you've gotten a 48 on an Advanced Placement U.S. History test.
- Don't ever fall in love with someone who is more than one thousand miles away from you. It usually doesn't work.
- Milk crates make boring pets.

- If it hurts, DON'T DO IT AGAIN!
- That which does not kill you will ultimately make you stronger.
- Speaking in public gets easier with practice.
- Don't sprint around a pool if you're trying to impersonate Jim from Huck Finn.
- Ten years from now most of what we freak out about won't make any difference.
- All that's gold doesn't glisten.
- Zits always pop up when you really can't afford for them to pop up.
- Always stay after class because that's where connections are made.
- When in doubt, duck. When certain, don't bother, 'cause you're already screwed.
- While driving a car through a gate, always, ALWAYS make sure the gate is open! The consequences might be fatal to your car.
- If you're not living (I mean really living), you're dead already.
- Never pierce your belly button in the dark.
- Just because someone flirts with you incessantly doesn't necessarily mean he or she likes you.
- If your calculus teacher tells you to quit talking after a test or he'll give you a zero for your test grade, he means it. Really.
- Sometimes smart people can do very, very stupid things.
- Being nice to people will get you far.
- The one person you can truly love is often right in front of you.
- Never, ever, EVER let a member of the opposite sex make you compromise your standards. Never.
- Nothing is ever too good to be true (said by Michael Faraday).
- If you start to like a girl, her roommate will immediately start liking you.

- Parents aren't around forever, and you need to treasure them while they are.
- Don't take the SAT twice if you already have a good score in the first place.
- Never do something if the risk is greater than the reward.
- Think carefully before you act.
- Dreaming and doing go hand in hand.
- Life moves fast, but not so fast that you can't slow down to enjoy it.
- Instead of waiting for life to get better, do something about it.
- You REALLY should do what needs to be done NOW, and not later. Procrastination is the easiest way, but not the most profitable.
- If your intuition is telling you not to do something, then don't. Your intuition is not stupid!
- Cereal is a vital staple food for all college students. Who cares how ridiculous you look eating it at 7:30 P.M.?
- If he doesn't respect you, then he's not worth any of your time.
- Learn to play an electric guitar: young women really dig it.
- Don't juggle knives unless you're really, really good at it.
- If at first you don't succeed, try again. Then give up. No sense being ridiculous about it.
- Sticking things up your nose isn't the smartest idea in the world.
- You can't light fireworks in the basement and not get caught.
- Hair is flammable. *Very* flammable.
- Never ever trust your friend with a pair of scissors against your hair.
- Dyeing hair strawberry blond that is already strawberry blond makes it turn strawberry pink.
- White dogs and black pants don't mix.
- God doesn't make junk!

- Someday you will look back on this and it will all seem funny.
- You never know when you're making a memory.
- The heart does heal and you will love like this again—except that when you do, you'll deny that you ever loved like this before.
- Nothing matters if you don't have loved ones to share it with. Your siblings are incredibly precious. If you don't know this now, you will—trust me!
- If you can laugh at yourself, you are going to be fine.
- If you allow others to laugh with you, you'll be great!
- Kissing is the most fun thing. Dancing is almost as fun.

Meredith Rowe

A Wider Classroom

Our white van meandered its way through the broken West Virginia landscape and pulled up alongside Jim's avocado-colored house. As the doors opened, we poured out with hammers in hand. We were eight teenagers on a week-long service project to repair the homes of the less fortunate residing in the Appalachian mountains. The area seemed to contradict itself, for it held so much beauty yet housed so much poverty. Maybe we hailed ourselves as being able to serve those people in need; I do not think we ever imagined that what they could give us would perhaps be more valuable then any services we could render.

We rotated jobs as we basked in the southern sun; some of us scraped and painted windows, while others stained the deck or worked on the roof. All the while Jim sat in a lawn chair observing us: the kindest of old men, only too sorry that he could not labor alongside us on the ladders. We passed the time with inside jokes and songs, truly enjoying ourselves regardless of the tedium of treating window after window as Jim just silently observed.

As the clock neared noon, we took our lunch break

in the shade of a small tree in Jim's front yard. Sam, our moderator, planted Jim's chair beside us and announced that since he was eager to help in any way possible, Jim would lead us in a before-meal prayer. He kept it succinct and we all began to eat.

"Let me tell you a story. . . ." he then began. And from the pit of his humble heart he began to unravel his eighty-some-odd years for us. He was a school teacher and a baseball coach who had a loyal dog named Pretty-Face. He told of old hunting expeditions in the mountains where his life was almost lost to a bear, and he talked of conquering a rattlesnake, even showing us the rattles.

Then his cavernous eyes just wandered off as if he was no longer talking solely for our benefit, but more for his own. He described that day his dog died, as fat tears rolled down his weathered cheeks and he gripped the end of his cane. He recalled her loyalty to the end as with one last thump of the tail, looking up at him, Pretty-Face passed on. He remembered his wife gazing up at him much the same way seconds before her death.

He always affectionately called his wife "Mama," and he told of how she'd always stayed up until the small hours of the morning to bake the bread for the next day, while he, often tired from a long day of teaching or hunting, would retire to bed.

"Why didn't I just stay up with her?" he said in a distant voice as his eyes gazed beyond us. "Why couldn't I have just taken that extra time? Why?"

I remember how profoundly those words rang inside of me. Here was a man brimming with wisdom and reflections on his life, telling me to make the most of mine, to take that extra time with those I love. I was inspired; I was mesmerized by this extraordinary old man that I had thought I was helping. Jim's house was not a job at all, it was a classroom.

Kate McMahon
Submitted by Olive O'Sullivan

Children's Eyes

What kind of world is it my friend
  that little children see?
I wonder if they see God first
  because they just believe?

Do they see strength in caring eyes
  who watch them as they play—
or maybe love through gentle hands
  that guide them on their way?

Do you think they dream of future times
  when they would be a king—
  or just enjoy their present life
  while with their friends they sing?

Do they see the acts of kindness
  done for people who are poor?
Is the very best in everyone
  what they are looking for?

And when the day is over,
  as they close their eyes to sleep,

do they look forward to tomorrow
with its promises to keep?

If this is what the children see,
then it should be no surprise,
the world would be a better place
if we all had children's eyes.

Tom Krause

China's Story

China was fourteen, she gave what she got
She had many friends, who loved her a lot.
She loved them back, too, and would always be there,
But at prettier girls, she could not help but stare.

You must understand, that this group was a sight,
With their Cover Girl masks, and their shirts way too tight.
The guys hung around them, as though in a trance,
They were always the first ones who were asked to dance.

They seemed so secure, knowing just what to say.
And they said what they said in *the* coolest of ways
They never were seen without smiles on their faces.
Their clothes were real tight in all the right places.

You can see what I mean, when I say they were cool.
They were by far the sexiest girls in the school.

So China dreamed on, by day and by night,
Wishing her shirts would fit her as tight.
She wondered what contest she would have to win.
For, she'd give up the world, and her life to fit in.

She kept it a secret, hoping nobody knew,
But her friends caught on fast, and they found it
was true.
They tried to warn her of their pretentious way.
But China grew more and more stubborn each day.

As cool as they were, and as hot as their show,
They struggled in school and their grades were
quite low.
The groups of girls smoked, and were known to
drink beer,
But this was not stuff China wanted to hear.

So China tried hard to fit in with the clique,
She giggled at jokes that she knew were just sick.
She gave her attention to these cool girls alone,
She dressed just like them, in a style not her own.

China's old friends feared her drifting away,
They were losing her slowly, and didn't know what
to say.
They told China the truth, that the group was all fake,
But their words of advice, China just wouldn't take.

Why aren't they happy for me? China thought,
I don't act like myself, but now look where I've got.
She thought her old friends were jealous and tart,
She was truthfully happy, deep down in her heart.

China laughed at her old friends, along with her new,
They made fun of so many and smiled at so few.
China's new friends were cool, she was in with the clan,
She was treated like they were, she was happy again.

China's old group of friends sadly melted away,
They left China alone, but watched close every day.
They longed for her friendship, the warmth in her smile.
And hoped she'd miss them, and come back in a while.

But the jokes kept on coming, so the group with a sigh,
Turned their backs on harsh China, and walked silently by.
The pain was too deep and the torture too hard,
Her old friend's poor hearts had been torn out and scarred.

As all this did happen, the cool did their thing,
They giggled and gossiped and made actions sting.
They mutated China, the best that they could,
And taught her to be like a glamour girl should.

China went to parties, she got into fights,
She became really cool, but during the night,
She tried to discover just what was the scoop,
Why she wasn't content in her newly found group.

Then one day it hit her, came into her head,
That the answer was one that she truly did dread.
She had run ahead quickly and back round the bends,
She had left her companions, she had ditched her true friends.

China realized her error, "This group's not a sight,
With their makeup done perfect and hair fixed just right.
That's not what they look like, it's a lie what you see,
It's the Maybelline models they wish they could be."

Then early one night, around seven o'clock,
A girl opened her door to the sound of a knock.
Out in the cold, standing there in the rain,
Stood teary-eyed China, her old self again.

Neither one spoke, as she ushered her in,
The girl knew from experience, where China had been.
She had also once felt that those girls were the best,
But those long-ago thoughts, she had put down to rest.

The girls sat up talking for a good length of time,
China knew in her heart that she would be just fine.
She couldn't believe just how much she'd been blessed,
That her loving dear friends would forgive her like this.

This tale ends happy, but not all stories will,
Some friends aren't so forgiving, they go in for the kill.

China was lucky, but you may not be,
So choose your friends wisely, and help others see.

The moral is not to have one group of friends,
From a particular table, with particular trends.
It's to teach of the truth, that those girls tried to
hide,
You will always be cool if it comes from inside.

Libby Barnes

*Accent*uating Difference

Julia and I met in math class—right before lunch. We soon realized that we both hated word problems, both loved egg salad sandwiches and both thought Bobby Bisbee was the only boy we could ever kiss. During recesses, we were inseparable. One Friday, Julia had an idea. "Hey, let's make plans for the weekend," she said. "We could have a sleep-over or something."

We were both so excited we couldn't sit still during math, or any other class. But when the bell sounded the end of school, I suddenly got very nervous.

"Hi, Talia. How was school today?" my mom asked with a smile. Today, her warm and caring hello did not sound comforting. Instead, all I heard in the loving syllables was her thick foreign accent.

I was so embarrassed. Julia and I were no longer the same. The sound of my mom's voice made me feel like an outsider. What would Julia think?

I didn't have to wait long to find out. From across the schoolyard, I saw Julia pulling her mother towards us.

"Hello, I'm Julia's mother. I hear the girls want to get together this weekend."

"Oh, that sounds wonderful," my mom replied.

But all I heard was the *v* replacing the *w* and the roll of the *r*: *vonderrrful.*

I was mortified. Were they staring? Had Julia changed her mind? Did I dare look into her eyes? I did. She answered my unspoken fears with an excited smile while our moms exchanged phone numbers. That Sunday we went to the movies.

Years later, Julia and I sit on my bed talking. Graduation is only days away. Julia has plans of becoming a math and physics major and I no longer like egg salad sandwiches. Neither of us has ever kissed Bobby Bisbee. (There are others who have left much more permanent marks on our hearts and our lips.) My mom comes into my room to see what we're up to. We tell her of our plans to spend the afternoon with friends at the beach, and maybe see a movie after dinner. "That sounds wonderful," she replies.

I no longer hear the *v* replacing a *w* in her speech. But I think it still does. Somewhere in the passing of math classes and lunch recesses, I realized that it is my mom's cheerful, compassionate nature that people hear, and love. She shares my excitements and frustrations with overflowing compassion, tender words and rolling *r*s. Sometimes, she still reminds me that I am different. But I think that differences between people are as valuable as similarities. As my mom closes the door, I look at Julia and smile. Our friendship has been strengthened not only by our shared interests but also by our distinctly differing ones.

Daphna Renan

7

TOUGH STUFF

The soul would have no rainbow had the eyes no tears.

John Vance Cheney

Eternal Light

No winter lasts forever; no spring skips its turn.

Hal Borland

Three years ago my best friend, Stephanie, was killed on her way to school in a head-on collision. The man who killed her did not have a driver's license and was under the influence. He was driving about sixty miles per hour and didn't even brake before he crossed into oncoming traffic and hit her. She died on impact. She was only sixteen. Painfully alone, somewhere between emotional inertia and complete despair, I struggled to navigate my suddenly unraveled reality.

When I received notice that my mother was at school to see me that foggy March day, my stomach sank. Something was terribly wrong. I immediately turned in my half-finished math test and rushed to the administration building to look for my mother. I found her sitting in the school's parlor. She asked me to sit—I stood. When she told me the tragic news, I could hear my heart pounding. The red walls seemed brighter then, and more fluid, as if they were swirling around me. A peculiar emptiness overtook me that afternoon in my mother's car as I repeated the words she had spoken to me earlier: *She died today. She died. She's dead.* I tried to make myself believe what I soon realized was the dark and horrific truth: Steph was dead, and she was never coming back.

There was a drastic change in my expectations and hopes for the future from that day forward. Never had I imagined that someone with whom I had cried, someone who had been a sister to me through everything from my parents' divorce to my first kiss—my future maid-of-honor—would no longer be in my life. All that was left of my future now were the questions. Who would give me those enormous, suffocating hugs and mischievous grins? What would I do at the times when her laugh was the only thing that could make me smile? Who would catch me when I fell? Who would be there for me when I endured the most crushing experience of my young life—the death of my best friend?

I had never felt so alone, and consequently I chose to look within myself for comfort and understanding. I hoped that somewhere, deep inside of me, she was still there and would guide me through the monumental changes occurring in my life. But as I began to peel back layers of my own consciousness, my feelings of isolation and desperation only grew. I had always considered myself a strong person, but I felt completely lost. I could not focus on my schoolwork or much else in my life except Stephanie's death. Most of my days were spent merely existing with little pleasure or interest in anything. I wrote poetry in math class and scrawled overly dramatic statements like "Have you ever lost yourself?" on my notebook during advanced placement biology. I never bothered or cared about the actual class discussion. I spent what seemed to be an eternity staring into the eyes of my favorite pictures of Steph. I had every lash and sparkle of those celestial blue eyes memorized, but I feared that my memory of the passion and charisma that I searched so intently for within them would fade. Although I didn't cry much, I thought a lot. I tried to figure out why she was gone, how someone could kill another person and have no remorse, what I was going to do with my life. Then, after much thought, I found something. Under all the layers of pain and frustration, something within me briefly twinkled.

A few months after Stephanie's death, her sister gave me a letter that she had found deep in one of her cluttered drawers. This letter was the healing catalyst I so desperately needed. She told me in the letter that she loved me always, that I was her best friend, and lastly, that I was her mentor. Like a piece of stardust, something deep inside of me began to illuminate my soul. Never in my life had I been so flattered, so touched, or felt so loved; it was as though she had left the letter behind to console and encourage me. She had always taken care of me before, and now I knew that her death did not change that. I realized that despite my suffering, I needed to take responsibility, use my talents and participate actively in my life's unfolding.

Now, whenever I'm worried, I ask her for guidance, and I swear that she has helped me profoundly. Whether she gives me the strength to call back after I've hung up on someone or the inspiration to trudge through my advanced placement language test with confidence and clarity, I know she helps me every day. Although it is impossible to verbalize such an abstract, warm confidence, I feel her presence inside of me as I succeed, and more importantly as I cry, longing for her sweet, warm embrace. It is with her strength and support that I am able to forge on in life. I have faith in her presence, and I have faith in myself.

Steph's death caused me to question myself and my

own position in life. I now feel that although I have endured an emotional darkness more intense and shattering than most eighteen-year-olds have, it is not the pain that has changed me, but rather Stephanie's love and confidence in me that has inspired my metamorphosis. I can feel her guiding light in my own life as it changes, and thus I have the courage and resilience to embark on a new chapter of my life. I emerge from the darkness as a confident, faith-filled young woman with an especially bright twinkle in her eye.

Anastasia

One Final Lesson

One rainy day I was at home playing on my computer when the phone rang. It showed up on my caller ID as one of my really good friends from across the state. I anxiously grabbed for the receiver and answered. But instead of the lively reply that I had come to expect from my friend, I heard nothing but sobbing. She was crying so hard she couldn't even talk. Finally, she got it all out. Two of her best friends had just died. Slowly over the next hour and a half I got the story piece by piece.

After I hung up I couldn't clear my mind of what I had just heard. It was a scenario I had heard too many times in my life. So I pulled the facts together and wrote a story of what happened. The following is what I came up with.

The last day of school is today. It couldn't be more perfect since today is also your seventeenth birthday. All that you and two of your buddies have planned is a night out on the lake.

For a couple of hours you and your friends sit in a little aluminum boat in the middle of the lake under the colorful skies painted by a setting sun. As you guys empty can after can from a case of beer, you talk about the usual: girls and your plans for the summer, and what it's going to be like when school begins and all three of you are finally seniors.

You don't notice the wind beginning to pick up, churning the calm, smooth lake into something dangerous. By the time you realize it's time to come in, the waves have already begun to thrash your little boat. Your friend gets the engine going and handles the steering while you work the throttle. As soon as he gets the engine started you open the throttle maybe just a little more than you should. With a jolt, the little boat is sent speeding across the waves. Halfway to the landing you helplessly watch in horror as you notice a huge wave coming at you from the side. Your friend turns the boat into the wind and toward the wave as you throttle down the engine for all you're worth, but not soon enough. The wave hits the boat at an angle, sending her off the crest and smashing down into its trough. All three of you are knocked against the side as the force of the wave capsizes the boat and sends you all into the lake.

You kick for the surface, but your legs feel heavy and sluggish. It feels as if something is pulling you down into the depths. Your boots, now weighted by the water, are pulling you deeper and deeper into the darkness. As much as you try, the light of the surface becomes more and more distant. As your last few seconds of consciousness pass, you desperately try to pull your boots off. You tear at the laces, but they won't come undone. You panic, thrashing wildly, doing anything just for a breath of precious air. Before blackness consumes you, images of your friends and family swim through your mind. *No,* you think to yourself. *This isn't happening to me. I'm only a teenager. I can't die!*

And then, almost as an answer to your thoughts, you miraculously find yourself on the sandy shore—dry, warm and sober. You see one of your friends swimming toward the beach. You call out to him, but he doesn't respond. He pulls himself out of the lake and he stands there shivering as water drips from his T-shirt, looking at the overturned boat. He calls out for you and your friend. "Hey!" you yell as you walk over to him. "I'm right here." But he doesn't seem to notice. He calls out again, and again you give him your same response: "Hey! I'm right here!" You step in front of him, but his frantic eyes look past you, around you, and even through you.

Oh, God, he says to himself. *What have I done?* He takes a few steps backward, then turns and runs up the road.

"Hey!" you yell. "Hey, where are you going?!" But it's almost as if you had said nothing at all. You watch helplessly as he continues to run until he disappears from sight.

For a time all is silent. Ten minutes pass, then twenty. After thirty, maybe thirty-five minutes, a siren pierces the silence. At first you don't notice. But within minutes ignoring it is impossible. Down the road come a multitude of emergency vehicles, followed in short succession by cars and trucks, some of which you recognize as belonging to friends. As people jump out of their cars, you notice that your parents are there also. Your father walks somberly, while your mother sobs endlessly in his arms. You run over to your parents, yelling out to them, but they don't seem to hear. They pull an officer aside to talk, to find out what is going on. As you get closer you hear the officer say, "Ma'am, I'm sorry but your son's body is missing. We have called in helicopters to search the beaches with searchlights. Men on horseback have gone up to scan the cliffs . . . divers will come in tomorrow."

"But you don't need all them!" you yell. "I'm right here! I'm not dead! It's not supposed to happen to me!"

As the night draws to a close, the lake fills with more

and more boats. People from all over your little town are out on the water with flashlights, calling out for you and your missing friend. And no matter how hard you yell, no one seems to hear you. You walk by groups of some of your best friends, and even some of those people with whom you never really got along. Some of them are trying not to cry, yet holding those who are.

You watch your girlfriend crying and calling out for you as her friends try to comfort her. "Don't cry," your soundless voice says to her. "I'm not dead. I can't be. I'm only seventeen. This can't happen to me."

Night gives way to morning and no one has left—instead, more have come. Your mother is out on the dock. She has been there for nearly five hours. You watch as your father and an officer walk out to her, and you hear your father whisper, "C'mon, honey, it's time to go now." She breaks into tears while you try desperately to hold back yours. She won't go. Not until the body of her son is found. The flood of emotions hits you like a brick wall when the police have to sedate her in order to move her from the end of the dock. *This shouldn't be happening,* you tell yourself. *I'm only a teenager. I can't be dead.*

The names of you and your friend, which have been called out by rescuers all night long, are drowned out by the high-pitched roar of two army helicopters. Immediately, their searchlights pierce the fading darkness and begin sweeping over the lake and the beaches that surround it.

One of the searchlights passes over you; you put your arms in front of your face as the blinding light engulfs you. And then is gone . . .

You lower your arms and look around. The helicopters are gone. As are the police, medics and firemen. They are all gone. The boats that once carried searchers and their flashlights bob gently in their moorings at the dock. Your friends no longer sit on the shore, crying at the realization that two of their companions are forever lost.

Instead, the sun rises over the clear and pristine lake. The sky is blue, with not a cloud in sight. Your clothes ripple as a cool west wind slips beside you.

In a clearing you can see a small congregation of people. As you walk closer, each and every one of them becomes familiar—each of them a friend or a family member. There are two sections of folding chairs, all of which are occupied. Before them, beside a little makeshift podium, propped above a pile of flower bouquets, are two pictures—one is of your friend whom you never saw after the boat capsized and threw all three of you into the lake. You hesitate to look at the other picture because you already know—it's you.

As one friend leaves the little podium, another stands and takes his place. She speaks about what the two of you meant to her and how much she will miss you. One by one, friends and relatives come up to speak, each emphasizing how much you will be missed. And you sit there and watch, all the time not believing that it happened to you. That you died, even though you were still a teenager.

Noah Campana

The Bus Stop

Waiting at the bus stop
I shivered from the cold.
When you walked up
it seemed as if
you were outlined all in gold.
You asked me if my shivering
was out of cold or fear,
I said the cold, I'm not afraid
for you to stand so near.

Then you removed your jacket
and handed it to me,
I shyly refused your jacket,
embarrassed so, you see.
You put the jacket on my shoulders
and back a step you took.
"I'm Anna," I said extending my hand.
"Tobias," you said. We shook.

Day after day we stood,
waiting for the bus,

Not a single word spoken
by either one of us.
Until one day I turned to you
and bravely started to say,
"I have a crush on you, Tobias,
and also, by the way—"

As I started to tell you what it was
that was burning on my mind,
You told me that you liked me, too,
but the words were hard to find.
I smiled a smile that seemed to stretch
to both of my two ears.
The smiling and the happiness
erasing all my fears.

And now, my friend, you're dying
and there's nothing I can do,
But sit with you and hold your hand
and be forever true.
Last night while you were sleeping,
your soul just slipped away,
The many words that filled my heart
were impossible to say.
As I was cleaning out the drawer
that stood beside your empty bed,
I found a letter addressed to me
and heard your voice speak as I read.

My darling I am sorry that
I will have to leave so soon,
You know how much I love you
and I know you love me, too.
I hope you won't forget me
but please do try to move on,

I hope that you won't cry too much
when I am dead and gone.

Two silent tears slid down my face
and moistened both my cheeks,
I won't get over the loss of you
not for days, and not for weeks.
I continued reading the letter
that I held in both my hands,
My fingers numb as if they had
been wrapped in rubber bands.

Now I'm standing at the bus stop
where two years ago we met,
And as I stand here in the cold
I feel my cheeks start to get wet.
I don't think I will get over you,
never, not in any way,
Our anniversary would have been
two years ago today.

And on this lonely bus ride,
I sit alone without you near.
I hear a voice that may just be
the voice I've longed to hear.
The voice is from an angel
and his words are sweet and strong.
He tells me, "Life's a treasure.
Learn to love again. Move on."

And through the words he whispers
I finally start to see,
That although I'll always love you—
It's time to set you free.

Anna Maier

Tomorrow Came Again

My sister was twelve. My parents were separated. As for myself, I was eight. I really did not have a clue what my family was going through until that horrible, cold January night. How could I have had a clue? I mean, I was only eight years old. All I cared about was my afterschool snack, the cartoons on television and trying to stay up later than eight-thirty on school nights.

I remember that night like it was only milliseconds ago. My mother had asked me to carry the towels upstairs to the linen closet. After I moaned, groaned and procrastinated for about ten minutes, I finally agreed. I remember trying to peer over the tower of towels to make my way up the steep stairs safely. When I got to the closet, which just happens to be next to my sister's room, I heard her crying. Being the most concerned third-grader I could be, I opened the door a little bit wider, and I asked, "Shelley, what's wrong?"

She just looked at my confused expression, and then asked me to give her a hug. I was pretty much into the charade of showing that you hated your siblings, so I refused her request. She persisted and asked me once more. My shaky response was, "Why?"

Shelley explained to me that she had just swallowed an entire bottle of over-the-counter pills. I was not exactly sure at that point in time if this was a dangerous move on her part. But, I realized it must have been pretty serious. I ran down the stairs to my mother, crying the whole way. I told her exactly, word for word, what Shelley had just explained to me.

My mother raced up the stairs, two at a time. She burst into my sister's room, and she begged Shelley to get out of bed to tell her what happened. Shelley refused to tell my mother anything. My mother forced her out of bed, told her to get dressed, and they hurried to the hospital. My neighbor came over, and I cried myself to sleep. All I remember after that is waking up, and my neighbor was still there.

I later learned that Shelley was going to be all right, after she had gotten her stomach pumped. And especially after she had spent three months of her seventh-grade year in a rehabilitation center for adolescents. I never knew exactly why she had attempted suicide, and I never want to ask her. But what I do know is that life is our most precious gift, and I will never again pretend that I do not love my sister.

Ashley Hiser

It Happened to Me

Cancer. It's a funny word. It has two meanings. One of those meanings is the life-threatening disease we all know about. The other meaning isn't as accurate. We take it to mean something that happens to someone else, something that happens to your friend's aunt or someone in the newspaper. It's not something that happens to us, and it's definitely not something that happens to our own sister. But it happened to mine.

When I was about eight, every once in a while my eyesight would become blurry. I'd blink a few times and my eyes would go back to normal. I was taken to the eye doctor, and then for a CAT scan and various testing, but no one could find anything wrong. Eventually, it went away.

When my sister, Naomi, was about eight, she claimed to go blind when I hit her in the eye with an old nightshirt. I got in trouble, but when she was taken to the eye doctor, he couldn't find anything either. Eventually, she stopped complaining.

But when my sister, Tali, was about eight, she too began to complain that it was getting harder and harder to see out of one eye. My parents made an appointment with the eye doctor for about a month later, but they weren't too concerned.

But when my sister's complaints began to worsen, my parents began to get worried and made the eye doctor appointment sooner. When the appointment came, my parents were informed that it was possible that Tali had a form of cancer called melanoma. One of the places that this can form is the eye, though there is no known reason why it forms in a particular person. To ensure that the disease is completely removed from the body, the part of the body infected with the disease must be removed. In this case, it would be her eye. If it was proven, for certain, that she had melanoma, the doctors would have to work fast, or the disease could travel from her eye to her brain.

It was not time to worry yet, though, because all that was the worst-case scenario, and melanoma is very rare among children anyway. Nevertheless, I remember my mom coming home from the eye doctor and crying, along with my grandmother and my aunt and trying not to let my sister see. I remember thinking, *This isn't really happening. She can't really die, this will all blow over.* Maybe I was in shock, but it didn't feel like it. It was more like I had never even heard it, never even tried to acknowledge it was happening. Maybe it was crazy to feel like that, but maybe it was better that way, because I, the "unshaken one," was able to be the shoulder to cry on for everyone else. It makes it sound as if I was the brave one, but sometimes if you don't show your feelings on the outside, it means you're the most scared inside.

Well, Tali went in for her tests, and her X rays, and it was confirmed that she had cancer. Her eye would have to be removed immediately. We knew that if even one cancerous cell was left, the disease could fully return.

The operation took place soon after. My mother waited in the hospital, while I stayed home and answered various phone calls. "No, we haven't heard anything yet," "Yes, she's still in surgery," "Yes, we'll notify you immediately." I still didn't believe it was happening. My sister was in surgery. . . . and I still thought I was dreaming.

We later got a call that she was out of surgery, and just awakening from the anesthesia. All had gone smoothly, and tests had shown that they probably got everything out. She would be fine.

Never during the entire experience did I acknowledge what was happening. People would stop to comfort me, and half the time it would take me a few seconds to realize why. Almost every day, I have people stop me in the halls and ask, "Hey, how's Tali doing?" and I answer, "She's fine, why do you ask?"

Even now, as I write this, she's jumping on the bed across the hall, screaming, "Hey Joanie, you done writing the wonderful story of my life yet?" And though it's a miracle, it seems quite normal that there is nothing wrong at all.

Joanie Twersky

I Am Not Alone

Here I stand, just another voice, lost in a crowd of noise. Though I am surrounded by familiar faces, I do not recognize anyone. I have never felt so alone. . . .

I am eighteen years old, and in love with the most wonderful person! He is cute, sweet and oh so charming. He makes me so happy. I have never felt so content. He is my best friend. When he looks in my eyes and says, "I love you," I just know we are forever. For us, life is a party.

Reality sets in and threatens to reveal the illusions of my fantasy world. *Where is he now?* I wonder desperately. *Where did I go wrong? Did I fall short of his expectations somehow? Or was he unable to meet mine? Was it that he never really loved me, and if so, did he lie? WHY?* The young man I thought I knew so well does not exist, is someone whose face I do not recognize. His voice sounds strange and distant. I see behind his disguise. I look past his smile and his promises. I see him for who he *really* is.

My stomach hurts lately, and I have trouble eating. I feel dizzy and nauseous. I get so tired, I can hardly stay awake. Yet even after a nap, I still feel cranky and irritable. Maybe it's just the flu. No, it is something else. I sense a truth I want to ignore.

My friend must know, too. I can tell by the way she watches me. I don't want to say anything because I am afraid. She brings me a pregnancy test and tells me, "You should take it just to be sure."

I pretend that I am not worried, that this is silly. "I know I am not pregnant." I keep saying it to reassure myself more than her. Then I go to the bathroom.

I watch two lines appear quickly. I can hardly breathe. I feel nothing really, except shock and denial. Tears will not come. I just stare in disbelief and then quietly call for my friend. I point at the test stick lying face up on the counter, the faint pink lines rapidly changing to a dark shade of maroon. As calmly as I can, I say, "This can't be right." She knows the test is right, and so do I. Tomorrow, I will go to the doctor. Right now, I just want to lie down.

"Positive. You are definitely pregnant." I look up and catch the nurse's eyes. It is real. There is no way to avoid the truth. She hands me a tissue as I cry. Now, my tears are endless. She listens as I lose myself in despair. I can't think. A million thoughts are colliding in my head, causing a mass of confusion. How will I tell him? He has to know.

I go to see him when I leave the clinic. He is sitting in his bedroom, with the light off. A small ray of light comes through the window, and casts shadows across his face. I turn my head away. I can't look him in the eye. I can feel my lips trembling as I try not to cry, but I will not allow him to witness the panic that grips me. I try to appear brave and unemotional as I tell this stranger I am carrying his child. He, too, seems unemotional. I feel his eyes upon me. Getting my words out is a struggle. I look up and try to smile, a weak attempt. This is not how I had imagined it would be. So, I wait for him to do, or say, something, anything to let me know I am not alone. Instead, his silence chills me. I know that things between us are changed forever; I turn and walk away. I want him to call to me, or run after me. I want him to hold me in his arms. As I am leaving, I vaguely hear him say, "I'm sorry."

I am outside now. The sun shines down upon me like a spotlight. I feel naked. The door shuts behind me, and I burst into tears. I cry for the young man on the other side of the door. I cry for the baby that is growing inside me. I cry because my heart is breaking. I suddenly feel my youth is ending.

Weeks go by, and every day I live in fear. I wish I had been more careful with my heart and my body. I wish I had never met him. I am too young to be a mother. I am scared. I feel sick and alone. Will my baby have a father? I sleep all day and cry all night. I wonder how it feels to laugh. I stare at myself in the mirror, looking for my smile, my happiness.

Now I see the beginning of this tiny creature on a screen. I hear a heartbeat separate from my own. I feel a new kind of love. A love that has confidence and guidance—the love of a mother. I lift my head up, and I stand strong for myself, for my unborn child and for the priorities instilled in me by my pregnancy.

Here I am amidst a crowd of noise, swimming against the current I have accepted as my reality, in a sea where familiar faces fade away, and I am not alone.

Sara Strickland

Visionary

When I was fifteen, I stood in front of my English class and read an essay I had written. I talked about how excited all my friends were to be taking driver's education and getting driver's licenses. I was jealous. I knew that I'd always be walking everywhere I went or else dependent on others to drive me. I am legally blind.

Since I was four years old, I have had a condition called dry-eye syndrome. While I do have some sight, I never know when I wake up in the morning exactly how much vision I will have that day. The reason for this is that my eyes do not produce enough tears to lubricate my corneas. As a result, my corneas are scarred. Glasses cannot help me.

There are many things I cannot do. I can't drive, read the blackboard in school or read a book comfortably. But there are far more things I can do.

In high school, I played varsity basketball. My teammates gave me oral signals and I learned to gauge where the ball was by the sound of their voices. As a result, I learned to focus extremely well. I earned the sportsmanship award my senior year.

In addition to basketball, I was a representative to the student council. I also participated in a Model United Nations program, traveling to Washington, D.C., with my class to see our legislators in action. I graduated from high school with a dual curriculum in Jewish and general studies.

After graduation, I studied in Israel for two years. Today, I am a sophomore at Yeshiva University. I plan to go to law school and maybe rabbinical school.

Do I wish I could see like other people? Of course. But being blind hasn't limited me in any of the ways I consider really important. I'm still me. If I've had to be more dependent on my friends, at least I've learned who my friends really are.

Because I've had to struggle to find ways to learn that didn't include sight, I've made superior use of my other senses.

I don't know why God chose to give me only a little vision. Maybe he did it so that I would appreciate what I do have even more. Maybe he did it so that I would have to develop my other capabilities and talents to compensate. Or maybe he gave me this special "gift" because I am, in every other respect, so normal that he wanted to push me to excel. It worked.

There are many different ways to look at life. This is how I see it.

Jason Leib

The Mom I Never Had

I still remember the first time I heard that my mom had been admitted to the hospital for drug-related problems. I was angry, scared, sad and confused, and I felt betrayed. Questions ran through my mind. How could she do this to me? How could she do this to her family? Was it my fault? I felt that it was; that I had done something wrong. As if I had fought with her too much the day before. As if I had rebelled enough to drive her over the edge.

I think back to when I was younger, and I don't really remember my mom being there when I needed her. I never talked to her about the guys I liked, or shared my feelings if I was upset. In turn, she never confided in me when she was sad or needed someone to talk to. My life was never "normal" like all the other girls in my class. Why didn't my mom take me shopping? Why didn't my mom ever come to basketball games, teacher conferences or orthodontist appointments? Then it hit me. My mother, an R.N. who worked in the emergency room for numerous years—a great nurse, and friend to all—was a drug addict. My dad tried to convince me that everything would be okay, that if she moved away for a while, we would all be fine. But I knew deep in my heart that I needed my mother.

The next few days while my mother was in de-tox were hell. It still hadn't sunk in. I had no one to talk to, and there were so many unanswered questions. I watched home videos of when I was a little girl and wished everything would be "normal." I know now that it was never normal.

Then my mom called from the hospital. I remember her voice so soft and weak. She said she was sorry for everything. I wanted to tell her to come home, that I loved her and everything would be okay from now on. Instead, I kept telling her that it wasn't her fault, and between my sobs I said good-bye. You see, I wasn't supposed to cry. I was supposed to be the strong one.

The next day, we went to visit her. I didn't want to be alone with her. I didn't want to talk to her because I was afraid of what she might say. It was weird having those feelings toward my own mother. I felt like she was a stranger, someone I didn't know.

She came home on a Tuesday. We talked for a while and she said she wanted me to come to meetings with her. I said that I would, not knowing what kind of people I would meet or what they would be like. So I went, and the meetings really helped me understand that what my mom was dealing with was a disease, and that no one was at fault. I also met some great people who helped me understand things even further.

I was still unsure, though. At meetings, I heard all this talk about relapse and how to prevent it. What if my mom relapsed? How would I deal with this a second time? I remember when my mom was using drugs, she would stay in her bedroom for long periods of time. One day, after noticing that my mom hadn't come downstairs for a while, I got frightened. I tried to tell myself that even if she slipped, we would get through it, but I didn't really believe we could. I forced myself to go upstairs and see what she was doing. I was scared as I opened the door to her bedroom, afraid of what I might see. But I wasn't disappointed. I found her in her bed, reading a prayer book. I knew then that my mom was going to make it!

She had pulled through, and because of it, we were able to begin the mother-daughter relationship that we never had. I finally had my mom.

Becka Allen

Train Tracks

"Alison, come on out and play," my best friend yelled through the screen door. Many summer mornings, I ran through the old house, my long red hair flying after me, to meet Manda on the rickety front steps.

"Watcha wanna do t'day?" she always asked.

"Oh, I dunno. Let's go play at the Ol' Station again."

The Ol' Station was once a train station in 1912, but it was no longer in use. The tracks were rusty, but trains used them all the same. A narrow gravel road cut through the old train tracks and was used to lead to the housing area in which Manda and I lived.

Playing at the Ol' Station was more than fun, it was an eight-year-old's dream. Imaginations ran wild, friendships blossomed, and the day's worries were forgotten at the Ol' Station. Manda and I loved to run down the train tracks searching for granite rocks and old money that might have been left from the station's productive days. When we were younger, we would dress in our mothers' clothes and pretend we were ladies of America's elite, waiting for a train of riches. When one of us became angry with the other, we would run down the tracks, either as far as we were allowed or until we couldn't breathe.

One day, in a fit of rage against Manda, I started sprinting down the tracks, when her foot caught and she tripped.

"Ouch! Oh my gosh, Alison, help me!"

I looked back to find Manda lying on the tracks, bawling like I'd never seen my tough friend bawl before. I ran back to her. "What's wrong? Are you okay?"

"I tripped and hurt my knee."

I looked at the badly skinned knee.

"It's just a little blood. Here, you hop on my back and I'll carry you home." So that's what we did—I gave her a piggyback ride home.

Over the years, Manda and I had gone our separate ways, but we still considered ourselves friends. Beginning our ninth-grade year, we had only one class together, and that was Algebra I. We both hated math with a violent passion and hated our teacher equally as much. Manda sat behind me, so I spent most of the class time passing notes to Manda that made fun of Mrs. Madlock, whom we'd nicknamed "The Green Heifer" due to her large build and green shirts.

"Guess what today is?" Manda asked me during class one day.

"September nineteenth?"

"Yeah, but today is soccer try-out day!" Manda had always wanted to play soccer. "I've practiced so hard, the coach would be an idiot not to put me on the team."

"Alison, turn around and shut up. You have all weekend to talk to Manda." Mrs. Madlock barked at me. Smiling at Manda, I turned around to learn about the exciting world of algebra.

That night, I went out of town to watch my brother's first football game of the season. I couldn't help but wonder if Manda had made the soccer team; after all, it had been her dream. I called Manda's house as soon as I got home from the football game, but no one answered.

Disappointed that Manda hadn't cared enough to call and tell me the results of the soccer try-outs, I went to the local car show alone. Aimlessly wandering through the maze of cars, wondering why Manda and I had grown apart, I heard a voice shout my name. I turned around to see Jenni Stovers, a girl I was friendly with from school.

"Alison, did you hear about Manda?" The look on her face was difficult to read.

"No," I said casually. "Did she make the soccer team?" Jenni's eyes swelled up with tears as she sympathetically looked at me.

"Alison, Manda was killed last night in an accident."

My mouth dropped and my stomach did a flip-flop, making me feel sick. "Wha . . . what happened?" I stammered.

"Her mother was driving her home from soccer try-outs, and the sun made it hard to see. They were crossing the tracks by your house, and a train smashed into them."

I looked at Jenni's sympathetic face and ran. I ran past Ol' Station, over the railroad crossing, and down the gravel road that seemed to stare angrily up at me like an evil monster ready to attack. I ran up the rickety porch step and through my house, my long red hair flying after me. Throwing myself upon my bed, sobbing into my pillow, I thought back to the carefree days of our childhood when Manda had tripped on the tracks.

"It's just a little blood. Here, you hop on my back and I'll carry you home."

Only this time, I couldn't carry her home.

Alison Hamby

Let's Go Dancing in the Rain

Spring break of 1999 was perfect—I got to spend the entire time with my friends just vegging and hanging out. Of course, there was that English project due the day I got back, which I put off until the Sunday before. I was sitting at my computer furiously making up an essay when my little sister walked in from softball practice eating a snow cone and laughing with a sticky smile.

"Whatcha working on?" she asked lightheartedly.

I smiled at her appearance and told her that it was just an English essay. I turned back and continued clacking away. From behind my shoulder she tried to start a conversation.

"So . . ." she began. "You know a kid in your grade named Justin? Justin Schultz?" She licked at a drip on her snow cone.

"Yeah, I know him," I replied. I had gone to elementary school with Justin. He had to be the greatest guy I knew. He never stopped smiling. Justin had tried to teach me to play soccer in the third grade. I couldn't get it, so he smiled and told me to do my best and cheer everyone else on. I'd kind of lost touch with him in the last year, but I told my sister yes, anyway.

"Well," she said, trying to keep her messy snow cone under control. "His church group went skiing this week." She paused to take a lick.

Lucky guy, I thought.

My sister swallowed the ice chips and continued, "So he went skiing and today he died."

I felt the blood drain from my face in disbelief. My hands froze on the keyboard, and a line of Rs inched across the screen. My jaw slowly dropped as I tried to process what she'd said. *Breathe,* something in my head screamed. I shook my head and whipped around to look at my sister.

She was still innocently munching on her snow cone, staring at it determinedly. Her eyes rose to mine and she leaned back, a little startled. "What?" she asked.

"Y-you're joking, right? Who told you that? I don't believe it. How? Are you sure?" I spit out a long string of questions.

"Claire," she stopped me. She began a little slower this time. "A girl on my softball team was house-sitting for them. Justin's parents called her today and told her, and she told me. Sorry, I didn't think you knew him." She sat very still waiting for my response.

Every memory I had of Justin flashed through my mind. I inhaled slowly. "No. No! NO!" I tried to scream. No words came out. I sat up clumsily and shakily ran from the room with my sister behind me yelling, "Wait! I'm sorry . . ."

I called one of our mutual friends right away. She told me between sobs that no one knew why he died. The thirteen-year-old was as healthy as a horse. He fell asleep on Saturday night in the hotel room, and when his roommate tried to wake him up Sunday morning, Justin wasn't breathing. I didn't want her to hear me cry, so I quickly got off the phone.

I went to school the next day and put on the same strong mask. The principal gave an impersonal announcement about Justin's death that morning and almost immediately I could hear sobs throughout the classroom. That was the worst week of my life. I tried to be a shoulder for others to cry on, but inside I was the one crying.

On Wednesday evening my friend gave me a ride to Justin's viewing. What surprised me when we walked into the room was that Justin's parents weren't crying. They were smiling and comforting everyone. I asked them how they were holding up, and they told me that they were fine. They told me they knew that he wasn't hurting now, that he was with God and would wait for them in heaven. I cried and nearly collapsed. Mrs. Schultz stepped forward to hug me, and I cried on her beautiful red sweater. I looked into her eyes and saw her sympathy for a girl who'd lost her friend.

I went home that night with a deep sadness in my heart for Justin. I wrote a letter to him that I planned on giving him at his funeral. In the letter I wrote to him about how sad everyone was, how much we missed him, how wonderful his parents were and the things he'd never get to do on Earth. I closed it with:

> *Somehow I've always believed that once in heaven, tangible things really don't mean that much anymore. Well, before you get too used to your new life, take these things with you. The smell of grass thirty minutes after it's cut. The feel of freshly washed sheets. The heat of a small candle. The sound a bee makes. The taste of a hot Coke just poured and swirling with ice—hot, but partially cold. The feel of raindrops on your soaked face. But if you take nothing else with you, take your family's embrace.*

I paused and stared into my candle. I rearranged my pen in my hand and continued writing. *Tell you what, Justin. When I die, let's go dancing in the rain.* I smiled through tears and slid my letter into an envelope.

The next day was Justin's funeral. At the last minute, my ride had to cancel because of a schedule conflict, and I was left to sit alone in my house crying. I glanced down at my letter and smiled, "How am I going to get this to you now, Justin?" I laughed through my tears and kept crying.

Sometimes strange thoughts pop into my head, as if from somewhere else. Sitting on my bed fingering a tissue, one of those thoughts told me how to get it to him. *Smoke is faster than dirt.* I was startled by this, but after thinking about it, I realized I was to burn the letter, not bury it. I cried for an hour as I carefully burned the letter. I'd burn a corner, then blow it out under the running water in the sink, afraid of the flames. Eventually, the letter was gone and the white smoke streamed from my window. I waved it away and prayed to God that Justin would someday read my words in the smoke.

That night I dreamt about death and awoke at 2:38 A.M. to hear rain tapping on my window. Rare are the visible words from heaven, but those precious raindrops were my answer. I had told Justin that I wanted to go dancing in the rain. The slow rhythm on my window told me that Justin had heard me. In that moment, I knew that he felt no pain and that we would see each other again. And on that day, we will go dancing in the rain together.

Claire Hayenga

Emergency 911

I never thought the day would come. You stop by me as I get on the tennis bus. "Would you like a ride to practice?" you ask.

"No, Stephanie—but thanks, anyway." My parents would freak if they found out I got into a car with a sixteen-year-old driver.

You drive away after promising to come to our tennis match tomorrow. I wave out of the bus window as you head down the hill.

Five minutes later, our bus is slowing down as we pass a crash on our left side. Crashes are really cool, especially if they are really bloody and gory. The car, a red Honda Civic, looks like yours, but there are lots here in Valley Center. The side is all bashed in, and everyone's faces are covered in blood. People are walking around with cell phones, calling 911. The bus moves on to tennis practice.

My mom is working at the hospital tonight. She calls home to say that two girls from my school are dead, and one is in critical condition. The other was released earlier. I blow it off. The next morning, my mom comes home. She says that you are dead, Stephie, and so is Jenn. I don't believe her and go to school. When I get to school, I suddenly believe her. I start crying as my friends look at each other in amazement. I never cry, at least I haven't in about three years. But this is real. They have a room open for people who can't handle classes. But I'm Danni. Of course I can handle them. But I can't. I can't last five minutes through first period before I start bawling.

I spend the day in the memorial room making cards for your families. Reporters come up to me and ask me how I feel. I say words not befitting a girl. Your family comes in, Stephanie. I am surprised by how much your sisters look like you. I almost mistook your older one for you. But you weren't there. I laid roses in the quad for you. I wrote countless poems and cried countless tears. Did you know you had so many friends?

The memorial service was held today. The song they played was "Lately"—a song about death and learning to live again. It was our favorite. As I step off of the bus back at Ramona High School, the last chords of "Lately" can be heard.

I won all of my matches for you today. I met a guy the other day. You sent him from heaven, didn't you? His name is Tyler. He helped me through this. I wanted to be with you, and almost succeeded. But he helped me realize that life is worth living to the fullest. After all, that's what you did.

Each day I forget a little more, but in my heart will always be the memory of your love and kindness. Oh, and Stephanie: I don't think crashes are cool anymore.

Danni Villemez

11:21 A.M.

[AUTHOR'S NOTE: ***I was a junior at Columbine High School and was in the choir room when the shootings began. I wrote this poem after the tragedy to help me deal with the pain and grief. My classmates and I are still struggling with the emotional trauma, but we continue to heal. We are so grateful to the officers, firefighters and others who saved people's lives that day. I would like to thank everyone throughout the world for their ongoing support and prayers as we begin to rebuild.*****]**

I lie on my bed
   numb,
   unemotional,
   non-feeling.
Fear stains my memories as I reflect
   on a placid morning in Littleton.
A usual day in choir.
We prepare for concerts,
   blithely indulging in normal routine.
Carefree . . . Content . . .
   Unaware. . . .

A sudden blast startles us.
A chemistry explosion?
Deafening eruptions penetrate "Ave Maria."
Sinuous voices now punctuated by gunshots,
  the demonic splintering the angelic.

The choir hushes
  to the rhythm of pounding hearts.
Students scream through halls
  as terror burns itself on innocent faces.

Tick, Tick, Tick—11:21—
  lives are forever changed.
Shock . . . Hysteria. . . .
  Why?
The sound of bombs ignite horror through our veins
  and send chills
  that pinch the skin like needles.

Some run.
Some stand paralyzed in shock,
  numbness engulfing all other emotions.
Billows of powder now blanket the hall,
  creating ghostly images.
I look through the delicate webs of cotton
  and see the fruits of hatred.
Bullets shatter glass
  and invade bodies,
  as malice sears the souls of the perpetrators.

A student prays;
  another hides in stunned confusion;
  a teacher bleeds.

Like children
  we are helpless,
  longing to be in mama's arms.

Screaming . . . Frantic . . .
  Why?

Two faces
  are plastered against the window.
The horror in their eyes strips away
  my consciousness.
My first instinct is to run;
  I duck as bullets spray the halls.

Our school is now the grounds of warfare—
  mortal fighting
  in a field of bombs and bullets.
Weapons that have fallen into the wrong hands
  have only one purpose and they
  are killing us and all I hear is gunfire.
Crackling, Crackling,
Humming, bursting, screaming, ringing, what
  now,
Too much
Too soon
Too young
So scared
Help us.

I struggle to escape but am slowed
  as if trudging through water.
Through the front doors I see milky clouds
  that absorb the sun;
I see golden light and sunburned pavement.
I cannot get there fast enough.

I am almost to the door.
A bullet ricochets off the pane.
The glass swirls like a droplet on water,
  creating rings that shiver and spread,

shattering as I dash through the door—
All is silent.
I have escaped hell.

There is a dark room
where ten broken bodies lie,
and where others play dead.
In the darkness of the library,
angels embrace the lifeless,
and their wings flicker light
against a wall of helpless shadows.
God now wraps His arms
around the school
and gathers the souls of the lost,
makes strong the souls of the weak,
cries for the violence on Earth.

Time picks up and I am
vulnerable, insecure.
A dog's bark screams like bullets.
Who to trust?
Our haven is destroyed,
and we are scattered.

I sit immobilized,
while anxiety and guilt wrap themselves around me
and consume me.
Angry . . . Numb . . .
Why?
Are there answers in silence . . . ?
Because I am asking you and you don't answer . . .

Or maybe the silence is just you listening.

Joanna Gates

Building Bridges

When written in Chinese, the word "crisis" is composed of two characters. One represents danger and the other represents opportunity.

John F. Kennedy

The day started out just like most other Tuesdays. I'm in a show choir called "Unclaimed Freight" at Columbine High School; we rehearse in the mornings before school. I got to school at 6:50 A.M., saw friends and said hello on my way in.

We went through the day normally until fifth period, which for me is Concert Choir. We were starting our warm-ups when a student in the choir came into the room and said there was a guy downstairs with a gun.

This student was known to be a jokester. But he had a pretty serious look on his face, and I saw kids running by when I looked out the window. The choir director told us all to chill out. He didn't want us to panic—there were 114 choir members. He was walking toward the door near the stairwell when two girls opened the door, and we heard two shotgun bursts. Half the choir hit the ground.

My first instinct was to run. I went out the opposite door that the two girls had come in, into a corridor that leads to the auditorium.

I saw a stampede of people running down the hallways. I heard screams. I decided I wasn't going to try and join the mob, so I ran into the auditorium. I stood at the back of the auditorium, wondering what refuge kids were finding behind plastic chairs. Then I heard the semi-automatic fire. At some point, somebody pulled the fire alarm down, so lots of kids in the east end of the school got out without a notion of what was happening.

I headed out the north door. I saw the fire doors at the north hallway—the main hallway—were closed, so I turned and ran for the front door. As I got closer I saw there were already bullet holes in the glass.

Seeing the bullet holes made me run even faster. I reached the front door and pushed it open. The bullets had weakened the glass, and shattered glass came showering out of the door all over me. I just kept running. I didn't even notice the blood all over me until much later. I later went to the hospital for stitches.

About fifteen kids followed me and got out the front door. I learned later that we barely made it out. Seconds later one of the shooters, Dylan, came into the main office and started spraying bullets.

I saw a friend, and we ran to her house. From her house we could see the front of the school. We watched the police, the firefighters, the paramedics, the SWAT teams from Denver and other areas, and the National Guard as they showed up. State patrolmen and sheriffs pulled up and got out of their cars with their guns. They stood behind trees and told kids to run.

The next few hours seemed to last forever. At first I thought a kid was in the school with a gun and that he may have shot a few kids, maybe injuring somebody, but

I hoped he hadn't caused much harm. As I watched the different teams of police show up and heard on the radio there were two gunmen, possibly three, I started to realize how big this really was.

A group of police drove a fire truck close to the building. They jumped out and ran inside. I found out later that lots of those guys weren't trained to be in the positions they were leading. They went in and risked their lives—they didn't even think about it, they just did it to save lives.

It scared me to death when later reports on the radio said that twenty-five kids were killed. I hadn't seen my best friend, Dustin, come out. I prayed he was all right. I didn't find out he was safe until much later. He had hidden in a bathroom in the kitchen and was evacuated with other kids who hid nearby.

It was a living nightmare. It was a bad day multiplied by the biggest number you can think of. The day seemed to go on for years—hours were days; everything was wrong.

The night of the shootings a lot of us went to a service at St. Francis Cabrini Catholic Church. It was really emotional for all of us because we knew our friends who should be there were gone forever. I couldn't even imagine that friends of mine—Cory, Rachel, Isaiah, Cassie—wouldn't be back at school. How could their lives end so violently? How could Eric's and Dylan's minds get so messed up?

For the longest time I didn't know what day it was, the day of the week, the date—it all just kind of ran together. I didn't eat anything for three days—I had a sick feeling inside. I kept crying. Every emotion ran through my head. I was sad, mad, confused, helpless and lost.

I spent a little time with my parents. I hugged them a lot and told them I loved them. But I needed to be with my friends, the people who had experienced this with me. People can say, "I know how you feel," but it's not true if you weren't there.

There were lots of counselors around. Media were everywhere. People showed up trying to get kids to come to their church. What touched me most were the people who came just to be available for us. They were there if we needed someone to talk to. They didn't force themselves on us at all.

We had lots of get-togethers on private property where the media couldn't get to us. We would just go and be together—the first week that's all we did. We didn't have to speak to each other—it was enough to share the silence with each other.

The first place that the faculty and students got back together was at a community church. The student body was sitting together waiting for the faculty. The choir decided we wanted to sing because before the tragedy we were practicing some very spiritual, very touching songs that had a high level of difficulty. We got up together and went up on the stage. The faculty still hadn't made it in, so I was "volunteered" to conduct.

We started singing "Ave Maria." I had chills and the hair on the back of my neck was standing up. We hadn't warmed up and the song has some very high notes for females. But they were just ripping them out—the sound was unbelievable.

As we sang "The Lord's Prayer," the faculty came into the sanctuary and started singing with us. Then the whole student body joined in. Here we were, together for the first time after a living nightmare, singing "The Lord's Prayer." As I conducted and heard the most beautiful sounds ever, I felt the love in that room. At that moment I knew we would be all right.

Charlie Simmons

Fire and Rain

Leslie had the most incredible voice. When she sang everyone would get very quiet as if making a sound would stop this beautiful angel from singing. She played the drums, the piano and was strikingly beautiful. Her presence captivated me. Every time I looked at her or heard her voice, I knew that Leslie was going to do wonderful things with her life.

We used to sit by the piano for hours singing James Taylor and Carly Simon songs. She taught me how to harmonize. When we sang together nothing else mattered. It was always a way for me to achieve instant happiness.

I remember when Leslie met Mike. "This one is different," she would tell me. "He is so grown up, very mature." He wasn't like the high-school boys she was used to dating. She was so excited that he had asked her to pick him up at the airport. He had been out of town visiting relatives, and he couldn't wait an extra minute to see her. She borrowed her parents' car.

I was told two days later that Leslie was dead. She had had a couple beers before leaving for the airport. She had a six-pack in the back seat. It was assumed the beers were for their reunion. She drove off the side of the road and hit a boulder. They didn't find her until thirty-six hours later, although the search had started immediately after Mike reported her missing.

Sometimes I sit quietly, scared to make a sound. I only wish I that I could hear her singing. I softly hum the tune of "Fire and Rain." I am alone. My beautiful angel must be singing somewhere else.

Anonymous

8

OVERCOMING OBSTACLES

The way I see it, if you want the rainbow, you gotta put up with the rain.

Dolly Parton

They always say that time changes things, but you actually have to change them yourselves.

Andy Warhol

Owning the World

Character cannot be developed in ease and quiet. Only through experience of trial and suffering can the soul be strengthened, ambition inspired, and success achieved.

Helen Keller

I slowly came to understand what had been said. Instead of the expected dismissal of my illness and being told to choke down a series of medications, I was told I had leukemia. It was June 27, 1997. The weather was pleasant, and I was calm. From the smaller hospital in Kitchener, my mom and I proceeded directly to London to begin my own personal hell.

As my mom, dad and I sat listening in a vague stupor, what we could come to expect was explained to us in the simplest and nicest way possible. That information was repeated a lot during the next little while. It was a great deal to take in while under such shock. However, I decided right away that my case would be different. I would not lose all my hair, I would not puff up from steroids, I would not get mouth sores, and the chemotherapy would not be so hard on me as it is on other people. I was wrong.

The next couple of days were the most difficult I had faced in my life. To that point, most of my life had been no problem. I could dismiss whatever was wrong within a couple of days and never face very severe or life-changing consequences. But leukemia was a big deal that I would have to live with for an indeterminate length of time. I decided to complete this temporary obstacle with grace, maturity and an understanding of how much people were helping me, and how much I had to be grateful for.

Meanwhile, back at home people were slowly hearing the news. I started getting lots of cards and gifts. I knew they were meant to cheer me up, but they made me sad. I didn't want to be the center of bad attention. I didn't want people to know I was even sick. I wanted to get the chemotherapy, go home and be happy without everybody knowing. But the gifts and cards piled up, each one a painful reminder of what a difficult and daunting task lay before me.

When it was around time for it to fall out, I cut my shoulder-length black curly hair short. I didn't really care that much; I was too weak from the leukemia and the first strong dose of chemotherapy. My hair fell out about a week later. For the first little while I wore a wig or a hat all the time because I was so ashamed. Eventually, I came not to care if the nurses or my parents saw me without hair. It took quite a while longer for me to show a select group of my friends. I kept in contact with two of my best friends. I didn't have the energy or the strength to reassure them all firsthand.

I spent most of July in the hospital, waiting for my blood counts to come back high enough that I could return home. I completed a number of paintings, finding that painting helped to keep my spirits high and my mood cool, calm and collected. It was amazing therapy. I went home for a week in early August. I needed a break. I had to stay out of the sun, didn't have as much stamina as usual and wore a wig, but other than that it was the closest I would feel to normal for quite a while.

The following cycle of chemotherapy was the worst I have ever experienced. I had no idea what was in store for me. Up until then, I had handled all the chemotherapy with flying colors. At the end of August I was back in the hospital, only this time in pain. It was the worst pain I had ever felt. I wasn't allowed to have pain relievers because the doctors had to know if the pain changed in any way. An endless bombardment of seemingly unimportant questions, which in reality were quite significant, drove me insane. They put a tube down my nose to drain the stomach acid, and I suffered severe nausea and stomach pain for the next month. I finally went home feeling better. My bone marrow transplant was scheduled for October, earlier than anticipated. I went shopping, had my friends over, and had a great time. It was a very well-deserved break.

I was very fortunate to have two donors to choose from. Both my brother and my sister were perfect matches. The doctors chose my brother. We went to Toronto's special bone-marrow transplant unit confident and full of hope that this was finally coming to a close. The round of chemotherapy was strong enough to kill me if I hadn't had my brother's marrow to back me up. I did quite well in isolation. Except for the nausea. It just never went away. Everything I ate just came back up again. I went home promising to eat and drink as much as I could or a minimum of one-and-a-half liters a day. That proved to be extremely difficult.

Within a couple of days I was back in the hospital to get

hydrated and for treatment for shingles. The nausea still hadn't gone away. I was angry with myself for letting everybody down. We all had such high expectations for me after the bone-marrow transplant, and I wasn't meeting them. No matter how hard I tried, I could not bring myself to eat. On top of it, I had to take a great number of pills, which just made me more sick.

Even though the nausea continued, I was able to return home. It was torture. I got bronchitis and sinusitis and had no idea how it could possibly get worse. After a CT scan and routine clinic visit, I found out I had relapsed. The chemotherapy and bone-marrow transplant didn't work. The leukemia was back. All I had just been through was for nothing. This bad news came ten times harder than it had the first time. I had already been through all this, suffered the consequences, and lived through the trials and tribulations.

When a patient with AML relapses, the chances of long-term remission, or cure, with conventional treatments is about 20 percent. That news just never left my mind. However, I was able to remain secure in knowing that I was getting the newest and latest treatment. I was the eighth pediatric patient to try this new treatment through Sick Kids' Hospital, and so far it had worked quite well in adults. So I told myself it would be all right and started it along with another program my dad had heard about.

The medication my dad found was an experimental organic medicine that is injected into the lymph nodes. I had to do that every day for three months. It was up to me when to stop. It was as if a great weight had been taken off my shoulders when I finally felt confident enough to stop.

The hospital treatment was quite different. I had to endure a round of chemotherapy, followed by a dose of my brother's white blood cells, hoping that they would identify the leukemia as foreign "bad stuff" and destroy it. The first chemotherapy and batch of my brother's white blood cells proved inadequate. When I got my bone marrow checked there were still signs of leukemia. I went through the chemotherapy once more, knowing that if it didn't work this time I was as good as gone. They gave me the remaining batch of white blood cells, this time many more of them. My brother and I are such a close match that the blood cells hadn't attacked me enough, so, with the second and final round, they gave me the entire batch.

I am proud to say that I no longer show signs of any leukemia.

Slowly, day by day, I approach summer, regain my strength and remind myself of how valuable and fragile *everybody* is. It has been a long, hard fight, but I would not trade the lessons I have learned in those ten months for the world. I have learned to be brave. I have learned to be strong. And, most important, I have learned to persevere.

Liz Alarie

[EDITOR'S NOTE: ***We received the following from the author's parents:***

Two months later, Lizzie relapsed for the last time. Shortly after, she died at home. Lizzie lived her fifteen months of illness with radiant grace, maturity and ever-present gratitude. She accomplished her greatness here on Earth as a teacher. "Her world" witnessed her valiant actions, kind deeds and motivating stories such as this one. Lizzie's wish for mankind was simple: Begin now to live your life to the fullest—it is possible!

***Ray and Mary Pat Alarie*]**

Voices

When she looks in the mirror
She doesn't see what you see
You see,
Skin and bones,
The sunken face,
And dark circles under her eyes.
She looks in the mirror
And sees just the opposite.
She sees a girl,
With too much fat here
And there
And her body figure just not perfect.
You tell her to eat,
And that she's way too thin.
The voices in her head
Are saying,
If she eats she will gain,
And be way too fat to be loved.
She has been told countless times over
You are special,
Unique,

And loved by all.
On the other hand
The strong voices shout,
You are worthless,
And plain,
You don't deserve any of their love.
This child
She needs your ever-lasting support,
And love.
Continue to tell her she is a special,
Worthwhile person
Undeserving of this terrible disease.
The road to recovery will be a bumpy one,
With many curves,
Steep hills,
And valleys.
With the love and support from all
She will again realize she is loved
And wanted.
You may feel your words
Of hopeful strength,
Are sounds she isn't listening to,
But your words will soon
Build up in her head
And conquer her evil thoughts.
She will soon blossom,
And live a life of
Love,
And laughter
Once again.

Micah Twaddle

I Just Wanted to Be Skinny

I couldn't believe that I hadn't let myself see how awful Colleen had become. I was so ashamed of myself at that moment, staring at her in her size zero sundress draped loosely over her. She looked like a little girl swimming in her mother's clothes. It was as if I was seeing her for the first time. Her adorable round baby face had become so gaunt, and her once bright eyes had become dull and faded, now just slightly sunken in as if all her desire for life had been sucked out of her. I began to panic as my eyes frantically scanned the rest of her body. But it was no use. With every glance, I saw skin and bone where there should have been the beginnings of womanly curves. Everything about her was so tiny and frail that she reminded me of a twig that could be snapped with the blow of a harsh winter wind. I was overwhelmed with guilt. I was supposed to be her friend. I was supposed to keep her from doing things like this to herself. I had promised I would always be there for her. And right then, I wanted to run crying from the store because I knew I had failed. Instead, I just stood there next to her, unable to say anything, while she critiqued herself about how fat she looked and how tight the dress was. How had this happened?

I later found out it began in the eighth grade, which was the year when attention on being thin became emphasized. Diets became an obsession for many girls. There was a new one to try every week, each promising better results than the last. They were "in style" the same way green nail polish or jelly sandals were. Colleen was always insecure about being fat, which surprised me because she had such a healthy looking body. But seeing those stick-figured girls talk about their diets only perpetuated Colleen's insecurity.

How could I have been so dumb and so blind? How could I not have realized that her reasoning for all the missed school lunches were just excuses, that she hadn't conveniently just eaten before she came over? And all the times my friends and I invited her to eat with us, how could we not have seen the pattern in her continuous declines, saying she would love to come . . . another time?

Colleen's parents took her to see a doctor, and he confirmed everyone's worst fear: He diagnosed her as anorexic. It sounded so weird to hear her called that; even though everyone knew she was, no one had ever actually said it before. Colleen was anorexic. It was almost as if I had to say it to myself a couple of times before I could really comprehend it. She weighed only eighty-six pounds at a height of 5'4" when she was admitted, and the doctors said that had she continued the destructive pattern much longer, there was a good chance she could have died of a heart attack. Imagine that—dying of a heart attack at age fourteen.

The doctors and psychologists asked Colleen repeatedly, "What made you decide to stop eating?" And she always answered sincerely and simply, "I just wanted to be skinny." This reply frustrated them. I guess they expected to hear a huge psychological reasoning behind her anorexia, like pressure from her parents, school or sports. I'm not really sure what they wanted to hear, but they couldn't seem to accept that Colleen starved herself because she just wanted to be thinner.

It's been a little over a year now, and I'm proud to say that Colleen has only been back to the hospital once. She has worked incredibly hard to gain back her normal, stress-free life, and it's been a difficult struggle. But I know she will win this battle in the end.

It bothers me, though, that Colleen's struggle could have been prevented. What is it that makes girls feel like they must look like waifs before they are considered beautiful? Some people might blame the media, others may fault the girl's lack of self-confidence, or the parents for not providing better examples. Maybe it's a little of all three. If only there were a way to tell each young, impressionable girl that women are *supposed* to be different shapes, that it's all those dozens of unique figures that make our world beautiful. If only there were some way to tell them that it's this variety that makes every woman truly beautiful. Then, maybe, cases like Colleen's could be prevented.

Laura Bloor

Inner Sustenance

All I ever wanted was to be popular. Have the coolest friends. Be in a hot rock band and date the best-looking men—simple wishes for a young girl. Some of my dreams even came true. I started a rock band. And the cutest guy at Melbourne High School even asked me out.

I answered yes of course, but within a week, he complained, "Your hips are too big. You need to lose weight to look thin like the other girls in your band."

Immediately, I tried several different diets to lose weight. For one, I ate grapefruit and vegetables only. That didn't work; I felt faint and had to eat. The second week I tried skipping breakfast and dinner. When I did that, I became so hungry by the time dinner came, I splurged and eventually started gaining weight. Ten pounds I added in a month trying to please my boyfriend. Instead of praising my efforts, he cut me down even more. "You look like a whale," he said, making me feel not as pretty as my other friends who wanted to date him. I felt self-conscious and didn't want to lose him as a boyfriend, so I desperately searched for another way to lose the pounds that were keeping him at bay.

I didn't even think that he was the problem: just me, it was just me. Whatever I ate made me fatter. Whatever I wore, I looked hideous. I was now 110 pounds, a complete blimp!

One evening after a date, I got so angry by his "whale" remarks that I ate an enormous piece of cake. The guilt made me want to try something I had seen other girls in my school doing at lunch break: throw up. I went to my bathroom and without even thinking of the consequences, stuck my finger down my throat and threw up in the toilet.

All I ever wanted was to be as pretty as a model. I wanted my boyfriend to look at me the same way as he did those bikini-poster girls.

It was so easy. That cake I just enjoyed didn't cost me any unwanted calories.

Once a day soon turned into three forced vomits. Becoming malnourished, I was constantly hungry, so I ate more, threw up more. It wasn't until I strangely gained another fifteen pounds and tried to quit a month later that I realized I couldn't stop. I fought to, for several weeks. As soon as I got up from the table, my stomach began convulsing. Now my own stomach somehow believed that's what it was supposed to do. I had to run from the table. I was throwing up without even sticking my finger down my throat or even wanting to!

I wasn't in control anymore. I was caught in a whirlwind. I thought bulimia would help me lose pounds but after the months of doing it, not only hadn't it controlled my weight, but the purging had opened up the pits of hell.

I needed help. My boyfriend's comments and my weight were the least of my problems now and I knew it. At age fifteen I didn't know what to do. Desperate for a solution, I broke down into tears and confided in the only person I could trust: my mom. Unsure, of how she would react and wondering if she'd stop loving me if she knew, I mustered up the courage to write the truth on a note and leave it on her dresser:

"Mom, I'm sick. I tried forcing myself to throw up to lose weight, now I am vomiting every day. I can't stop. I'm afraid I'm going to die."

I locked myself in my room the entire night. My mother knocked on my door several times. I could hear her crying. The next morning she pounded harder and told me she had made a doctor's appointment for me. "Get out here before we're late!" she said.

I opened the door. Instead of a hard and loud scolding, I received a hug. Being in her understanding arms, I had the confidence to go to the doctor with her.

The first meeting with the doctor, I'll never forget. He told me that by using bulimia to lose weight I was actually retaining water, losing hair, ruining the enamel on my teeth and was now developing a very serious stomach condition called gastritis. He informed me I was malnourished and in danger of losing my life. He strongly recommended that I check myself into a hospital for treatment.

Knowing that I would be apart from my friends and my mother, I didn't want to agree. Going to the hospital seemed to be a way of walking away from everything I've ever known. I was terrified about leaving home. I'd never been away from my house, my school or my friends before. I was wondering if anyone would even stay my friend or if they all would think I was a freak. I thought about telling the doctor I wouldn't even consider it, but my conscience reminded me, *If I don't go I'll be spending the rest of my days, however many more I have left, throwing my life away, literally down the toilet.* I told the doctor I would go.

The first day and night were the hardest. Nurses gave me a study schedule for both educational and counseling activities. I would attend six different classes each day: math, English, science, group counseling, PE and a personal session with my doctor. All the people were complete strangers. Most of the patients my age weren't there for eating disorders but for severe mental illnesses or violent behaviors. In my first class, math, I sat down and said hello to the girl sitting next to me. She turned her head and ignored me. I shifted in my chair and waved to the girl on my left and asked what her problem was. She didn't answer and mumbled something about needing medicine. I quickly learned that the other patients were hard to relate to or on heavy medication. They didn't seem to have any desire to make friends. That night, I cried myself to sleep, feeling more alone than I ever had.

The next morning, I was told that my blood work reported that I was not only dehydrated but also starving. The doctor said he wouldn't release me until I was strong inside and out. Months passed like this and I continued attending classes with screaming, irrational kids. I felt so isolated. The doctors tried several types of medicines; none of them seemed to be working to keep my food down. They started feeding me intravenously. A needle was stuck in the top of my hand and stayed there, taped, twenty-four hours a day. It was so gross, having a big needle sticking out in my hand. Every morning they would attach a liquid-filled bag that dripped nutrients into my bloodstream. Each night they gave me pills that made me nauseous and want to throw up. I was becoming more and more discouraged. *Will I ever be normal again?* I wondered. Still, I wouldn't give up. I knew what I had to do and I tried yet another medication.

When that didn't seem to do anything, a nurse came into my room, took that morning's medication out of my hand and suggested that I stand in front of the mirror one hour after each meal and repeat to myself these words,

"Yes, I am perfect because God made me."

I thought she was nuts! If modern medicine couldn't work, how could saying a few words do the trick? Still, I knew I had to try it. It couldn't hurt and if it got me off the feeding tube, it was worth it no matter how crazy it sounded. Beside, if it didn't work, I could tell the nurse that it wasn't the cure and that at least I tried.

The next meal, I said the words for several minutes. Religiously. I said them for an entire week extending the time every day. After a while, I realized I began saying them as if I meant them and I had been keeping my food down. My bulimia was becoming under control because my mind stopped focusing on throwing up, and started focusing on saying those words! Within a week I stopped needing to be fed through tubes, my stomach had stopped rejecting food and my compulsion to vomit ceased. My mind had been tricked into more positive thinking!

With the support of my counselors and nurses, I continued searching for ways to bolster my self-esteem, so that I would never again be so vulnerable to the judgments of others. I began to read self-esteem books and the Bible to further my self-image. By then, my boyfriend had dumped me. Most of my friends had stopped coming to see me. Even on the day I celebrated my newfound ability to keep my food down, I called my brother to tell him the good news and he said, "You're making all this up for attention, aren't you?"

I can't tell you how much that hurt. Still, I wouldn't let the outside world's cruelty diminish my victory or my newly found self-esteem of loving myself no matter what my weight was. Finally, I realized with this new strength, I was well.

I began feeding myself and choosing to be full—literally, spiritually, emotionally and physically. My self-esteem strengthened as I ate, repeated those words, and learned to love myself. By gulping down food, I became the vessel God had created me to be. I was special regardless of what others thought. And, I saw that old boyfriend for what he really was: shallow, close-minded, inconsiderate, and not even worthy of my love in the first place.

It had taken months in the hospital with nurses and counseling to learn a lesson I'll never forget. Being popular is just an illusion. If you love yourself you are in the "in" crowd. You are an individual gift from God to the world. It's comforting to know joy comes from being who I am instead of trying to become somebody else's perfect model.

My first day back to school, my ex-boyfriend actually came up to me and asked me out again. "Wow, you look great. You're so thin! You want to go to the football game on Friday?"

"No," I answered, without regret. "I'd rather date someone who loves my heart."

Me! Accepting me suddenly became a daily celebration of life. I love me! Those three words sound so simple, but living them, believing them makes living so tantalizingly delicious!

Michelle Wallace Campanelli

I Am Not Alone

Here I stand, just another voice, lost in a crowd of noise. Though I am surrounded by familiar faces, I do not recognize anyone. I have never felt so alone. . . .

I am eighteen years old, and in love with the most wonderful person! He is cute, sweet and oh so charming. He makes me so happy. I have never felt so content. He is my best friend. When he looks in my eyes and says, "I love you," I just know we are forever. For us, life is a party.

Reality sets in and threatens to reveal the illusions of my fantasy world. *Where is he now?* I wonder desperately. *Where did I go wrong? Did I fall short of his expectations somehow? Or was he unable to meet mine? Was it that he never really loved me, and if so, did he lie? WHY?* The young man I thought I knew so well does not exist, is someone whose face I do not recognize. His voice sounds strange and distant. I see behind his disguise. I look past his smile and his promises. I see him for who he *really* is.

My stomach hurts lately, and I have trouble eating. I feel dizzy and nauseous. I get so tired, I can hardly stay awake. Yet even after a nap, I still feel cranky and irritable. Maybe it's just the flu. No, it is something else.

I sense a truth I want to ignore.

My friend must know, too. I can tell by the way she watches me. I don't want to say anything because I am afraid. She brings me a pregnancy test and tells me, "You should take it just to be sure."

I pretend that I am not worried, that this is silly. "I know I am not pregnant." I keep saying it to reassure myself more than her. Then I go to the bathroom.

I watch two lines appear quickly. I can hardly breathe. I feel nothing really, except shock and denial. Tears will not come. I just stare in disbelief and then quietly call for my friend. I point at the test stick lying face up on the counter, the faint pink lines rapidly changing to a dark shade of maroon. As calmly as I can, I say, "This can't be right." She knows the test is right, and so do I. Tomorrow, I will go to the doctor. Right now, I just want to lie down.

"Positive. You are definitely pregnant." I look up and catch the nurse's eyes. It is real. There is no way to avoid the truth. She hands me a tissue as I cry. Now, my tears are endless. She listens as I lose myself in despair. I can't think. A million thoughts are colliding in my head, causing a mass of confusion. How will I tell him? He has to know.

I go to see him when I leave the clinic. He is sitting in his bedroom, with the light off. A small ray of light comes through the window, and casts shadows across his face. I turn my head away. I can't look him in the eye. I can feel my lips trembling as I try not to cry, but I will not allow him to witness the panic that grips me. I try to appear brave and unemotional as I tell this stranger I am carrying his child. He, too, seems unemotional. I feel his eyes upon me. Getting my words out is a struggle. I look up and try to smile, a weak attempt. This is not how I had imagined it would be. So, I wait for him to do, or say, something, anything to let me know I am not alone. Instead, his silence chills me. I know that things between us are changed forever; I turn and walk away. I want him to call to me, or run after me. I want him to hold me in his arms. As I am leaving, I vaguely hear him say, "I'm sorry."

I am outside now. The sun shines down upon me like a spotlight. I feel naked. The door shuts behind me, and I burst into tears. I cry for the young man on the other side of the door. I cry for the baby that is growing inside me. I cry because my heart is breaking. I suddenly feel my youth is ending.

Weeks go by, and every day I live in fear. I wish I had been more careful with my heart and my body. I wish I had never met him. I am too young to be a mother. I am scared. I feel sick and alone. Will my baby have a father? I sleep all day and cry all night. I wonder how it feels to laugh. I stare at myself in the mirror, looking for my smile, my happiness.

Now I see the beginning of this tiny creature on a screen. I hear a heartbeat separate from my own. I feel a new kind of love. A love that has confidence and guidance—the love of a mother. I lift my head up, and I stand strong for myself, for my unborn child and for the priorities instilled in me by my pregnancy.

Here I am amidst a crowd of noise, swimming against the current I have accepted as my reality, in a sea where familiar faces fade away, and I am not alone.

Sara Strickland

Four Kisses

I am thirteen and going to a baseball game with my father. I bring binoculars, a little Dutch-boy haircut, my glasses, insecurity, a love for the game and a lack of serotonin in my brain. The fog is twisting around Candlestick Park, leaving the feeling of dampness, dirty water on my jacket and wetness on my glasses, making my perspective skewed like a funhouse mirror. My father wants more than anything else to teach me to keep score, but I am desperately trying to never learn anything new again, because the things I have learned in the last year have been all-around destructive: that I am clinically depressed, that a school day is too long, that I have obsessive-compulsive disorder, and that I am losing even more weight, and am down to eighty-five pounds.

My father grabs my hand. "Did you see that pitch? Right on the money, right on the money. Whoever says they're not going to take it all the way . . ." Asleep in the car on the way home, I can only vaguely hear the music he has on softly so as not to wake me. Something about going home, going home, going home. Mom is asleep in their bed with her red-and-gray quilt that smells just like she does.

My father stops in my room on his way to his. "Good night, Kater." He is standing in the one spot in my doorway where everything echoes. "Good night, Daddy. I love you. Can I have four kisses?" I need four of everything, because obsessive-compulsive disorder has me believing in plastic number power, power I can't have in other arenas. So I make my bed sixteen times and wash my hands until I have slammed the door to the cabinet under the sink just so, so that nobody dies or gets in a car wreck.

My father notes that I have been sleeping wildly. I am usually a still sleeper, the biggest moves I make are a shift from one side to the other, so that I go to sleep staring at the green light from my clock, and wake up with my face towards the wall. But starting last year, I have been waking up having kicked my quilt off, with my stuffed animals relegated unconsciously to the coldness of the floor.

The next day my father says, "Maybe you're getting better." He tries.

"I just want it to end."

"I know you do."

"But I really, really need it to end. Dad, I can't deal with it."

"You know how when you're cleaning out your desk or your room, you have to empty everything out, spread it all over the floor?"

"I guess." I wipe the tears from my face. I hate not being able to see.

"Well, you're there right now."

I hadn't noticed until now how foggy it is. We are walking across the street from a mortuary on the way back from my therapist. It is a Tuesday.

"What?" I asked, not understanding his point.

"Katie, you have everything spread out all over the floor. You have to wait, to pick it all up." This only makes me cry harder, because I am frustrated by the reality of the metaphor blown up, enlarged, unreachable.

My father and my mother are constant reminders to me of what I leave when I go to school for abbreviated days. They are what I stand to lose.

Graduation day. My father and my mother sit in the white plastic chairs; I am on an elevated platform. It is wood painted brown, and parts of it have chipped off so that the chairs that my eighth-grade class sits on are tipping and making plastic-to-wood noises through hollow speeches. Somewhere in the middle, I start to cry. For once it's okay, nobody jeers. I am leaving a part of my life on an uneven platform with my above-the-ears-but-growing-out haircut, bangs clipped back with golden barrettes, a white dress and wonderful parents.

My father drives me to my first day at high school. I haven't been to the therapist in three months. I am walking on legs and feet and ankles that I trust. A senior tells my older sister that I am strutting around school. I keep my bangs pulled away from my face. I hate not being able to see.

My father and I have begun to fight. He does not want me staying out too late. He is upset that my grades are lower than he expected. He always wants to know when I'll be home. When I argue with him, and he leaves, I almost don't know what to do with myself. My obsessive-compulsive power is gone. I am empty so that I can start over.

"Fall came today," my dad says, his first words to me that morning. Since the recent death of my friend's brother, I think of first words and last words more carefully than I should. There have been other first words on other mornings, mostly about the weather or the Giants and how they blew it in the seventh with two runners on, one of them in scoring position. I nod. I'm ineffectual with him that way, letting him bounce off me, because if I let him in, I would be admitting to something. I have thoughts now. And they are mine. My insides and my breaths and my friends and my words, they are all mine. I cling to them more and more.

When my father and I fight, it is loud and articulate. There's something cleansing about it, and it makes me shake. He tells me that he's proud of how well I can argue, that I can always get my point across. My father blames me when my mother gets sick, because it's the stress that I cause, manifesting itself in her.

I am finally sixteen. I have a best friend and contact lenses, a father, a mother and a past. I have beaten something. And that is what I have inside me: strength. I realize, midway through the first quarter of my junior year, that I don't know who bats cleanup for the Giants. I realize that the mortuary across from my old therapist was torn down to build a parking lot. I realize that I haven't talked to my father, sat down and talked to him, since I went away this summer by myself and came back with crisp white inspiration.

I finally have enough serotonin in my brain. I know what I need. I have respect for myself and what I went through. It used to be inexplicable. My father, my mother, a dry bedspread, a song about going home and the National League champion Giants went through it with me. I had built a fresh new me, but I had lost my father. And I wasn't willing to give him up.

I hear his sweaty-feet footsteps coming up the stairs in the house. I lie in my bed tonight, a sixteen-year-old at 110 pounds with long hair, a daughter, home by curfew. Warm and whole, stubborn, stronger, older, and I ask my father for one solitary kiss.

Kate Reder

Mark's Choice

The question is not whether we will die, but how we will live.

Joan Borysenko

"What's wrong?" I still remember asking that question to my teammate as he sat in front of his locker more than twenty years ago. We had just finished polishing off another opponent our senior year and there he sat—head in hands—alone—in pain. He was tough, seventeen years old and a great athlete. His name is Mark Overstreet. The rest of our teammates had showered and left for home, but Mark was still fully dressed in his football uniform. When he raised his head to speak, I saw tears in his eyes. Now I knew something was wrong. This was a young man who took pride in making the opponents cry on the football field. "I don't know," he said silently. "It's as if all the injuries I've ever had are coming back. My whole body hurts. My legs feel like they weigh a hundred pounds each."

A week or so before, an outbreak of the swine flu had swept through our community. One by one, students lined up to take the vaccine to prevent the spread of the illness. I remember we all took the shot and thought nothing of it. When Mark received the vaccine, however, his body developed a very rare allergic reaction to the drug—so rare that his sudden illness was never correctly diagnosed until ten years later.

The next morning after our conversation in the locker room, Mark awoke to find his right foot asleep. No matter how much he tried to rub the foot to alleviate the "pins and needles" feeling, the circulation never returned. Concerned, Mark's mother decided to take him to the doctor. Mark's life was about to change forever.

Baffled by what he saw while examining Mark, the doctor somberly exclaimed, "I don't know what's wrong with you, Mark, but you are going to lose that foot." Shocked, his mother backed up against the wall. Stunned, Mark said, "What are you talking about? What's wrong with me?" The doctor did not know the answer and admitted Mark into the hospital for further tests.

While in the hospital, Mark's left foot fell asleep and, just like the right one, never woke up. Now, not only were both feet losing circulation, but things were getting worse. Finally, after many failed tests, the doctor entered his room to tell him the news. "Mark, whatever it is, it is killing you. It's spreading up to your heart. We have one plan. To hopefully stop the spread we want to amputate both your legs just below the knee. If that doesn't work, you have two weeks."

Two weeks. Two weeks for a young man who had never been sick a day in his life. "What is wrong with me?" Mark again asked. "We don't know," responded the doctor. Mark prepared for the operation not knowing his chances.

When the operation was over, Mark awoke to find the doctor by his bed. "I've got some good news and some bad news," he said. "The good news is, whatever it was, it's gone. The operation was successful. You are going to live. The bad news is, you are probably going to be in a wheelchair your whole life and in and out of hospitals, as well. I'm sorry."

It was at that moment that Mark made a decision—a choice that would shape his whole future. "No!" he responded. "I'm not staying in hospitals—I'm not staying in wheelchairs. I'm going to walk and I'm going to live life! This is just the beginning—not the end."

It took a year, but after learning to use wooden legs, Mark walked out of the hospital for the last time. Later, he decided that since he would never play football or baseball again, he would coach and teach others to play. While in college, Mark met Sharon and fell in love. Sharon didn't mind Mark's wooden legs. She loved him for who he was. After graduation they married and Mark began his first job teaching handicapped students and coaching high school football. Today, Mark and Sharon have four beautiful children and a lovely home. He is a high-school principal in southwest Missouri and my boss. Every morning Mark gets up, puts on his legs and goes to school to greet students and teachers alike. You would never know if he has had a bad day because he would never tell you.

The choice was his. He could still be back in that wheelchair, in and out of hospitals, feeling sorry about the bad break he suffered in high school, but, instead, he is changing lives and living a blessed one himself.

Tom Krause

Ability

Ability is to look at a blank page,
And create a poem.
Ability is to stare into the eyes of fear,
And come out stronger because of it.
Ability is to walk into a room of strangers,
And come out with friends.
Ability is to admit you are wrong,
When you are wrong.
Ability is to get back up,
When you fall down.
Ability is to believe,
When everything seems lost.

Ability—a simple word, with a complex meaning.
For many, ability is never found, but for all ability is within.
Ability stares everyone in the face at one time or another.
Whether your ability is how well you shoot hoops,
How well you flip at dancing,
How smart you are at school.
You have ability.
For some, ability is lost by never trying.

Whether never trying to shoot one more time,
Never trying to bend a little more,
Or never trying to score higher in school.

Ability is within.
Ability is yours.

Selina E. Matis

The Final Game

No pessimist ever discovered the secret of the stars or sailed to an uncharted land, or opened a new doorway for the human spirit.

Helen Keller

Before the final game, life was an ordinary, daily routine. Each day, I awakened with a mental list of the tasks I had to complete before the end of the day. My routine wasn't too complicated: class, soccer practice, studying and sleep. Oftentimes, I returned home from endless hours on the soccer field only to have to study until the early hours of the morning.

Having adapted well to my daily routine, I never imagined it would be altered. However, my life changed the day of the final game. It was the last game of the tournament, and the winner would capture the championship. Not only had my team been under vigorous physical training for the past four years in anticipation of this day, but emotionally, we were ready as well. I was ready. I entered the game with the mindset that the title was in our hands. We deserved it because our desire to win was so great, and we were *hot!*

"Captains!" called the referee. I approached the center of the field, and with confidence, looked my opponent in the eyes while giving her a powerful handshake, wishing her luck. As I took my position on the field, I knew it was time for the final game to begin. I took a deep breath and reassured myself that I would give this game my all, displaying the best of my abilities as if it were the last game I ever played.

"Goalie, Goalie," yelled the man dressed in black and white. The two goalies simultaneously raised their right hands in the air, indicating that they were ready. The game could begin. This was it. The whistle sounded, and the ball was soon kicked in my direction. I received the ball and crossed it twenty feet toward the goal, just in time for my teammate to meet it and pound it right into the net. "Goal!" everyone shouted. The game had started out well.

But the momentum of the game soon grew intense as the opposing team came right back at us with a goal to tie the game at one to one. The game continued at an extremely competitive level throughout the first half and into the second. The score was still tied at one to one, until I received the ball with one minute to go. I needed to put the ball in the net, and I did just that, making the final score two to one. But it didn't go exactly as planned.

In an attempt to block my shot, my opponent challenged me in midair. But instead of heading the ball, her body slammed into mine, leaving me unconscious in the middle of the field, while my teammates shouted cries of victory and horror at the same time.

When I regained consciousness, I found myself in a hospital bed, surrounded by family, friends and teammates, with a huge cast on my right leg. Also at my side were doctors, the determiners of my future. In a matter of moments, they would tell me the severity of my injuries.

To my dismay, I had torn every tendon in my ankle and would have to undergo an extremely rare surgery that had only been performed a limited number of times in the United States, with a mere 50 percent success rate. After hours of contemplation, I decided to chance the surgery, knowing that either way, many challenges would await me. Would I be able to finish the semester? What effect would it have on my social life, my grades, my GPA? These questions circled my head, and unfortunately, only time would provide answers.

After the surgery, I was no longer the independent person I had once been, for I had to depend on my boyfriend, Jordan, to assist me in even the simplest tasks. It was going to be a long, tough road to recovery, and I knew I couldn't get through it without a positive attitude. Needless to say, I engaged in many mind exercises, which helped me attain the positive attitude that would aid in my adjustment to the changes in my life. I began to realize that I didn't have to give up my old life completely, and I focused my energy on a favorite pastime: writing.

Even though it was necessary for Jordan to accompany me everywhere I went, I was still able to produce works of art in the silence and solace of my mind and spirit. Although I was not in physical control of half of my body, I still had control of my mind.

Looking back on the situation in its entirety, I am glad that the final game was, in fact, my final game. I have no regrets. I said I would give it 110 percent and play as if it were my final game. I did just that, and ultimately, I came out a winner. Although my accident robbed me of my physical abilities, it left me with the power of mind and forced me to discover my inner self. That final game, in retrospect, couldn't have been more rewarding. Not only did we win, but I was able to discover a new level within. I guess I gained two victories that day.

Kelly Harrington

Winner

You can complain because roses have thorns, or you can rejoice because thorns have roses.

Ziggy

I am a winner.

I have beaten odds to get where I am today.

I have felt some pain every time I have walked another step forward, yet after having taken even one step back, I have known that regression and giving up were not options for me. I have felt the emptiness of separation as I have moved in the wrong direction.

I have learned the arts of persistence, tenacity and dedication. I know how it feels to watch my world and dreams shatter to a million pieces at my feet. I know what it is to run until there is nothing left inside of me, and then run some more.

I know how it feels to be loved, and I know how it feels when that love grows hard and cold.

I know how to be happy. I know how to smile and spread joy into lives of others with that same smile.

I have learned that one conversation can make or break

a fragile mind and heart, and thus I have learned to choose my words carefully.

I know that enthusiasm is the key to everything, and yet I know how it feels to completely lack enthusiasm.

I have learned that winning is not everything, but sometimes it feels like it is the most important thing. I have learned that other color ribbons only prove to make that blue so much sweeter. I know that my chief competitor is always myself.

I know that sometimes my best isn't good enough for others and that people can be cruel. I know that sometimes I get frustrated with myself, especially when others are frustrated with me.

I know how it feels to have something mean so much to me that it *is* me. I have experienced wrath, outrage and fury, but have still made it through the storm a survivor.

I know what it is to love. I know how to spread joy and how to extract it from even the darkest situations.

I know what hope is, and I rely on it as my last refuge. I know that darkness must exist if only to make those tiny bits of light seem that much brighter.

I know that success is self-made, and that luck is a relative term.

I know that I am strong.

I know that miracles do exist, angels do find us in our hour of need, and there is always something behind me, pushing me forward.

I believe in myself at all times, even when I think that I don't and even when I feel like no one else does.

I know how it feels to be lost. I also know how it feels to be picked out of a crowd. What it is like to be the winner, and how it feels when, for one moment, you are the star of the show.

Above all, though, I know that all of this has made me ME.

I know that being a winner is not about winning whatever race faces me in the moment. I recognize I am winning just by pushing myself every day and by waking up each morning feeling blessed by the day that lies ahead of me. Through this I am winning in the most important race ever, the race I entered at birth—this race we call life.

Amy Huffman

9

MAKING A DIFFERENCE

It's important to be involved and stand up for what you believe in.

Ione Skye

The Leader

If only they knew how hard it is for me.
I'm turning sixteen, the world I begin to see.
My friends begin to change, right before my eyes,
and now they seem to laugh, and tell all sorts of lies.
They hang around together in groups of three or four;
the language they use . . . it isn't gentle anymore.
The kids that seem most lonely wind up in their pack,
and those that stand alone, they talk behind their back.
Somehow I feel rejected because I don't conform.
Those that step to their own beat don't seem to be the norm.
I've watched a few just fade away, with drugs and alcohol;
and many more have given up, too many to recall.
Alcohol is an option for everyone in my school.
I've lost a friend to booze again; I will not be a fool.
And sex, it seems so open, for everyone to explore.
Three girls I know that came to school don't come here anymore.
If only I could make a difference, what could I do or say?
I would go to school and try my best each and every day.
There is one thing I'd like to do before I graduate.
I'd like to touch them one by one before it is too late.

Tony Overman

Turning Up Your Light

Those who bring sunshine to the lives of others cannot keep it from themselves.

James M. Barrie

More than three decades ago, I was a sophomore at a large high school in Southern California. The student body of 3,200 was a melting pot of ethnic differences. The environment was tough. Knives, pipes, chains, brass knuckles and an occasional zip gun were commonplace. Fights and gang activity were weekly events.

After a football game in the fall of 1959, I left the bleachers with my girlfriend. As we walked down the crowded sidewalk, someone kicked me from behind. Turning around, I discovered the local gang, armed with brass knuckles. The first blow of the unprovoked attack immediately broke my nose, one of several bones to be broken in the pounding. Fists came from every direction as the fifteen gang members surrounded me. More injuries. A brain concussion. Internal bleeding. Eventually, I had to have surgery. My doctor told me that if I had been hit in the head one more time, I probably would have died.

Fortunately, they did not harm my girlfriend.

After I recovered medically, some friends approached me and said, "Let's go get those guys!" That was the way problems were "resolved." After being attacked, evening the score became a priority. A part of me said, "Yes!" The sweet taste of revenge was clearly an option.

But another part of me paused and said no. Revenge did not work. Clearly, history had demonstrated time and again that reprisal only accelerates and intensifies conflict. We needed to do something differently to break the counterproductive chain of events.

Working with various ethnic groups, we put together what we called a "Brotherhood Committee" to work on enhancing racial relationships. I was amazed to learn how much interest fellow students had in building a brighter future. Not all bought in to doing things differently. While small numbers of students, faculty and parents actively resisted these cross-cultural exchanges, more and more individuals joined in on the effort to make a positive difference.

Two years later, I ran for student body president. Even though I ran against two friends, one a football hero and the other a popular "big man on campus," a significant majority of the 3,200 students joined me in the process of doing things differently. I will not claim that the racial problems were fully resolved. We did, however, make significant progress in building bridges between cultures, learning how to talk with and relate to different ethnic groups, resolving differences without resorting to violence and learning how to build trust in the most difficult of circumstances. It's amazing what happens when people are on speaking terms with one another!

Being attacked by the gang those many years ago was clearly one of my toughest life moments. What I learned, however, about responding with love rather than returning hate has been a powerful force in my life. Turning up our light in the presence of those whose light is dim becomes the difference that makes the difference.

Eric Allenbaugh

The Most Mature Thing I've Ever Seen

Every student at Monroe High School knew about it. Nobody did it. Nobody.

Lunchtime at Monroe High School was consistent. As soon as the bell that ended the last morning class started ringing, the students swarmed toward their lockers. Then those who didn't eat in the cafeteria headed with their sack lunches toward the quad. The quad was a large, treeless square of concrete in the center of campus. It was the meeting-and-eating place.

Around the quad the various school cliques assembled. The druggies lined up on the south side. The punkers were next to them. On the east side were the brothers. Next to them were the nerds and brains. The jocks stood on the north side next to the surfers. The rednecks were on the west side. The socialites were in the cafeteria. Everybody knew their place.

This arrangement did create some tension. But for all the tension generated on the perimeter of the quad at lunchtime, it was nothing compared with the inside of the quad.

The inside was no-man's land.

Nobody at Monroe walked across the middle of the quad. To get from one side to the other, students walked around the quad. Around the people. Around the stares.

Everybody knew about it, so nobody did it.

Then one day at the beginning of spring, a new student arrived at Monroe. Her name was Lisa. She was unfamiliar to the area; in fact, she was new to the state.

And although Lisa was pleasant enough, she did not quickly attract friends. She was overweight and shy, and the style of her clothes was not . . . right.

She had enrolled at Monroe that morning. All morning she had struggled to find her classes, sometimes arriving late, which was especially embarrassing. The teachers had generally been tolerant, if not cordial. Some were irritated; their classes were already too large, and now this added paperwork before class.

But she had made it through the morning to the lunch bell. Hearing the bell, she sighed and entered the crush of students in the hall. She weaved her way to her locker and tried her combination three, four, five times before it banged open. Standing in front of her locker, she decided to carry along with her lunch all of her books for afternoon classes. She thought she could save herself another trip to her locker by eating lunch on the steps in front of her next class.

So Lisa began the longest walk of her life—the walk across campus toward her next class. Through the hall. Down the steps. Across the lawn. Across the sidewalk. Across the quad.

As Lisa walked she shifted the heavy books, alternately resting the arm that held her light lunch. She had grabbed too many books; the top book kept slipping off, and she was forced to keep her eye on it in a balancing act as she moved past the people, shifting the books from arm to arm, focusing on the balanced book, shuffling forward, oblivious to her surroundings.

All at once she sensed something: The air was eerily quiet. A nameless dread clutched her. She stopped. She lifted her head.

Hundreds of eyes were staring. Cruel, hateful stares. Pitiless stares. Angry stares. Unfeeling, cold stares. They bore into her.

She froze, dazed, pinned down. Her mind screamed, No! This can't be happening!

What happened next people couldn't say for sure. Some later said she dropped her book, reached down to pick it up, and lost her balance. Some claimed she tripped. It didn't matter how it happened.

She slipped to the pavement and lay there, legs splayed, in the center of the quad.

Then the laughter started, like an electric current jolting the perimeter, charged with a nightmarish quality, wrapping itself around and around its victim.

And she lay there.

From every side fingers pointed, and then the taunt began, building in raucous merriment, building in heartless insanity: "You! You! You! YOU!"

And she lay there.

From the edge of the perimeter a figure emerged slowly. He was a tall boy, and he walked rigidly, as though he were measuring each step. He headed straight toward the place where the fingers pointed. As more and more students noticed someone else in the middle, the calls softened, and then they ceased. A hush flickered over the crowd.

The boy walked into the silence. He walked steadily, his eyes fixed on the form lying on the concrete.

By the time he reached the girl, the silence was deafening. The boy simply knelt and picked up the lunch sack and the scattered books, and then he placed his hand under the girl's arm and looked into her face. And she got up.

The boy steadied her once as they walked across the quad and through the quiet perimeter that parted before them.

The next day at Monroe High School at lunchtime a curious thing happened. As soon as the bell that ended the last morning class started ringing, the students swarmed toward their lockers. Then those who didn't eat in the cafeteria headed with their sack lunches across the quad.

From all parts of the campus, different groups of students walked freely across the quad. No one could really explain why it was okay now. Everybody just knew. And if you ever visit Monroe High School, that's how it is today.

It happened some time ago. I never even knew his name. But what he did, nobody who was there will ever forget.

Nobody.

Chris Blake
Submitted by Leon Bunker

Broken Wing

You were born with wings. Why prefer to crawl through life?

Rumi

Some people are just doomed to be failures. That's the way some adults look at troubled kids. Maybe you've heard the saying, "A bird with a broken wing will never fly as high." I'm sure that T. J. Ware was made to feel this way almost every day in school.

By high school, T. J. was the most celebrated troublemaker in his town. Teachers literally cringed when they saw his name posted on their classroom lists for the next semester. He wasn't very talkative, didn't answer questions and got into lots of fights. He had flunked almost every class by the time he entered his senior year, yet was being passed on each year to a higher grade level. Teachers didn't want to have him again the following year. T. J. was moving on, but definitely not moving up.

I met T. J. for the first time at a weekend leadership retreat. All the students at school had been invited to sign up for ACE training, a program designed to have students become more involved in their communities. T. J. was one of 405 students who signed up. When I showed up to lead their first retreat, the community leaders gave me this overview of the attending students: "We have a total spectrum represented today, from the student body president to T. J. Ware, the boy with the longest arrest record in the history of town." Somehow, I knew that I wasn't the first to hear about T. J.'s darker side as the first words of introduction.

At the start of the retreat, T. J. was literally standing outside the circle of students, against the back wall, with that "go ahead, impress me" look on his face. He didn't readily join the discussion groups, didn't seem to have much to say. But slowly, the interactive games drew him in. The ice really melted when the groups started building a list of positive and negative things that had occurred at school that year. T. J. had some definite thoughts on those situations. The other students in T. J.'s group welcomed his comments. All of a sudden T. J. felt like a part of the group, and before long he was being treated like a leader. He was saying things that made a lot of sense, and everyone was listening. T. J. was a smart guy and he had some great ideas.

The next day, T. J. was very active in all the sessions. By the end of the retreat, he had joined the Homeless Project team. He knew something about poverty, hunger and hopelessness. The other students on the team were impressed with his passionate concern and ideas. They elected T. J. co-chairman of the team. The student council president would be taking his instruction from T. J. Ware.

When T. J. showed up at school on Monday morning, he arrived to a firestorm. A group of teachers were protesting to the school principal about his being elected co-chairman. The very first communitywide service project was to be a giant food drive, organized by the

Homeless Project team. These teachers couldn't believe that the principal would allow this crucial beginning to a prestigious, three-year action plan to stay in the incapable hands of T. J. Ware. They reminded the principal, "He has an arrest record as long as your arm. He'll probably steal half the food." Mr. Coggshall reminded them that the purpose of the ACE program was to uncover any positive passion that a student had and reinforce its practice until true change can take place. The teachers left the meeting shaking their heads in disgust, firmly convinced that failure was imminent.

Two weeks later, T. J. and his friends led a group of seventy students in a drive to collect food. They collected a school record: 2,854 cans of food in just two hours. It was enough to fill the empty shelves in two neighborhood centers, and the food took care of needy families in the area for seventy-five days. The local newspaper covered the event with a full-page article the next day. That newspaper story was posted on the main bulletin board at school, where everyone could see it. T. J.'s picture was up there for doing something great, for leading a record-setting food drive. Every day he was reminded about what he did. He was being acknowledged as leadership material.

T. J. started showing up at school every day and answered questions from teachers for the first time. He led a second project, collecting 300 blankets and 1,000 pairs of shoes for the homeless shelter. The event he started now yields 9,000 cans of food in one day, taking care of 70 percent of the need for food for one year.

T. J. reminds us that a bird with a broken wing only needs mending. But once it has healed, it can fly higher than the rest. T. J. got a job. He became productive. He is flying quite nicely these days.

Jim Hullihan

To Track Down My Dream

It was the district track meet—the one we had been training for all season. My foot still hadn't healed from an earlier injury. As a matter of fact, I had debated whether or not I should attend the meet. But there I was, preparing for the 3,200-meter run.

"Ready . . . set . . ." The gun popped and we were off. The other girls darted ahead of me. I realized I was limping and felt humiliated as I fell farther and farther behind.

The first-place runner was two laps ahead of me when she crossed the finish line. "Hooray!" shouted the crowd. It was the loudest cheer I had ever heard at a meet.

"Maybe I should quit," I thought as I limped on. "Those people don't want to wait for me to finish this race." Somehow, though, I decided to keep going. During the last two laps, I ran in pain and decided not to compete in track next year. It wouldn't be worth it, even if my foot *did* heal. I could never beat the girl who lapped me twice.

When I finished, I heard a cheer—just as enthusiastic as the one I'd heard when the first girl passed the finish line. "What was that all about?" I asked myself. I turned around and sure enough, the boys were preparing for their race. "That must be it; they're cheering for the boys."

I went straight to the bathroom where a girl bumped into me. "Wow, you've got courage!" she told me.

I thought, "Courage? She must be mistaking me for someone else. I just lost a race!"

"I would have never been able to finish those two miles if I were you. I would have quit on the first lap. What happened to your foot? We were cheering for you. Did you hear us?"

I couldn't believe it. A complete stranger had been cheering for me—not because she wanted me to win, but because she wanted me to keep going and not give up. Suddenly I regained hope. I decided to stick with track next year. One girl saved my dream.

That day I learned two things:

First, a little kindness and confidence in people can make a great difference to them.

And second, strength and courage aren't always measured in medals and victories. They are measured in the struggles we overcome. The strongest people are not always the people who win, but the people who don't give up when they lose.

I only dream that someday—perhaps as a senior—I will be able to win the race with a cheer as big as the one I got when I lost the race as a freshman.

Ashley Hodgeson

From Crutches to a World-Class Runner

A number of years ago in Elkhart, Kansas, two brothers had a job at the local school. Early each morning their job was to start a fire in the potbellied stove in the classroom.

One cold morning, the brothers cleaned out the stove and loaded it with firewood. Grabbing a can of kerosene, one of them doused the wood and lit the fire. The explosion rocked the old building. The fire killed the older brother and badly burned the legs of the other boy. It was later discovered that the kerosene can had accidentally been filled with gasoline.

The doctor attending the injured boy recommended amputating the young boy's legs. The parents were devastated. They had already lost one son, and now their other son was to lose his legs. But they did not lose their faith. They asked the doctor for a postponement of the amputation. The doctor consented. Each day they asked the doctor for a delay, praying that their son's legs would somehow heal and he would become well again. For two months, the parents and the doctor debated on whether to amputate. They used this time to instill in the boy the belief that he would someday walk again.

They never amputated the boy's legs, but when the bandages were finally removed, it was discovered that his right leg was almost three inches shorter than the other. The toes on his left foot were almost completely burned off. Yet the boy was fiercely determined. Though in excruciating pain, he forced himself to exercise daily and finally took a few painful steps. Slowly recovering, this young man finally threw away his crutches and began to walk almost normally. Soon he was running.

This determined young man kept running and running and running—and those legs that came so close to being amputated carried him to a world record in the mile run. His name? Glenn Cunningham, who was known as the "World's Fastest Human Being," and was named athlete of the century at Madison Square Garden.

The Speaker's Sourcebook

The Power of a Smile

There is so much in the world to care about.

Laura Dern

Waiting tensely in the small, single room of the Portland Blanchet House, I could hardly control the knot of nervous excitement forming in my gut. It was my first time here with the church youth group to help feed the homeless, and I'd been given the hardest job of all. Nineteen tables in careful rows crowded the room, and it was my job to stand in the center, where I could see every table, telling new people to come in and fill the seats as they emptied.

I was thrilled and eager to be actively doing something directly to help people in the community, but I was also very nervous and curious. What would these people be like? I knew I was doing good and that I could learn a lot from hands-on work, but along with that zealous enthusiasm to broaden my perspective there tugged the urgent voice of a sheltered little suburban girl, whispering for me to hide.

There was no turning back now; it was time. People trudged in, a huddled line of bundles and packs. Red or blue patches of near frozen skin showed here and there beneath ragged scarves and overcoats, muffled eyes peered around the room with an air of bewilderment.

The seniors, who were always the first to be served, quickly occupied the seats farthest from the draft coming from the open door. They immediately started filling the complimentary plastic bags with portable food items such as cookies and rolls. I watched with a kind of naive awe, searching their faces, wondering what were their reasons for living this way, imagining what it would be like to live on the city streets twenty-four hours a day.

I was fidgety, having little to do at this point except wait for the first round of people to finish their meal, so I focused on the advice of the house director: "Lots of 'em come here as much to see a friendly face as to eat the food, so don't be afraid to smile."

This I could handle. Smiling the warmest, most sincere smile I could muster, I caught the eyes of every person I could, and though few smiled back, I felt good about it.

One old man with flyaway tufts of white hair kept looking at me with an expression of far-off wonderment. Vague gray-blue eyes shone amidst the wrinkled sand-paper of his face, and a not-quite-all-there smile beamed out with childlike simplicity. I was greatly touched by his evident pleasure at alternately swallowing a spoonful of ice cream and staring at my face. When he motioned me to come over closer to him, I was only a little alarmed. His speech was slurred and gentle, and he appeared mildly senile. As he reached out one thick-skinned hand to take mine, I felt no threat in his grandfatherly presence.

"I just wanted to ask you," he murmured sweetly, "how much do I owe you for your smile?"

In a laughing rush, I told him, "nothing," and that aged

smile grew even more wide and amazed.

"Well, in that case, may I have another?"

I complied with a helpless blush. He told me that as long as he remembered that smile, he'd be doing just fine.

I thought, *Me, too.* Sometimes that's all it takes.

Susan Record
Submitted by Mac Markstaller

Pay Attention

Jason came from a good family with two loving parents, two brothers and a sister. They were all successful academically and socially. They lived in a posh neighborhood. Jason had everything a boy could desire. But he was always into some kind of mischief. He wasn't a bad kid who caused trouble, but he always wound up in the thick of things.

In first grade, Jason was labeled Special Ed. They tried to keep him out of the regular classes. In middle school, he was the "misfit troublemaker." In high school, although never officially tested, Jason was tagged with having attention deficit disorder (ADD). More often than not, his teachers kicked him out of class. His first report card had one C and the rest Ds.

One Sunday the family was enjoying brunch at the country club when a teacher stopped and said, "Jason is doing so well these days. We're pleased and delighted."

"You must be mixing us up with another family," said the father. "Our Jason is worthless. He is always in trouble. We are so embarrassed and just can't figure out why."

As the teacher walked away, the mother remarked,

"You know, honey, come to think of it, Jason hasn't been in trouble for a month. He's even been going to school early and staying late. I wonder what's up?"

The second nine-week grading period was finally up. As usual, Jason's mom and dad expected low grades and unsatisfactory marks in behavior. Instead, he achieved four As and three Bs and honors in citizenship. His parents were baffled.

"Who did you sit by to get these grades?" the dad asked sarcastically.

"I did it all myself," Jason humbly answered.

Perplexed and still not satisfied, the parents took Jason back to school to meet with the principal. He assured them that Jason was doing very well.

"We have a new guidance counselor and she seems to have touched your son in a special way," he said. "His self-esteem is much better and he's doing great this term. I think you should meet her."

When the trio approached, the woman had her head down. It took a moment for her to notice she had visitors. When she did, she leaped to her feet and began gesturing with her hands.

"What's this?" asked Jason's father indignantly. "Sign language? Why, she can't even hear."

"That's why she's so great," said Jason, jumping in between them. "She does more than hear, Dad. She listens!"

Dan Clark

Joe Camel

"I don't believe it. They are actually taking it down!"

"We really do make a difference!"

As we sit in the bleachers of our high school stadium, we're feeling elated as the huge Joe Camel billboard, positioned directly in sight of our school, is being disassembled—and we did it!

Have you ever raised your hand simply to be part of something, and then have it turn into a life-altering event? That's exactly what happened to Eddie, Marisol and me. We belong to a school club called Friday Night Live, which promotes alcohol- and drug-free friendships and activities. It's not easy resisting the temptation to drink and smoke when, wherever you turn, advertising companies are using big money trying to hook us into using their products. The message is loud and clear: Use this stuff and you are cool, beautiful and popular.

During one of our FNL meetings, Eddie said, "It really makes me mad that everywhere I go on this campus, I can see the Joe Camel billboard, and yet the big tobacco companies tell everyone they are not targeting teens. Yeah, right!"

There are other billboards, but this is the only one you

can see from our school. Our counselor, Ms. Bambus, asked if anyone would be interested in writing to the billboard company and asking them to take it down. What followed was an amazing process that landed us on the *Today* show, CNN and many local TV shows.

We did some research and found out that there was a group called Human Health Services. We asked them if there were any other groups that had done this before and what they did. They gave us a few examples and recommended writing a polite letter to the billboard company. It seemed like it would be more fun if we just marched over and ripped up the billboard, but logic won out and we contacted the company and simply explained our concerns. We also cited the code that does not permit tobacco and alcohol advertisements within sight of a school. The vice president of the company said he couldn't see that the billboard was doing any harm.

Eddie wrote an article about it for the school newspaper, which was picked up by the local city paper. From then on, we had national media coming to our campus. One day, when I was on my way to lunch, Channel 10 came up to me and said, "Irene, we've been looking for you. We heard you and your friends are taking on Joe Camel." They asked for permission to film us talking about how we got started and what we hoped to accomplish.

Five months after all the excitement, the billboard came down. It was replaced by an ice cream advertisement. We were glad that it was all over and were looking forward to getting on with just being teens.

During the time we were involved with this, my grandfather—a smoker who started in his teens—was diagnosed with cancer. Maybe there was a higher power calling me to raise my hand to help write the letter that day. I believe if we help people not to start smoking, that's one family that won't have to watch a loved one die from it. That's a big deal!

Meladee McCarty

Anything Is Possible

It's funny how life works out. One day I was a regular high school student worried about landing the right career, and a year later, I was the owner of a company committed to changing the world, one teenager at a time. You see, my whole life I have been driven, to do something, to be something. I've always wanted to succeed, and I've never let anything come in the way of my goals.

It all started when I was eight years old. I felt like my life was over. My dad had just told me that he was no longer going to live with us; he and my mom were getting a divorce. That night, my loneliest night ever, my whole life changed. I became the man of the house. Although I felt a lot of pain when he left us, my new, important role in the family left me no choice but to move on and assume new responsibilities. Because my dad's leaving left us broke, I knew that my first job would be to earn some money for the family. As an eight-year-old, making money was not such an easy task. But I was a determined kid and not easily dismayed. I partnered with my best friend to start a lawn mowing company. I was director of marketing and he was director of labor. Our instant success gave me newfound confidence.

My ambitions to be successful did not end with the grass-cutting business in my childhood years. My drive to achieve my goals carried with me into my teenage years, where I first began exploring various career possibilities, confident that my explorations would unleash a hidden passion and begin the path to my future career. I attacked each possibility with intensity and determination. But neither medicine nor archaeology left me satisfied, so I continued to search for my passion.

During the time that I spent devoted to discovering my career, I also took some time to help a friend, five years older than I, learn to read. While my career searches left me unsatisfied, I felt an extreme sense of accomplishment in helping my friend. For the first time in my life, I became consciously aware of the power of helping others, and it was an experience that changed my life forever, although I didn't realize it at the time.

Still frustrated by the lack of career direction in my life, I decided that the stock market held my future and once again jumped head first into exploring this profession. Luckily, this one stuck. Before I knew it, I had landed myself an internship at a successful stock brokerage and eventually, after a great deal of hard work and commitment, I was offered many positions throughout the country.

Excited about my offers, but not wanting to ignore my education, I put my job offers on hold to attend classes at the University of Texas. It was during one of my classes that I was forced to reexamine my money-driven career choice. A successful young entrepreneur, Brad Armstrong, asked me what I wanted to do when I "grew up," a question many teenagers are asked and never want to answer. Feeling confident I replied, "I'll graduate when I'm nineteen or twenty, work in New York or Chicago, and retire young—like you." My teenage American dream.

Then he said, "Fantastic! Let's say you make lots of money and retire old, say age thirty-five. What are you going to do then?"

Without hesitation I replied, "See the world!"

He smiled and said, "Okay, let's say you see the world and you're thirty-eight. What are you going to do with the rest of your life? What is your *goal in life*?"

I suddenly flashed back on the experience I had teaching my friend to read and remembered the great sense of accomplishment that I had felt. It was at that moment that I realized what my goal was. I wanted to help others. And I wanted to do it in a way that I knew how.

"Brad," I said thoughtfully. "I want to write a book and help my peers." I am always so frustrated with the unfair portrayal of all teenagers as lazy, unintelligent and violent. What about the millions of us who work hard to get through school, hold steady jobs, support our families and stay clear of trouble?

He replied, "So, why don't you write now? Share with them the methods you've learned to succeed. You can help a lot of people. Share your knowledge."

That night I couldn't sleep. Brad's question about my life mission kept repeating in my head. I made the toughest decision of my life. I decided to follow my heart and jump into life not knowing where I would land.

After a great deal of research and hard work, my book about a career and life success for young people was complete. But I still had a problem. I realized that the very people I would be trying to sell my book to, would probably not be able to afford it. To solve this problem, I created an educational publishing company, designed to get my book into schools across America, where students could read the book at no cost and learn the skills needed to reach their dreams.

While I was not an overnight success, I am happy to say

that my book did eventually catch on with students, educators and business leaders. It is most rewarding to know that I got to help so many people realize what they can do to make their lives successful, especially teenagers, who have been constantly reminded of their weaknesses.

I've learned firsthand that every person holds limitless potential and passion waiting to be unleashed, and I am living proof that goals really can be achieved. Truly anything is possible when you follow your heart. The sky is no longer the limit.

Jason Dorsey

A Challenge That I Overcame

I was nervous as I sat waiting in the hospital room, unsure of what Dr. Waites, the pioneer of diagnosing developmental dyslexia, was telling my parents about the test results.

It all began when I moved to Dallas in the fourth grade, and I noticed that I was behind in my reading at Saint Michael's School. Reading out loud, I had difficulty with half the sentences. My teacher, Mrs. Agnew, said my reading comprehension and ability to pronounce words was at a lower lever than other fourth graders. I was scared every time she called on me to read aloud because, although I would try my hardest, she would always have to help me with the words. Mrs. Agnew suggested that I be tested for dyslexia.

At first I was confused about why I was being tested; I had been in all honors classes at the public school I had previously attended. The test made me feel uncomfortable, and I was scared to answer the questions, in fear of facing failure.

The test results showed that I had developmental dyslexia. At first I felt discouraged by this diagnosis, but eventually, I became determined to master my disability. I got tutors and speech therapy. I even tried to conquer the disability myself. I would read difficult books, hoping to increase the confidence I had in myself. I began to read and comprehend the readings better. I even began to love reading, which is kind of ironic since I had once detested it so much.

I had finally overcome my learning disability. Dr. Waites confirmed this when I was tested again. He said that my dyslexia was at a minimum. I was overjoyed. But even though I had conquered one of the biggest challenges in my life, I still felt like something was missing.

The missing link was filled when I put on my candy-striped uniform for the first time and walked down the halls of the hospital as a volunteer, the same hospital where I had once sat, nervous and confused. Because I felt so lucky to have had access to this facility that had helped me so much, I wanted to give back by being a volunteer.

One day a little girl in a wheelchair asked me to read a book to her. I read the book very slowly so that she could understand the story and the words. When it became time for me to leave, the girl thanked me for reading to her. I walked out of her room with a huge smile on my face. Eight years ago I would have hesitated in reading a book to this little girl, but now I was confident. I had overcome my disability and was helping others to overcome theirs. I am determined to succeed in life, and in the process, help others face and conquer the challenges that I have overcome.

Arundel Hartman Bell

Teenagers Today

I can't count how many times people have uttered, while shaking their heads in obvious disappointment, "I just don't know what is with teenagers today."

The other day I was in my car on my way to the farmers market with my friend Jan when we passed two teens standing by the side of the road with a car wash sign. My car was filthy and my heart was full, so I pulled over. There were teenagers everywhere. There was a group directing the cars and another group spraying them down. As sponges were wiped over every square inch of my dirty car, I sat enjoying the little water battles and the many silent scenarios that were so obviously taking place. I couldn't help but wonder how many crushes, how many new friendships and how many little insecurities were in the air on this beautiful Saturday afternoon. I was amazed at how forty to fifty teenagers had devoted their Saturday to washing cars, and I was curious what their motivation might be.

At the end of the assembly line I handed them a twenty-dollar bill and asked what they were raising money for. They explained to me that a friend of theirs, C.

T. Schmitz, had recently died of cancer. He was only fifteen years old and six-feet-two. He had gone to school with a lot of the teenagers who were there that day and each of them had memories of a boy sweeter than any they had known. His friend Kevin had decided to put this car wash together because he wanted to honor his friend and also bring together his classmates with his boy scout troop. He told me that they wanted to plant a tree in front of their school and if they raised enough money they would put a plaque there also. Both would be in memory of their friend C. T.

They handed me a bag of homemade cookies with my receipt and we drove away. I asked Jan to read to me what the tag that was tied to the bag said. It said simply, "Thanks for helping us plant a tree for C. T."

Yeah! I don't know what *is* with teenagers today!

Kimberly Kirberger

Mark's Choice

The question is not whether we will die, but how we will live.

Joan Borysenko

"What's wrong?" I still remember asking that question to my teammate as he sat in front of his locker more than twenty years ago. We had just finished polishing off another opponent our senior year and there he sat—head in hands—alone—in pain. He was tough, seventeen years old and a great athlete. His name is Mark Overstreet. The rest of our teammates had showered and left for home, but Mark was still fully dressed in his football uniform. When he raised his head to speak, I saw tears in his eyes. Now I knew something was wrong. This was a young man who took pride in making the opponents cry on the football field. "I don't know," he said silently. "It's as if all the injuries I've ever had are coming back. My whole body hurts. My legs feel like they weigh a hundred pounds each."

A week or so before, an outbreak of the swine flu had swept through our community. One by one, students lined up to take the vaccine to prevent the spread of the illness. I remember we all took the shot and thought nothing of it. When Mark received the vaccine, however, his body developed a very rare allergic reaction to the drug—so rare that his sudden illness was never correctly diagnosed until ten years later.

The next morning after our conversation in the locker room, Mark awoke to find his right foot asleep. No matter how much he tried to rub the foot to alleviate the "pins and needles" feeling, the circulation never returned. Concerned, Mark's mother decided to take him to the doctor. Mark's life was about to change forever.

Baffled by what he saw while examining Mark, the doctor somberly exclaimed, "I don't know what's wrong with you, Mark, but you are going to lose that foot." Shocked, his mother backed up against the wall. Stunned, Mark said, "What are you talking about? What's wrong with me?" The doctor did not know the answer and admitted Mark into the hospital for further tests.

While in the hospital, Mark's left foot fell asleep and, just like the right one, never woke up. Now, not only were both feet losing circulation, but things were getting worse. Finally, after many failed tests, the doctor entered his room to tell him the news. "Mark, whatever it is, it is killing you. It's spreading up to your heart. We have one plan. To hopefully stop the spread we want to amputate both your legs just below the knee. If that doesn't work, you have two weeks."

Two weeks. Two weeks for a young man who had never been sick a day in his life. "What is wrong with me?" Mark again asked. "We don't know," responded the doctor. Mark prepared for the operation not knowing his chances.

When the operation was over, Mark awoke to find the doctor by his bed. "I've got some good news and some bad news," he said. "The good news is, whatever it was, it's gone. The operation was successful. You are going to live. The bad news is, you are probably going to be in a wheelchair your whole life and in and out of hospitals, as well. I'm sorry."

It was at that moment that Mark made a decision—a choice that would shape his whole future. "No!" he responded. "I'm not staying in hospitals—I'm not staying in wheelchairs. I'm going to walk and I'm going to live life! This is just the beginning—not the end."

It took a year, but after learning to use wooden legs, Mark walked out of the hospital for the last time. Later, he decided that since he would never play football or baseball again, he would coach and teach others to play. While in college, Mark met Sharon and fell in love. Sharon didn't mind Mark's wooden legs. She loved him for who he was. After graduation they married and Mark began his first job teaching handicapped students and coaching high school football. Today, Mark and Sharon have four beautiful children and a lovely home. He is a high-school principal in southwest Missouri and my boss. Every morning Mark gets up, puts on his legs and goes to school to greet students and teachers alike. You would never know if he has had a bad day because he would never tell you.

The choice was his. He could still be back in that wheelchair, in and out of hospitals, feeling sorry about the bad break he suffered in high school, but, instead, he is changing lives and living a blessed one himself.

Tom Krause

10

SELF-DISCOVERY

Who in the world am I? Ah, that's the great puzzle.

Lewis Carroll

Minimaxims for My Godson

The purpose of life is a life of purpose.

Robert Byrne

Dear Sandy,

Your nice thank-you note for the graduation present I sent you a few weeks ago just came in, and I've been chuckling over your postscript in which you say that such presents are great but you wish someone could give you "half a dozen foolproof ideas for bending the world into a pretzel."

Well, Sandy, I must admit, I don't have any very original thoughts of my own. But through the years I've encountered a few ideas of that kind—not platitudes but ideas sharp-pointed enough to stick in my mind permanently. Concepts that release energy, make problem-solving easier, provide shortcuts to worthwhile goals. No one handed them over in a neat package. They just came along from time to time, usually from people not in the wisdom-dispensing business at all. Compared to the great time-tested codes of conduct, they may seem like pretty small change. But each of them has helped to make my life a good deal easier and happier and more productive.

So here they are. I hope you find them useful, too.

1. *If you can't change facts, try bending your attitudes.* Without a doubt, the bleakest period of my life so far was the winter of 1942 to 1943. I was with the Eighth Air Force in England. Our bomber bases, hacked out of the sodden English countryside, were seas of mud. On the ground, people were cold, miserable and homesick. In the air, people were getting shot. Replacements were few; morale was low.

   But there was one sergeant—a crew chief—who was always cheerful, always good-humored, always smiling. I watched him one day, in a freezing rain, struggle to salvage a fortress that had skidded into an apparently bottomless mire. He was whistling like a lark. "Sergeant," I said to him sourly, "how can you whistle in a mess like this?"

   He gave me a mud-caked grin. "Lieutenant," he said, "when the facts won't budge you have to bend your attitudes to fit them, that's all."

   Check it for yourself, Sandy. You'll see that, faced with a given set of problems one man may tackle them with intelligence, grace and courage; another may react with resentment and bitterness; a third may run away altogether. In any life, facts tend to remain unyielding. But attitudes are a matter of choice—and that choice is largely up to you.

2. *Don't come up to the net behind nothing.* One night in a PTA meeting, a lawyer—a friend and frequent tennis partner of mine—made a proposal that I disagreed with, and I challenged it. But when I had concluded what I thought was quite a good spur-of-the-moment argument, my friend stood up and proceeded to

demolish it. Where I had opinions, he had facts; where I had theories, he had statistics. He obviously knew so much more about the subject than I did that his viewpoint easily prevailed. When we met in the hall afterward, he winked and said, "You should know better than to come up to the net behind nothing!"

It is true; the tennis player who follows his own weak or badly placed shot up to the net is hopelessly vulnerable. And this is true when you rush into *anything* without adequate preparation or planning. In any important endeavor, you've got to do your homework, get your facts straight and sharpen your skills. In other words, don't bluff—because if you do, nine times out of ten, life will drill a backhand right past you.

3. *When the ball is over, take off your dancing shoes.* As a child, I used to hear my aunt say this, and it puzzled me a good deal, until the day I heard her spell out the lesson more explicitly. My sister had come back from a glamorous weekend full of glitter, exciting parties and stimulating people. She was bemoaning the contrast with her routine job, her modest apartment and her day-to-day friends. "Young lady," our aunt said gently, "no one lives on the top of the mountain. It's fine to go there occasionally—for inspiration, for new perspectives. But you have to come down. Life is lived in the valley. That's where the farms and gardens and orchards are, and where the plowing and the work are done. That's where you apply the visions you may have glimpsed from the peaks."

   It's a steadying thought when the time comes, as it always does, to exchange your dancing shoes for your working shoes.
4. *Shine up your neighbor's halo.* One Sunday morning, drowsing in a back pew of a little country church, I

dimly heard the old preacher urge his flock to "stop worrying about your own halo and shine up your neighbor's!" And it left me sitting up, wide-awake, because it struck me as just about the best eleven-word formula for getting along with people that I've ever heard.

I like it for its implication that everyone, in some area of life, has a halo that's worth watching for and acknowledging. I like it for the firm way it shifts the emphasis from self to interest and concern for others. Finally, I like it because it reflects a deep psychological truth: People have a tendency to become what you expect them to be.

5. *Keep one eye on the law of the echo.* I remember very well the occasion when I heard this sharp-edged bit of advice. Coming home from boarding school, some of us youngsters were in the dining car of a train. Somehow the talk got around to the subject of cheating on exams, and one boy readily admitted that he cheated all the time. He said that he found it both easy and profitable.

Suddenly, a mild-looking man sitting all alone at a table across the aisle—he might have been a banker, a bookkeeper, anything—leaned forward and spoke up. "Yes," he said directly to the apostle of cheating. "All the same—I'd keep one eye on the law of the echo, if I were you."

The law of the echo—is there really such a thing? Is the universe actually arranged so that whatever you send out—honesty or dishonesty, kindness or cruelty—ultimately comes back to you? It's hard to be sure. And yet, since the beginning of recorded history, mankind has had the conviction, based partly on intuition, partly on observation, that in the long run a man does indeed reap what he sows.

You know as well as I do, Sandy, that in this misty area there are no final answers. Still, as the man said, "I think I'd keep one eye on the law of the echo, if I were you!"

6. *Don't wear your raincoat in the shower.* In the distant days when I was a Boy Scout, I had a troop leader who was an ardent woodsman and naturalist. He would take us on hikes, not saying a word, and then challenge us to describe what we had observed: trees, plants, birds, wildlife, everything. Invariably, we hadn't seen a quarter as much as he had, nor half enough to satisfy him. "Creation is all around you," he would cry, waving his arms in vast inclusive circles, "but you're keeping it out. Don't be a buttoned-up person! Stop wearing your raincoat in the shower!"

   I've never forgotten the ludicrous image of a person standing in the shower with a raincoat buttoned up to his chin. The best way to discard that raincoat, I've found, is to expose yourself to new experiences in your life *all your life.*

All these phrases that I have been recalling really urge one to the same goal: a stronger participation, a deep involvement in life. This doesn't come naturally, by any means. And yet, with marvelous impartiality, each of us is given exactly the same number of minutes and hours in every day. Time is the raw material. What we do with it is up to us.

A wise man once said that tragedy is not what we suffer, but what we miss. Keep that in mind, Sandy.

Your affectionate godfather,

Arthur Gordon

No Longer a Child

Jordana was a twelve-year-old girl like every other; she worried about her clothes, hair and boys. She always had a smile on her face and a warm hug to share. What most people did not know about her was that this little girl had some very grown-up problems. Her father caused these problems. He had sexually abused her when she was five and physically abused her for years after. The emotional scars left her in hidden shambles. Her mother and father divorced when Jordana was eight, leaving her mother with sole custody.

When we met in seventh grade, years after the abuse had stopped, she seemed like every other twelve-year-old girl. We became instant best friends, gossiping about movie stars, rock bands and boys. Jordana seemed happy living with her mother and stepfather, and when I asked about her father she only told me that she did not see him anymore.

One June day, I found out one of her biggest secrets. It was hot that day after school, and we went in Jordana's backyard to tan in tank tops and shorts. It was then that I noticed cuts on her arms, mirrored by scars of cuts that had already healed. When I asked her where she received the cuts, she turned to me and began to cry stories of the past, horrors flowing from her lips as fast as the tears fell from her eyes. Jordana told me that she had cut herself because she felt so much anger towards her father. She told me about the nights of terror, about beatings and the bruises. I didn't know what to do so I just listened, consoled and counseled to the best of my ability.

Not until I had gone home did I realize what had just happened. Jordana had trusted me with information that she had hidden deep inside for a dozen years. She had chosen my hand to reach out to and pleaded silently for me to reach back.

As the weeks went on the cuts became more frequent, as if she was using her body as a personal canvas. I became increasingly scared. I was too young to handle this myself. I realized soon that I did not have the means to help her, and my decision lay before me like a shallow grave. That day after school when Jordana was at basketball practice I went to her house and knocked on the door and reached out the only way I knew how, "Mrs. Brown, I have something I have to tell you." It was then that I realized I was no longer a child.

Hilary E. Kisch

Finding a Vision

Six years ago, I went blind. Due to a severe herpes simplex virus in my eyes, I lost one of my most precious possessions: my eyesight. Tiny cold sores covered the surface of my eyes, scarring my cornea. I wasn't allowed to stand in direct sunlight or even in a brightly lit room. The light would penetrate my eyelids and cause too much pain. At the age of seventeen, I was unprepared to find myself in a dark world. Who would I be without my ability to see?

All I wanted throughout the entire summer was to be able to see people. What new cute bathing suit styles was everyone wearing? Who had cut their hair or dyed it purple? I would have a conversation with someone and realize that I had no idea what facial expressions he was making. I no longer had the ability to make eye contact, a privilege I had taken for granted before. I longed to talk with my eyes. I just wasn't whole without my vision.

My parents became my sole support system. Hoping for a miracle, they took me to an eye specialist every day. No one was sure if I would ever completely recover, and if so, how long the healing process would take. Meanwhile, Mom and Dad adjusted their own lives in order to keep my spirits up. They would take me to baseball games and out to dinner—anything to get me out of the house. However, going places was difficult. I had to wear eye patches and dark sunglasses to ease the pain of bright light. As a seventeen-year-old, this wasn't exactly the fashion statement I was trying to make.

My parents had to take care of me everywhere. At restaurants they ordered my food, arranged it on the table, and then explained where everything was on my plate so I could finally eat it. My fifteen-year-old brother took this opportunity to rearrange the food on my plate. My mom was amazing. Each day she would brush my hair and lay out a decent looking outfit so I could walk out of the house with a little bit of pride. She was determined to keep my self-esteem as high as possible. I relied on my mom to make me feel pretty. At an age when I should have been gaining my independence, I found myself becoming increasingly dependent on my parents.

I wasn't able to drive or visit my friends. Movies were completely out of the question. Life seemed to just go on without me, as if I was never there. Fortunately, I had a wonderful friend who knew how to make me feel special. Donny and I had dated a couple of times before I lost my vision, but at that time we were just friends. He would come to my house to sit and talk with me. If the TV were on, he'd watch and I'd listen. One time, Donny took me to a baseball barbecue and introduced me to all of his friends. I had never been so happy in my entire life. He didn't care that I couldn't see his friends. He held my hand proudly and led me around. I may not have been able to see all the people I met that day, but their voices are clear in mind. I can still separate whose laughter belonged to whom. When I close my eyes now and try to remember that day, I mostly see darkness. But I can still smell the sausage and brisket cooking on the grill. I can hear the happiness around me and Donny's voice saying, "This is my girlfriend, Talina."

I slowly began to make progress toward the end of the summer. Little by little, I was able to open my eyes. My vision was still blurred but this achievement called for a celebration. My parents were still concerned and Donny continued to stay by my side. Then I began to worry, *Will I have to start my senior year wearing my thick glasses that everyone still refers to as Coke bottles?* I didn't want to think about it. August crept up on me, though, and I started school with limited vision and thick glasses. As I walked through the halls, I struggled to look confident. I had a harder time cheering at pep rallies and football games. My lack of clear vision and concern with my physical appearance took the fun out of everything that I used to love. My level of self-confidence had diminished to an unrecognizable point.

At a time in my life when I expected my only concern to be to have fun, I was learning a powerful lesson. I could no longer rely on appearance to make me feel better about myself. I had to go deeper. With the support of my family and friends, I realized that feeling good about who I am on the inside is far more important. Believing that I can overcome the obstacles that I face is crucial. My identity wasn't my thick glasses. My identity was my inner strength. This inner strength allowed me to love life even when I was unable to see it. Losing my eyesight could not take away my ability to hear the voices of the people who love me. It could not steal away the fresh smell of morning or the lingering aroma of my mom's cooking. Most important, my loss could never take from me the feel of my boyfriend's hand around my own.

Six years later, I continue to need steroid eyedrops to keep the virus from reoccurring. The scar tissue is slowly improving. Recently, I began to wear both contacts, which is a huge accomplishment. A day doesn't go by that I am not thankful for my progress and the lesson I learned. I am incredibly thankful for my special friend who visited me, introduced me as his girlfriend and is now my husband.

I am currently preparing for my first year of teaching. I think about which of my personal qualities I might be able to share with my students. I know how difficult it is to grow up and I want my students to believe that I understand them. If I can't teach them anything else, I hope I can get across the lesson that changed my teenage experience: True beauty is not about what you *see* on the outside but what you feel, sense and love from within.

Talina Sessler-Barker

No More What Ifs

It was August 2, 1999, a day I would never forget. Indeed, it was my dad's fifty-third birthday, but something else about that day was also very special. I called my dad up to see if he would like to have lunch together for his birthday. He agreed, and half-an-hour later I arrived at his school. (He's an elementary principal.) He ordered us BLTs at a nearby restaurant.

We walked together to the small fast-food restaurant. As we neared the door, two young girls walked in: two beautiful goddesses. They recognized my father, and approached us. "Hey Mr. Margheim," they happily chimed.

My dad had been their elementary-school principal, so he introduced us. "Chance, this is Stephanie."

"Uh, hi," I said. I didn't catch her friend's name. I was under the assumption that they were both college students. My dad must have read my mind because he asked them their ages. Embarrassed, I rubbed my hands over my face, paranoid. *Do they know that I'm interested, am I obvious?*

"Juniors," they said in unison. *Perfect,* I thought. I am a senior.

The conversation pretty much ended there, unfortunately. They were both working, so I figured that it would be best not to talk to them too much. My dad and I sat down. He ate, I couldn't. My stomach was doing flips; I was secretly waiting for Stephanie to approach me, hair blowing, eyes sparkling . . .

I guess we waited for some time before my dad gave me the old nudge. "Gotta get back to work," he whispered.

As we left, Stephanie gave me the usual, "Bye, nice to have met you."

"You, too," I crooned, lowering my voice.

The car ride back was silent. I am usually the conversation starter, but I was too deep in thought. I stared out the car window, thinking. I thought to myself as I got out of the car and walked into my father's office. After much contemplation, I decided, I was going to ask this girl out! I gave my father a hug, wished him a happy birthday and left.

My mind was asking a million questions. *No more what ifs,* I said to myself. *I am tired of what ifs.*

I pulled into the parking lot of the fast-food restaurant, and sat in my car for a good half-hour, contemplating my move. I was nervous, very nervous, heart-popping-out-of-my-chest nervous. I literally felt like I was having a heart attack! I took a deep breath, prayed and walked into the restaurant. She was talking to someone, so I waited by the counter. Her eyes met mine, and she walked over to me. After what seemed like an hour of staring at her, I opened my mouth and let the words fall out.

"Umm, I know this is gonna sound crazy, but would you like to go out sometime?"

What a relief! I finally asked someone out! I studied her face, reading her reaction.

"Awww, that's nice, but I am serious with someone right now."

"Oh, yeah, okay, don't worry about it," I said, "that's fine."

"It was a good try though, right?" We both laughed. Our chat ended with a friendly handshake, and a "see you later."

Surprisingly enough, I wasn't disappointed. True, I would have loved to come home that night telling everyone that I finally had a date; and yet, I felt great! I had finally faced my fear and bit the bullet. I was prouder of myself at that moment than I had ever been in my life.

For the first time in seventeen years, I had faced my fear. I went home that day, and for once, I didn't have to ask myself, *what if?*

Chance Margheim

All the More Beautiful

At seventeen, I wanted desperately to be an adult, and believed I was making progress. I shaved almost every other day, and had my own wheels. The only thing I needed was the girl.

I saw her from a block away. She was tall, with long brown hair. We went to the same public school, but she often wore this plaid skirt, like a private-school girl. I drove up from behind, in my car, the only place I didn't feel short, and something amazing happened. She looked back at me. It felt just like one of those cheesy movies, slow motion, hair flowing, a halo of light surrounding her. She followed me with her eyes as I passed. That day, I felt tall wherever I went.

My luck didn't stop there. It turned out that she and my cousin were friends. He gave me her name and number. That afternoon, my sweaty, shaking hand picked up the phone, and I spoke to Kristen for the first time. That weekend, I drove down the same street where our eyes first met, to pick her up for our first date, my first real date ever.

I pictured myself sitting next to this perfect girl, in her

perfect living room, being interrogated by her perfect parents. I arrived, and all my expectations began to be challenged. There was no playful dog in the front yard, and no white picket fence to keep him from running away. Before I could knock on the door, Kristen opened it just enough to slip out. Then she smiled and all was perfect again. We went miniature golfing and laughed together for the first time.

After that night, we were inseparable, sickening all our friends. She made me feel like a big man, even though she called me her little guy. I had never felt so close to anyone before. But some mornings, when I'd pick her up for school and she'd slip out her door, something was different. She wouldn't have that perfect smile. She'd stare out the window and she seemed lost. I'd ask her what was wrong, and she'd say, "Nothing."

No answer could have been worse. It drove me crazy. I wanted to help. I wanted her to smile. Most of all, I wanted to be let inside. If I was an adult, it was time to start acting like one.

I confronted her; told her I knew there was something wrong. I knew she had problems at home, and I knew I could help if she'd just let me. Then she started to cry. I felt utterly helpless.

She put her arms around me and pressed her face into my chest. I felt her hot tears seeping through my shirt.

I soon learned that Kristen suffered from anxiety and depression. At home, she couldn't escape her past. Outside, with me, she could pretend all was perfect. When she started crying, she stopped pretending, and let me inside. I also stopped pretending. There were times when I didn't feel strong, when I didn't feel wise. There were times when I didn't feel like an adult.

During these past six years, Kristen and I have shared many laughs and tears together. I have had time to study her smile. I realize it is not perfect and, therefore, all the more beautiful. She continues to challenge and surpass all my expectations, teaching me more about life than I ever imagined there was to know. We talk about marriage and a family of our own, but we're in no hurry to grow up.

Marc Gaudioso

Return to High School

Don't be afraid to take a big step. You can't cross a chasm in two small jumps.

David Lloyd George

On September 15, 1998, two landmark events occurred that I'd been anticipating my entire life: I turned eighteen, and I began college. When my parents, my sister, our dog, four boxes, three oddly shaped duffel bags and our gray station wagon drew near to the university where I would spend the next four years of my life, I was terrified.

I fidgeted, played with my clothing and my hair, then tried to distract myself by passing a lost ant from hand to hand for fifteen minutes, before releasing it safely by the side of the road as we pulled up to the dorm. My ant-gazing left me nearly cross-eyed and largely unconsoled. By the time we reached the front steps, my fear had left an "anxiety wrinkle" in my forehead, one that I swear I can still see today.

Meanwhile, orientation passed in a blur, like racing down a water slide, from which I plunged into the first day of classes. I went to the wrong building for three of my classes and the wrong side of campus for another. As I race-walked from class to class, I kept thinking I saw high school classmates, and had to remind myself that most of them were now living on the other side of the country.

Only six months later, on the occasion of my sister's debut in the school musical, I would return home for spring break and revisit high school; again, I felt terrified. As a freshman in high school, I had felt like a shadow-person until I found my place on the stage, where the true me found expression in drama. In one of the great ironies of my high school years, I felt the freest when my words were scripted and my gestures rehearsed. Offstage, and out of the classroom, I had felt like an outcast before the unforgiving eyes of my peers. Now, as a visitor from college who had not quite escaped the ghosts of high school past, I was going to watch my sister act, dance and sing on stage.

I arrived at my old high school two minutes before the musical was to begin, intending to sneak in and out, like a shadow in the night. But I'd forgotten that the shows always started late, that there was an intermission, and that I'd have to wait for my sister at the end to congratulate her. I would see everyone, and in the garish light of the lobby, everyone would see me. I escaped temporarily into the ladies' bathroom and practiced relaxed smiles, only to discover that as the corners of my mouth went up, the anxiety wrinkle in my brow deepened. With a sigh, I went out to watch the show.

Taking my seat as the lights and sound dimmed and the overture began, I tried to sit serenely. But I fidgeted, just as I had during the last few minutes of that two-hour drive to college, only this time, I had no ants to save. As I watched my sister perform, I couldn't help feeling as though I should be up on that same stage. And in that moment, I genuinely missed high school, the place where, as a senior, I had finally nearly fit in. Now I was a freshman all over again.

When the musical ended, I wove through the crowd, hugging classmates who had never really known me, searching for my sister. As I passed several of my former classmates, I looked them over carefully. Like me, they looked pretty much the same, as uncomfortable as I. One of them, a girl who might have become a good friend if social status had not divided us, asked me if I felt out of place, no longer a high school student, no longer a member of the cast. "Of course," I wanted to say, but now this seemed trivial. In high school, I'd almost always felt out of place. Only now had the sensation become manageable, like holding your breath under water, knowing that any second, you can pop back up and take a deep breath of air.

So I laughed and said, "Tonight I'm just the sister." She laughed too, but it was an awkward laugh. Now, she also understood what it was like to feel out of place, and suddenly I understood something about her, about the rest of my classmates. That night, the last night of our past together, we were all the same. I squeezed her hand, and, then, I had no trouble smiling a real smile, with both forgiveness and regret, before saying good-bye.

As I left the theater, I saw a few figures in the distance. Thinking I recognized them, I raised my arm and prepared to call their names. Then one figure turned toward me; realizing my error, I laughed. I had mistaken my sister's classmates for two of my college friends. In that moment, I knew where I belonged. Taking a fond last look at my high school, and my past, I walked through the gates to my car. A streetlight rose from behind a hedge, and my shadow pulled back and let me by.

Sierra Millman

Inspirations

Courage is the discovery that you may not win.
and trying when you know you can lose.

Honor is standing for what you believe—
not for what you know.

Life isn't about living without problems.
Life is about solving problems.

If you plow the field every day—
the only thing that grows is resentment.

Compassion is passion with a heart.

The only thing in the whole universe people need to control are their attitudes.

How a person wins and loses is much more important
than *how much* a person wins and loses.

If you only do what you know you can do—
you never do very much.

There are no failures—
just experiences and your reactions to them.

Getting what you want is not nearly as important
as giving what you have.

Going on a journey with a map requires following
directions—
going on a journey without one requires following
your heart.

Talent without humility is wasted.

If you don't want it bad enough to risk losing it—
you don't want it bad enough.

When life knocks you down you have two choices—
stay down or get up.

Tom Krause

Growing

I'm leaving now to slay the foe—
Fight the battles, high and low.
I'm leaving, Mother, hear me go!
Please wish me luck today.

I've grown my wings, I want to fly,
Seize my victories where they lie.
I'm going, Mom, but please don't cry—
Just let me find my way.

I want to see and touch and hear,
Though there are dangers, there are fears.
I'll smile my smiles and dry my tears—
Please let me speak my say.

I'm off to find my world, my dreams,
Carve my niche, sew my seams,
Remember, as I sail my streams—
I'll love you, all the way.

Brooke Mueller

The Two Roads

There was a path
Deep in the woods.
Once it forked—
The bad, the good.

I chose to take
The left-hand path,
I did not know
I had no map.

Now this road that I travel
Is dirty and battered.
It's littered with dreams
That are broken and tattered.

Paved with wrongdoings
And dotted with hearts,
That were taken from people
And just torn apart.

Pain and regret
Are common here.

wherever you turn,
They're always near.

I want to cross
To the other path,
And leave behind
This painful wrath.

I thought I was forever
doomed to walk.
And all the gates
were tightly locked.

But as I continued,
A footbridge I could see.
A Bridge of Hope
called out to me.

Slowly I crossed
to the path of good.
Finally I was on the path
Of which I thought I
should.

Now hidden deep
Within the woods.
The one that forked;
Paths bad and good.

I once was wrong,
But now I'm right.
And before me
Glows a guiding light.

Altered by
A little step.
So close to falling
In darkened depths.

But I was finally
Pulled to hope.
I found that footbridge,
And learned to cope.

My simple mistake
Following the crowd.
Ignoring the heart
That speaks so loud.

The choices you make
Can change your life.
One will bring happiness,
The other brings strife.

Following the crowd,
Won't lead you to right.
If you follow your heart,
You'll be guided by light.

There was a path,
Deep in the woods.
Once it forked—
The bad, the good.

Heed my warning,
Because I know.
Follow your heart—
You know where to go.

Whitney Welch

Image Isn't Everything

On the first day of school, after I got out of my mom's car and mumbled a good-bye, I stared in awe at the huge buildings that seemed to tower over my head. This high school was definitely bigger than the one I had previously attended. Over the summer I moved from Midland, Texas, to St. Louis, Missouri. I had lived in Midland all my life, until the move.

This was my second year of high school, but my first year of school in St. Louis. I was really nervous about starting a new school and having people like me. I had decided the night before, while lying in my bed trying to fall asleep, that I would be much happier in a new school if I made friends that were so-called "popular." Getting in with the right group of people would make my life a whole lot better. I had to project the right image to the people at this school. I didn't care how much money it cost me, I was determined to buy an outfit everyone else would want to have. I bought a new outfit, new make-up, got a manicure and had my hair styled just so the first day would be perfect. I had the chance to start over in a new school, make new friends and build an image for myself. I wasn't going to waste this opportunity.

Scared, yet anxious to begin my new life, I walked up the stairs to the front door. The halls were packed with kids yelling and laughing and telling stories of their summer adventures. I found my way to the main office where I was to receive my schedule and fill out forms. I was on my way. *My first class was geometry, but where was that?*

I was standing in the hall looking confused, when a short, blond girl wearing glasses came up and asked, "Are you new? You look lost. Do you want me to help you find your class? My name is Diane. What's yours?" Even though she seemed a bit strange, definitely not the kind of person I wanted to be associated with, I decided to answer her anyway. I was, after all, lost.

After exchanging names, I followed her up the stairs and down a hallway on the right, making polite conversation the whole way.

When we reached my room she said, "Well, here you are. It was nice meeting you. I hope I see you again. Welcome to JFK, and I hope your day goes all right."

I said thanks and waved good-bye. Once inside the classroom, I saw one big group of people huddled around someone who seemed to be telling some sort of story. I walked over and got close enough to overhear. All eyes were glued to the guy in the middle of the circle who was wearing a letter jacket covered with patches. I decided that this guy was popular. He was talking about how he and some of his friends had gone up to someone's ranch outside of St. Louis and done some pretty wild and crazy things. A few minutes later the teacher told everyone to break it up and go find a seat. I managed to get one right next to the guy wearing the letter jacket. I said, "Hi, my name is April and I'm new here." He said, "Hi, I'm Johnny."

That class dragged on and on. Finally the bell rang. I turned to him and asked, "I'm not sure where my next class is, could you help me find it?" He looked at me and then said a quick no, turned back to his friends, and walked out of the classroom. As they were walking out I heard him say, "Did you guys see that new girl trying to get into our group? That outfit was way too weird." They all laughed and some of them turned around and stared at me. I slowly gathered my stuff, not believing what had just happened. I walked out of the classroom and found my next class, bewildered that I could have cared so much.

The same type of thing happened all day in all of my classes. At lunch, I ended up sitting by myself because I had snubbed people who had been nice to me and I had been snubbed by people who I had tried to be nice to. I didn't realize it then, but I had been really shallow just wanting to be friends with popular people.

Finally, sixth period came around and I was ready to go home and never come back. Before class started, someone came up behind me and said, "Hi, again. How was your first day?" It was that same girl who had showed me to my first class.

I told her my day had not been so great. She said she was sorry and offered to walk me outside. At that moment I realized how wrong I was in wanting to only be friends with popular people. Those people weren't even going to consider being my friends, but there were some other people who I'd already met today and liked and they liked me. Maybe I shouldn't decide whether a person is worth being my friend or not by their reputation, but by who they are. I said, "Thanks, I'd like that. I'm sorry I was kind of rude this morning." She said it was okay, she was new at school once, too. Walking with Diane made me realize how nice it would be to have a friend like her. On the way to class she asked me if I wanted to go out after school to hang out with some of her friends and get to know them better. I did go out with Diane and had a lot of fun.

As time went on I made friends with lots of different people, some of them from "the popular crowd" and some not. My standards were different though. The people I sought out for friends were the nice ones—period.

Jamie Shockley

Hi There, Ugly!

It wasn't easy to pay attention in French class. Our yearbooks had just been passed out, so while the teacher droned on, we were quietly signing books and passing them around the room.

Mine was somewhere at the back of the class. I couldn't wait to get it back. What would my friends say of me? Would there be words of praise? Admiration? When class was over, I quickly found my yearbook and flipped through it with anticipation. And then it caught my eye: Someone had written large words across the last page of my book: HI THERE, UGLY!

I had never really considered whether or not I was 'good looking,' but now I knew. I was ugly. If someone at the back of that grade-seven class thought I was ugly, there were probably many others who agreed. I studied myself in the mirror: big nose, pimples, slightly overweight, not muscular. Yes, it must be true, I thought. I'm ugly. I told no one any of this. There seemed to be no need. It was a fact: I was ugly.

Years went by. I married a woman who is a very beautiful person—inside and out. I would tell her, "You're the most beautiful girl in the world!" and I meant it. She would reply, "And you're so handsome." I never looked her in the eyes when she said this. I felt it was one of those things wives "have to say" to their husbands. I would simply look down and remember that the true verdict on my looks was tucked away in my grade-seven yearbook.

Finally one day my wife asked, "Why is it that you never look at me when I say that you're handsome?" I decided to tell her about the yearbook and my conclusions. "You can't believe that! It's wrong! Somebody who didn't even know you in grade seven can't be taken that seriously! I know you, I love you and I chose to marry you. I think you're handsome and I think I've proved that." So, was I going to believe my wife . . . or that old graffiti?

I thought about that question for a long time and about how God doesn't make junk. Who was I going to believe? I chose to believe my wife and God.

I still have a big nose. At age thirty-four, I even still get pimples! My hair has begun to recede and you could probably find people who would say that I am ugly. But I'm not one of them! As time goes on and I listen more and more to those who love me, I know that I am beautiful . . . or should I say, handsome.

Greg Barker

Just Me

From the time I was little, I knew I was great
'cause the people would tell me, "You'll make it—just wait."
But they never did tell me how great I would be
if I ever played someone who was greater than me.

When I'm in the back yard, I'm king with the ball.
To swish all those baskets is no sweat at all.
But all of a sudden there's a man in my face
who doesn't seem to realize that I'm king of this place.

So the pressure gets to me; I rush with the ball.
My passes to teammates could go through the wall.
My jumpers not falling, my dribbles not sure.
My hand is not steady, my eye is not pure.

The fault is my teammates—they don't understand.
The fault is my coaches—what a terrible plan.
The fault is the call by that blind referee.
But the fault is not mine; I'm the greatest, you see.

Then finally it hit me when I started to see
that the face in the mirror looked exactly like me.

It wasn't my teammates who were dropping the ball,
and it wasn't my coach shooting bricks at the wall.

That face in the mirror that was always so great
had some room for improvement instead of just hate.
So I stopped blaming others and I started to grow.
My play got much better and it started to show.

And all of my teammates didn't seem quite so bad.
I learned to depend on the good friends I had.
Now I like myself better since I started to see
that I was lousy being great—I'm much better being me.

Tom Krause

Winner

You can complain because roses have thorns, or you can rejoice because thorns have roses.

Ziggy

I am a winner.

I have beaten odds to get where I am today.

I have felt some pain every time I have walked another step forward, yet after having taken even one step back, I have known that regression and giving up were not options for me. I have felt the emptiness of separation as I have moved in the wrong direction.

I have learned the arts of persistence, tenacity and dedication. I know how it feels to watch my world and dreams shatter to a million pieces at my feet. I know what it is to run until there is nothing left inside of me, and then run some more.

I know how it feels to be loved, and I know how it feels when that love grows hard and cold.

I know how to be happy. I know how to smile and spread joy into lives of others with that same smile.

I have learned that one conversation can make or break

a fragile mind and heart, and thus I have learned to choose my words carefully.

I know that enthusiasm is the key to everything, and yet I know how it feels to completely lack enthusiasm.

I have learned that winning is not everything, but sometimes it feels like it is the most important thing. I have learned that other color ribbons only prove to make that blue so much sweeter. I know that my chief competitor is always myself.

I know that sometimes my best isn't good enough for others and that people can be cruel. I know that sometimes I get frustrated with myself, especially when others are frustrated with me.

I know how it feels to have something mean so much to me that it *is* me. I have experienced wrath, outrage and fury, but have still made it through the storm a survivor.

I know what it is to love. I know how to spread joy and how to extract it from even the darkest situations.

I know what hope is, and I rely on it as my last refuge. I know that darkness must exist if only to make those tiny bits of light seem that much brighter.

I know that success is self-made, and that luck is a relative term.

I know that I am strong.

I know that miracles do exist, angels do find us in our hour of need, and there is always something behind me, pushing me forward.

I believe in myself at all times, even when I think that I don't and even when I feel like no one else does.

I know how it feels to be lost. I also know how it feels to be picked out of a crowd. What it is like to be the winner, and how it feels when, for one moment, you are the star of the show.

Above all, though, I know that all of this has made me ME.

I know that being a winner is not about winning whatever race faces me in the moment. I recognize I am winning just by pushing myself every day and by waking up each morning feeling blessed by the day that lies ahead of me. Through this I am winning in the most important race ever, the race I entered at birth—this race we call life.

Amy Huffman

So I Am Told

I'm a fourteen-year-old girl with moss-colored hair, sparkles and funny clothes, who feels lonely sometimes.
I do not ask to be understood because *I* can't even understand myself.
I ask to be accepted,
I ask to be accepted as I am.
I do not want to be told what potential I have, or what my future holds.
I do not want to be told that I'm going nowhere in life because I skipped a math test.
I question my existence, my meaning.
I question what the "Real World" is, and why I'm not there.
I feel happy with no shoes on.
I feel lonesome in a crowded room.
Sometimes my heart bleeds and I cry,
Laughter echoes in my mind.
I am told to be different,
To be myself.
But then I am told what to wear and how to act.

I like to write and rumors hurt.
I don't know how to dance, but I try to anyway.
Please don't try to understand me, nor judge me too
  quickly.
My name doesn't matter,
My heart is open.

Alexei Perry

Finding a Vision

Six years ago, I went blind. Due to a severe herpes simplex virus in my eyes, I lost one of my most precious possessions: my eyesight. Tiny cold sores covered the surface of my eyes, scarring my cornea. I wasn't allowed to stand in direct sunlight or even in a brightly lit room. The light would penetrate my eyelids and cause too much pain. At the age of seventeen, I was unprepared to find myself in a dark world. Who would I be without my ability to see?

All I wanted throughout the entire summer was to be able to see people. What new cute bathing suit styles was everyone wearing? Who had cut their hair or dyed it purple? I would have a conversation with someone and realize that I had no idea what facial expressions he was making. I no longer had the ability to make eye contact, a privilege I had taken for granted before. I longed to talk with my eyes. I just wasn't whole without my vision.

My parents became my sole support system. Hoping for a miracle, they took me to an eye specialist every day. No one was sure if I would ever completely recover, and if so, how long the healing process would take. Meanwhile, Mom and Dad adjusted their own lives in order to keep my spirits up. They would take me to baseball games and out to dinner—anything to get me out of the house. However, going places was difficult. I had to wear eye patches and dark sunglasses to ease the pain of bright light. As a seventeen-year-old, this wasn't exactly the fashion statement I was trying to make.

My parents had to take care of me everywhere. At restaurants they ordered my food, arranged it on the table, and then explained where everything was on my plate so I could finally eat it. My fifteen-year-old brother took this opportunity to rearrange the food on my plate. My mom was amazing. Each day she would brush my hair and lay out a decent looking outfit so I could walk out of the house with a little bit of pride. She was determined to keep my self-esteem as high as possible. I relied on my mom to make me feel pretty. At an age when I should have been gaining my independence, I found myself becoming increasingly dependent on my parents.

I wasn't able to drive or visit my friends. Movies were completely out of the question. Life seemed to just go on without me, as if I was never there. Fortunately, I had a wonderful friend who knew how to make me feel special. Donny and I had dated a couple of times before I lost my vision, but at that time we were just friends. He would come to my house to sit and talk with me. If the TV were on, he'd watch and I'd listen. One time, Donny took me to a baseball barbecue and introduced me to all of his friends. I had never been so happy in my entire life. He didn't care that I couldn't see his friends. He held my hand proudly and led me around. I may not have been able to see all the people I met that day, but their voices are clear in mind. I can still separate whose laughter belonged to whom. When I close my eyes now and try to remember that day, I mostly see darkness. But I can still smell the sausage and brisket cooking on the grill. I can hear the happiness around me and Donny's voice saying, "This is my girlfriend, Talina."

I slowly began to make progress toward the end of the summer. Little by little, I was able to open my eyes. My vision was still blurred but this achievement called for a celebration. My parents were still concerned and Donny continued to stay by my side. Then I began to worry, *Will I have to start my senior year wearing my thick glasses that everyone still refers to as Coke bottles?* I didn't want to think about it. August crept up on me, though, and I started school with limited vision and thick glasses. As I walked through the halls, I struggled to look confident. I had a harder time cheering at pep rallies and football games. My lack of clear vision and concern with my physical appearance took the fun out of everything that I used to love. My level of self-confidence had diminished to an unrecognizable point.

At a time in my life when I expected my only concern to be to have fun, I was learning a powerful lesson. I could no longer rely on appearance to make me feel better about myself. I had to go deeper. With the support of my family and friends, I realized that feeling good about who I am on the inside is far more important. Believing that I can overcome the obstacles that I face is crucial. My identity wasn't my thick glasses. My identity was my inner strength. This inner strength allowed me to love life even when I was unable to see it. Losing my eyesight could not take away my ability to hear the voices of the people who love me. It could not steal away the fresh smell of morning or the lingering aroma of my mom's cooking. Most important, my loss could never take from me the feel of my boyfriend's hand around my own.

Six years later, I continue to need steroid eyedrops to keep the virus from reoccurring. The scar tissue is slowly improving. Recently, I began to wear both contacts, which is a huge accomplishment. A day doesn't go by that I am not thankful for my progress and the lesson I learned. I am incredibly thankful for my special friend who visited me, introduced me as his girlfriend and is now my husband.

I am currently preparing for my first year of teaching. I think about which of my personal qualities I might be able to share with my students. I know how difficult it is to grow up and I want my students to believe that I understand them. If I can't teach them anything else, I hope I can get across the lesson that changed my teenage experience: True beauty is not about what you *see* on the outside but what you feel, sense and love from within.

Talina Sessler-Barker

No More What Ifs

It was August 2, 1999, a day I would never forget. Indeed, it was my dad's fifty-third birthday, but something else about that day was also very special. I called my dad up to see if he would like to have lunch together for his birthday. He agreed, and half-an-hour later I arrived at his school. (He's an elementary principal.) He ordered us BLTs at a nearby restaurant.

We walked together to the small fast-food restaurant. As we neared the door, two young girls walked in: two beautiful goddesses. They recognized my father, and approached us. "Hey Mr. Margheim," they happily chimed.

My dad had been their elementary-school principal, so he introduced us. "Chance, this is Stephanie."

"Uh, hi," I said. I didn't catch her friend's name. I was under the assumption that they were both college students. My dad must have read my mind because he asked them their ages. Embarrassed, I rubbed my hands over my face, paranoid. *Do they know that I'm interested, am I obvious?*

"Juniors," they said in unison. *Perfect,* I thought. I am a senior.

The conversation pretty much ended there, unfortunately. They were both working, so I figured that it would be best not to talk to them too much. My dad and I sat down. He ate, I couldn't. My stomach was doing flips; I was secretly waiting for Stephanie to approach me, hair blowing, eyes sparkling . . .

I guess we waited for some time before my dad gave me the old nudge. "Gotta get back to work," he whispered.

As we left, Stephanie gave me the usual, "Bye, nice to have met you."

"You, too," I crooned, lowering my voice.

The car ride back was silent. I am usually the conversation starter, but I was too deep in thought. I stared out the car window, thinking. I thought to myself as I got out of the car and walked into my father's office. After much contemplation, I decided, I was going to ask this girl out! I gave my father a hug, wished him a happy birthday and left.

My mind was asking a million questions. *No more what ifs,* I said to myself. *I am tired of what ifs.*

I pulled into the parking lot of the fast-food restaurant, and sat in my car for a good half-hour, contemplating my move. I was nervous, very nervous, heart-popping-out-of-my-chest nervous. I literally felt like I was having a heart attack! I took a deep breath, prayed and walked into the restaurant. She was talking to someone, so I waited by the counter. Her eyes met mine, and she walked over to me. After what seemed like an hour of staring at her, I opened my mouth and let the words fall out.

"Umm, I know this is gonna sound crazy, but would you like to go out sometime?"

What a relief! I finally asked someone out! I studied her face, reading her reaction.

"Awww, that's nice, but I am serious with someone right now."

"Oh, yeah, okay, don't worry about it," I said, "that's fine."

"It was a good try though, right?" We both laughed. Our chat ended with a friendly handshake, and a "see you later."

Surprisingly enough, I wasn't disappointed. True, I would have loved to come home that night telling everyone that I finally had a date; and yet, I felt great! I had finally faced my fear and bit the bullet. I was prouder of myself at that moment than I had ever been in my life.

For the first time in seventeen years, I had faced my fear. I went home that day, and for once, I didn't have to ask myself, *what if?*

Chance Margheim

Return to High School

Don't be afraid to take a big step. You can't cross a chasm in two small jumps.

David Lloyd George

On September 15, 1998, two landmark events occurred that I'd been anticipating my entire life: I turned eighteen, and I began college. When my parents, my sister, our dog, four boxes, three oddly shaped duffel bags and our gray station wagon drew near to the university where I would spend the next four years of my life, I was terrified.

I fidgeted, played with my clothing and my hair, then tried to distract myself by passing a lost ant from hand to hand for fifteen minutes, before releasing it safely by the side of the road as we pulled up to the dorm. My ant-gazing left me nearly cross-eyed and largely unconsoled. By the time we reached the front steps, my fear had left an "anxiety wrinkle" in my forehead, one that I swear I can still see today.

Meanwhile, orientation passed in a blur, like racing down a water slide, from which I plunged into the first day of classes. I went to the wrong building for three of my classes and the wrong side of campus for another. As I race-walked from class to class, I kept thinking I saw high school classmates, and had to remind myself that most of them were now living on the other side of the country.

Only six months later, on the occasion of my sister's debut in the school musical, I would return home for spring break and revisit high school; again, I felt terrified. As a freshman in high school, I had felt like a shadow-person until I found my place on the stage, where the true me found expression in drama. In one of the great ironies of my high school years, I felt the freest when my words were scripted and my gestures rehearsed. Offstage, and out of the classroom, I had felt like an outcast before the unforgiving eyes of my peers. Now, as a visitor from college who had not quite escaped the ghosts of high school past, I was going to watch my sister act, dance and sing on stage.

I arrived at my old high school two minutes before the musical was to begin, intending to sneak in and out, like a shadow in the night. But I'd forgotten that the shows always started late, that there was an intermission, and that I'd have to wait for my sister at the end to congratulate her. I would see everyone, and in the garish light of the lobby, everyone would see me. I escaped temporarily into the ladies' bathroom and practiced relaxed smiles, only to discover that as the corners of my mouth went up, the anxiety wrinkle in my brow deepened. With a sigh, I went out to watch the show.

Taking my seat as the lights and sound dimmed and the overture began, I tried to sit serenely. But I fidgeted, just as I had during the last few minutes of that two-hour drive to college, only this time, I had no ants to save. As I watched my sister perform, I couldn't help feeling as though I should be up on that same stage. And in that moment, I genuinely missed high school, the place where, as a senior, I had finally nearly fit in. Now I was a freshman all over again.

When the musical ended, I wove through the crowd, hugging classmates who had never really known me, searching for my sister. As I passed several of my former classmates, I looked them over carefully. Like me, they looked pretty much the same, as uncomfortable as I. One of them, a girl who might have become a good friend if social status had not divided us, asked me if I felt out of place, no longer a high school student, no longer a member of the cast. "Of course," I wanted to say, but now this seemed trivial. In high school, I'd almost always felt out of place. Only now had the sensation become manageable, like holding your breath under water, knowing that any second, you can pop back up and take a deep breath of air.

So I laughed and said, "Tonight I'm just the sister." She laughed too, but it was an awkward laugh. Now, she also understood what it was like to feel out of place, and suddenly I understood something about her, about the rest of my classmates. That night, the last night of our past together, we were all the same. I squeezed her hand, and, then, I had no trouble smiling a real smile, with both forgiveness and regret, before saying good-bye.

As I left the theater, I saw a few figures in the distance. Thinking I recognized them, I raised my arm and prepared to call their names. Then one figure turned toward me; realizing my error, I laughed. I had mistaken my sister's classmates for two of my college friends. In that moment, I knew where I belonged. Taking a fond last look at my high school, and my past, I walked through the gates to my car. A streetlight rose from behind a hedge, and my shadow pulled back and let me by.

Sierra Millman

Inspirations

Courage is the discovery that you may not win,
and trying when you know you can lose.

Honor is standing for what you believe—
not for what you know.

Life isn't about living without problems.
Life is about solving problems.

If you plow the field every day—
the only thing that grows is resentment.

Compassion is passion with a heart.

The only thing in the whole universe people need to
control are their attitudes.

How a person wins and loses is much more important
than *how much* a person wins and loses.

If you only do what you know you can do—
you never do very much.

There are no failures—
just experiences and your reactions to them.

Getting what you want is not nearly as important
as giving what you have.

Going on a journey with a map requires following
directions—
going on a journey without one requires following
your heart.

Talent without humility is wasted.

If you don't want it bad enough to risk losing it—
you don't want it bad enough.

When life knocks you down you have two choices—
stay down or get up.

Tom Krause

The Days of Cardboard Boxes

Enjoy yourself. These are the good old days you're going to miss in the years ahead.

Anonymous

Cardboard boxes played a significant role in my childhood days. Don't get me wrong; toys were wonderful, too, but nothing could out-do a cardboard box and a few kids to go along with it—especially my two best neighborhood friends, Chris and Nick, brothers who lived three blocks away.

Summer was always the perfect time to have a cardboard box. The long, lazy days offered sufficient time to experience the true essence of a box and to truly bond with it. However, in order to bond with a box, we first had to find one. The three of us would pile into the back of my parents' truck, briefly jockeying for the coveted wheel seats, then sing the "Na Na Na" song (any song we only knew some of the words to but sang anyway) while we waited for my mom to find her keys. None of us dared to suggest that we ride in the front of the truck; that was for sissies.

Finally, after an infinite number of "Na Na Na" songs, Mom drove us to a box place, and there it was! The most beautiful box we had ever seen. It was a refrigerator box, most definitely the best kind to have. Refrigerator boxes could journey to far better places than any other box, and their ability to be anything was simply phenomenal. The furniture warehouse/showroom had thrown this glorious bounty out the back door like it was useless. We had arrived in time to rescue it from the nefarious jaws of a trash truck.

We watched with anticipation as Mom slid the box to the back of the truck. We crawled into the box for the ride home, sheltered from the wind and the bugs that seemed to aim right for the tonsils during mid-"Na."

Arriving back in the neighborhood was an experience that made our heads swell. Everyone who was outdoors could see us, and word would soon spread that Nick, Chris and Eva possessed a refrigerator box. You see, anyone who owned a refrigerator box held an esteemed position. We would be legends. We would take our box where no kids had ever gone before.

We unloaded our treasure and carried it with great care into the back yard. Chris said we should spend a few minutes of quiet time to gather our thoughts, and then we could discuss our ideas for this magnificent being. We did so for about five seconds. Then suddenly, as if an unknown force opened our voice boxes, we broke into song:

Na na na na
Our box is groovy
Na Na Na
And so are we!

Okay, it was a short song. But it was beautiful. And I'm sure it would have touched the hearts of those fortunate enough to hear it.

It was time to make our decision. "Let's go to Zo in our box," I said.

"Who?" Nick and Chris gave me one of their looks.

"Where to go or where not to go, that is the question," I retorted.

Nick told me I didn't make any sense, and I explained that it was all very simple, that he and Chris just needed to learn how to think backwards. Chris decided Nick was right—I didn't make any sense.

"Zo is Oz backwards, you ignorant little twerps! We wanna go to Zo and do everything Dorothy does in Oz, but backwards." I was hollering at them because I knew they had better sense than they were using.

Chris looked first at me and then at the box as he contemplated my bright idea. I wondered if Chris and Nick were seriously ill because they should have known by then, from all our past experiences, that boxes (especially this one) could take us anywhere. We could be or do anything we wanted because of the power of the almighty refrigerator box. And we could be backwards about it too.

"You know, Eva is right," Chris said. "We have never done anything backwards before, so let's make this the first time. But we can go *anywhere* backwards, not just Zo."

At that moment in our young lives we understood clearly that we were going to go down in history. People all over the world would be talking about "The Three Backwards Box Kids." Other children would attempt to go where we had gone, but none of them could ever be like us because their imaginations were inferior to ours.

We made a solemn declaration that our box would be a time machine. We swore on chocolate peanut butter cups that this backward idea was here to stay (at least until the next box). And anyone who broke a promise made over chocolate peanut butter cups was basically considered immoral.

After we had traveled several years back in time, we were faced with a dilemma. We were visiting with a singer named Elvis who inquired about how we got to Graceland. We told him about our time machine, the backwards idea, the chocolate-peanut-butter-cup promise, and how we were going to go down in history. Elvis was all shook up about us, and he said that we were pretty neat kids . . . but . . .

"But what?" we pressed.

He wanted to know how we were eventually going to get home again if we could only go backwards.

In all our days, we had never been faced with a predicament such as this. We had also never broken a chocolate-peanut-butter-cup promise. We were, you know, up a creek. We could not capitulate. Life always had its ups and downs—this was just one of the very big downs that would take a long night of pondering. Luckily, our parents would not let us stay out all night to play our make-believe games.

Soon my mom called out the back door, breaking us out of our imaginary world and landing us abruptly in the backyard again. It was time for Nick and Chris to go home. The three of us quickly made plans to meet at eight o'clock the next morning to discuss solutions to get us out of the disaster we were in. As I ran the few feet to my back door, Nick and Chris took off running the three blocks toward their home. Time could not be squandered. We only had until morning before we would be back in the reality of our imaginary world again.

At 7:33 the next morning, the phone broke the silence, and I stumbled out of bed with a hangover from thinking too much. When I answered the phone, Nick demanded to know if I had covered the box with plastic the night before like we were supposed to do, in case of rain. I looked out the window to see that it had rained, a very hard and drenching rain. With deep regret in my heart, I told Nick I hadn't, but the responsibility belonged to all of us, so it wasn't completely my fault.

Nick and Chris came over, and silence replaced our usual banter. Our box had only been with us for one day. Now we were stuck in the real world because our box was dead.

The soggy cardboard couldn't just be left out in the yard to rot away. It had been a good box while it lasted, and it deserved proper respect. So we dragged it to the side of the street where the garbage was picked up. The day before we had saved it from a trash truck that would have taken its life too early; now it was time for our box to go. Although it was a natural death, it could have been prevented. This reality would be a weight we would carry for all our childhood days.

The three of us sat next to our dead box so we could be there when the trash truck came. We even made up a "Na Na Na" requiem, and we sang with all our might as the truck hauled our box away. No one could have put more sincerity or emotion into a song than we did that day. Although we were mourning our box, we knew we must go on. We must find another box, and we must build another imaginary world with it.

I miss the cardboard-box days. However, just as we had to go on after the demise of our box, I had to go on and grow up. But my childhood imagination will always be a part of me. I will always believe in cardboard boxes.

Eva Burke

11

GROWING UP

There came a time when the risk to remain tight in a bud was more painful than the risk it took to blossom.

Anaïs Nin

The Need for Speed

Nobody told me what to expect during my teenage years. But what I was most unprepared for was loss. Not just loss of childhood, but loss of innocence and simplicity, too. I felt like I was standing between two continents, childhood and adulthood, in some in-between, nowhere zone.

So I started doing crazy things that involved speed. Like clinging to the roof of a car while my buddy T. J. gunned the engine and spun in circles in an empty parking lot at night—knowing full well if I were to slip or let go, my life would be over. Or like skiing or biking down steep hills so fast I could barely stay in control—all without a helmet. Was it that the speed made me feel alive? Or was I trying to get away from everything around me?

Although by all accounts I was a normal, soccer-playing, sixteen-year-old suburban kid on the north shore of Chicago, with a B-plus average, a doctor for a father and a housewife for a mother, everything seemed to be going haywire around me. I started losing friends in dramatic ways, one after another.

First there was my friend Nick, the basketball team captain, the football quarterback, the guy every guy wanted to be and every girl had a crush on. One sunny suburban day, Nick crashed his motorcycle into a truck. The next day he was paralyzed from the waist down for life. *For life?* I couldn't fathom the notion. I tried to stay friends with him, but the Nick I knew was gone.

Next was John, the lead guitarist in the coolest band, the guy who would shut his eyes on stage, lean back, bathed in a magenta glow, and let his fingers scatter up the frets, effortlessly, while everyone gawked. He got heavy into drugs, invited his girlfriends to climb the tree outside his window to his bedroom where they'd have sex, and then he'd help them down the tree before dawn. Very Romeo and Juliet, he thought. I'd been friends with John forever and knew that there was something basically good in him that had gotten buried. But whenever I saw him his eyes were glazed over and he could barely walk, and I soon realized there was nothing left between us. He tried suicide a few times in a few different ways, and one frigid January Sunday, his parents had the men in white take him, yelling and screaming, to a psychiatric clinic.

Then my friend Heather, who had always been a great student, suddenly became obsessed over perfecting her homework. She wrote and rewrote term papers, staying up all night, going to sleep just before dawn, walking zombielike through school corridors, lost, often bewildered, always postponing handing in papers so she could make changes. In class, she began plucking hairs from the crown of her head. Her parents sent her away, too.

Those were the dramatic losses. But I felt everyone was pulling away, growing faster, doing more, knowing more, being smarter, moving quicker, getting more grades, girls, glamour. I couldn't get a handle on it. And nobody seemed to be paying any attention to those of us who were left behind.

One day, T. J. asked me to go winter camping about two

hours north in Wisconsin. He had the whole thing figured out: We'd snowshoe in with backpacks, a gas stove, sleeping bags and a tent. We'd stay a weekend, then miss a day of school. That was the part that intrigued me: It was a statement to everyone at school that I was different, not interested in the usual stuff, the kind of guy who could take care of himself. "What if there's a freak storm and we freeze?" I asked. He looked at me as if to say, *Danger is what we're after, right?* Against all odds, my parents, after hours of haggling, let me go with him.

So there I was, leaning against the hood of T. J.'s car, strapping on snowshoes. "I never used these," I said. "Just like walking," he replied. But it wasn't. For me, it was more like floating—above the world, above my worries. I liked the slow pace, the tracks I left behind me and the untouched snow ahead.

It wasn't that night, when we made a partial igloo, pitched our tent, melted snow to make water, cooked a pathetic astronautlike meal and fell into deep sleep. Nor was it on the second day, when we melted more snow and fretted about the need for water and the threat of dehydration. But on our last day, it warmed by ten degrees and everything around us started to melt. T. J. was going on about new dangerous stuff we could do back home: laying down on streets so startled drivers would have to stop; climbing up roofs of cheerleaders' houses and tapping on their windows; throwing iceballs at cars as they drove down a lonely ravine, hoping the drivers might chase us . . . when he spotted an iced-over pond and dared me to touch the center. A voice said, *No.* The more he urged me on, the more I had to get away. I began to snowshoe up a ridge, and then I continued until there was no sign of T. J., where the only sounds were my breath and snow falling in clumps off pines.

Suddenly, inexplicably, a surge of sadness seemed to

pulse through my feet, up my legs, through my arms and right out my skull. It wasn't like crying, more like an eruption . . . and it felt good, natural, sane. And when it ceased, some time later, I realized it was just me in the world, but that was a gift, not a curse. My life was mine to make or break. It was my show, my ball game. I couldn't control everything. But I realized I'd lost more than just friends: I'd temporarily lost myself. The speed I'd been seeking by clinging to the top of cars in parking lots hadn't helped me find myself. One-step-at-a-time snowshoes had.

James D. Barron

On Shame and Shadowboxing

Nothing is so strong as gentleness, and nothing is so gentle as real strength.

Ralph W. Sockman

That summer I spent my days with a group of young men whose long, stringy hair was bleached from sun and saltwater. This was in Corpus Christi, Texas, on the Gulf Coast, and the boys went surfing in the mornings then returned in the afternoons to play football on my parents' lawn. My parents warned me about them. They knew about cars and smoked cigarettes, and when they took off their shirts for our games, their chests and arms were hard with muscle that came from paddling out into the ocean before dawn. Girls fawned over them, and that summer I idolized them, too. I've forgotten all but one of their names, Barry, though maybe another was called Todd. Always in this ever-present gang of boys there is one named Todd.

My father didn't like the boys smoking around me or their long hair, and he didn't like things he'd heard about them, things he wouldn't tell me. But he wanted me to spend more time outside and must have figured that since the games took place in our front yard, the shadow of our house would protect me from them, from their influence.

Earlier that year my father had taught me to throw a football, and by summer I could pass the length of two, sometimes three, lawns. These were high, arching throws that should not have come from the small arms of a boy who preferred books to ball games. Every time I heaved the football, I expected it to veer off course into a window or under the tire of a passing car, but instead it almost always went where I wanted it to, into that pocket of my father's chest and arms. "Perfect," he would say. "Right in the numbers." When I played football with the boys, I was "All-Time Quarterback," which meant that I threw for both teams and got sacked a lot.

In addition to teaching me how to throw long bombs, my father also taught me how to fight. He stressed that I should never throw the first punch, but once it's thrown, I shouldn't hold back. My father had fought a lot: In his youth, in the army and once in a pool hall after a man made a vulgar innuendo toward my mother. He taught me how to shadowbox and how to hit someone, how to twist my fist just as it made impact so that it cut the skin. He encouraged me to bite, scratch and pull hair, to use sticks or attack from behind, to kick whoever had started the fight in the shins or between the legs, or to stomp the bridges of his feet. I nodded as my father told me these things, but I knew if the time came, I would worry that hitting someone would only make him hurt me worse. In the pool hall, my father had hit the man in the knee with a pool cue, and when I asked him if it had broken, he said, "The stick or his leg?"

Maybe I wanted so badly for Barry and Todd and the boys to accept me because each of them seemed more like the young man my father was than I did. And maybe, too, that's why my father worried about my time with them and taught me how to fight. He thought the boys would bully me, take advantage of my adoration, and he knew I would not snitch on them. I would suffer their insults and mockery because I feared bringing trouble to anyone, and he saw that these boys thrived on trouble, as probably he had.

But in the summer when I was fourteen, the boys tolerated me because of my quarterback abilities and my parents' long, even lawn. The target of their harassment that summer was a boy named Robert, but they called him Roberta. They called him Roberta because of a high voice and the feminine lightness in his stride, something like a prance. For three months, he stayed with his grandmother who lived across the street from my family. Robert usually left on his bicycle in the mornings and returned in the afternoons while we played football. When he rode past, the boys acted as if they were going to peg him with the football. Although they never actually threw it, every time one of them dropped back and took aim with the ball, Robert flinched. Sometimes he fell off the bicycle and turned red. If his grandmother tottered outside, the boys waved at her and asked Robert if he wanted to join the game. He never did.

I felt sorry for him and hated to see him turn the corner on his bicycle because I knew Barry and Todd would start insulting him. He made an easy target, and for all of their muscle and mouthing off, for all of their bragging and bravado, they were weak, insecure boys. But I never interfered with their cruel impressions of his prance or tried to silence the jokes they made about his voice; I just waited for the game to resume. As much as I wanted them to lay off of Robert, there was always the great sense of relief that the insults weren't being hurled at me.

After almost an entire summer of enduring their threats and slurs, something happened on a hot August afternoon. I'm not sure what changed that day; maybe they'd finally pushed him too far, or maybe he'd been planning it all summer. Maybe he'd been scouting our games like a coach from an opposing team, looking for weaknesses, trying to identify the player who would fumble or fall most easily. When Barry and Todd started in on Robert when he returned from his bike ride, he didn't retreat. Instead of sulking away, he stood flat-footed in his grandmother's driveway and started insulting me. I can still hear his high, girly voice coming across the street, across all of these years.

I hoped the boys would rush to my defense, but as Robert marched into my yard, they only laughed, their eyes boring into me as if it were the showdown they'd been waiting for all along. My knees trembled as they did when I had to speak with girls. With everything Robert said, the boys cackled louder. He fed off their laughter, his words growing louder and more harsh, and soon the boys rallied behind him and egged him on. They listened to him as a football team listens to its quarterback.

That afternoon when he gathered the courage and confidence to insult me, I did the one thing that would have disappointed my father: I threw the first punch. I whipped a hard, perfect spiral into Robert's face. Then as he brought up his hands, I exploded across the yard like a fullback charging for a touchdown, barreled into his chest and knocked him to the ground. The boys closed in around us, yelling and laughing. Robert and I grappled with each other—he was much stronger than I would have anticipated—then I managed to mount and straddle his chest. Aside from an awkward, frantic slap that bloodied my nose, I owned the fight. My fists flurried on his face, and his pale, freckled flesh tore between my knuckles and his cheekbones.

Soon my father broke through the boys around us and pulled me off him. Because he never learned the truth behind the fight—Robert, like me, would never tell—I knew he was proud of me. I felt ashamed, and even then wished I had the strength to walk into my house and leave the boys in the sun. The truth is, while I've grown to resemble my father in many ways—his stubborn optimism, his broad, round shoulders and his inclination to protect those he loves—on that day in the yard, I was the weak one. I think Robert understood this. He saw me as an outsider in the group, someone like himself who would never quite fit in, and he knew the boys would turn on me. If his eyes would have been open, he would have seen that I winced with each strike, and was as scared and ashamed and in as much pain as he was. It was as if I were shadowboxing, throwing blows at my own image, and with each swing, I came that much closer to connecting.

Bret Anthony Johnston

Spare Change

Life has no limitations except the ones you make.

Les Brown

I'm seated in the back row of Mrs. Andrew's sixth-grade class. I wriggle tightly in the stiff-backed, wooden desk/chair combination, which is unfairly constructed for a right-handed world. I hold my pencil firmly in my left hand and try to conform to the ill-fitting desk. I'm not just different because of my anti-dexterity; there are many things that make me peculiar to the world.

First of all, there are my clothes. My dad's blue-collar salary limits my fashion ability. No penny is spent frivolously. In my family's nightly ritual, Dad hauls down the four-liter jug from the shelf over the kitchen sink. Into the glass he empties both pockets. Pennies, dimes and nickels sing out the tinkle of a poor man's wallet. We are a family of coin rollers. My mom's purse is not filled with singles or tens; it is weighted down by rolls of change, as though she were ready at a moment's notice to hit the Vegas slot machines. Oh, how carefree it must feel to line your pockets with paper currency as unencumbered as air.

You would think by looking at my clothes that we're back in 1975. My mom uses words like "retro" to try and convince me that my clothes are cool. Kids at my school shop at thrift stores for cool vintage T-shirts; they buy their jeans at the Gap. But not me. I'm branded with the wardrobe of a victim. It's like wearing a neon sign that reads: All future psychotics take out frustrations and misplaced anger right here! As you will find in most schools, there is that one classification of child—the bully—who immediately reads the signs and moves in for the kill. Many adults claim that the bully is himself a "victim" of his own self-hatred. However, all this means little to those of us who have been subjected to the bully's misunderstood and misspent anger.

While in class, it is my sole intention to innocently blend in with the herd—little chance of that. Carefully, I press my pencil against the workbook page. The numbers blur into one huge, fuzzy black caterpillar. My mind is a thousand miles away from these division problems. Instead, I'm thinking about my pencil—of all things. I'm trying to write with it ever so lightly, so I don't snap the point. A visit to the pencil sharpener would mean a certain run-in with my bully, who conveniently sits alongside it and the exit door. It is only a matter of time before my lead or my bladder give out.

Then comes the moment when I am forced to visit the sharpener. My pencil in one hand, I begin turning the crank. I don't get very far before his hand reaches out and grabs my arm, spinning me round roughly to face him.

"Going somewhere, Dog Face?"

I try to answer him, but all that issues from my mouth is a tightly choked whisper, "No."

As if strengthened by my weakness, his laughter becomes the public-address system that calls the others. "Where'd you get that bird's nest you call hair—the circus?" he asks, pointing to my huge sprouts of long frizzy tendrils. Each wiry brown strand defies entrapment by any elastic scrunchee. "Did you stick your hand in an electric socket, Dog Face?" His comments raise not only the pitch of laughter around the room, but the pressure I feel building behind my eyes. Finally, like an engorged geyser, tears burst forth and the bully's victory is assured.

Tears are the blood that bullies savor. They're proof of dominance among the herd. It's hard to explain how deeply he can hurt me with his simple words. It's a pain that can choke my windpipes and strangle my heart. He tells me I'm ugly, and inside I agree. Is it possible I hate myself for crying more than I hate him?

I run away from my bully and the laughter, and head for the girls' bathroom. Inside these walls I still believe it's possible to wash away all suffering and tears. While water may wash away most tear-stained traces, it can never bathe the anguish that grips so tightly at my heart.

But all this happened to me many years ago, when I was a younger and different person. Now, I'm seventeen and headed for college. In the years since, my dad got a new job, and we moved to another town. I have not seen my bully in over five years, and there have been no other bullies to take his place. I have grown not only outside, but inside as well. In my new school I've made friends who accept me, and I've grown not only to accept, but even like myself. Though times are better for us financially, my dad still keeps that jug filled with change—just in case. I'm no longer ashamed of my family. Instead, with maturity, I have learned to respect their strength and tenacity.

Now I am standing in line waiting to sign up for classes for my first semester of college. The room is packed with others like me, nervously anticipating what lies ahead: meeting new people, trying a new life on for size. Suddenly, I notice my bully standing in a corner of the room looking as puzzled and threatened as anyone else—but he doesn't see me. I panic at the sight of him. I recognize the slant of his smile and the furl of his brow. He can still set ripples of acid swirling through my belly.

I can't believe he's going to the same school as me. In that short moment, two scenarios run through my mind: I can run over, slap him in the face, shake him and demand to know why he made my life a living hell. But what would happen if I run over and slap him, and then he slaps me back and we both end up getting hauled away by campus security?

This is what really happened: I looked over at him, and then I looked over at the long line for names A to H, and that's when it hit me. Why waste my time living in the past? That bully *was* my history, and now it was time to turn toward my future. I couldn't move ahead until I came to terms with that simple concept. So I got in line and registered, and then I got in the next line, and the next, and the next. This bully meant nothing to my present life or dreams. There was nothing I needed to say to him anymore, because he no longer meant anything to me. He appeared so much smaller to me now. With this realization, my mind's eye shrank him down further, until there was nothing left of him that mattered now at all.

That day I let go of my bully who, I thought, held power over me for so long, and all it took was a conscious decision to do so. It wasn't the bully who kept me prisoner—it was my own spirit. I realized that I must live each day in the present, and not allow myself to sink into the murkiness of a lost childhood. Each day is like a brand-new penny, which I value and spend wisely. At night I toss them inside a kind of glass jug in my mind. As they hit bottom they resonate with the splendid tinkling of a life filled with possibilities.

Alyssa Morgan
As told to C. S. Dweck

The Rumor Was True

I do not think much of a man who is not wiser today than he was yesterday.

Abraham Lincoln

Junior-high school was probably the worst time in my life. My body was changing daily, and I spent most of my time trying to fit into a mold that my peers had formed for me. Gone were the days of Elmer's glue, crayons and those tiny scissors with the rounded edges. From here on out, I had my own locker, carried my books to each class and started making my own decisions about which classes to take. Oh yeah, I almost forgot: I had to take showers in front of my peers. Naked. That was dreadful.

What I remember most about junior high, however, was the incredible pain and heartache that students inflicted on one another with their words and actions. There were students who seemed to have it all together and made those around them feel as if they didn't measure up. It wasn't until much later that I learned that those who ripped on others suffered from a terrible self-image, so in order to make themselves feel better, they tore others down. In fact, they were usually a totally different person from the one they presented to the outside world.

I didn't have the best self-image in junior high, and there were two things that I fell back on to be accepted—athletics and humor. I have always been a decent athlete, which brought a certain confidence to my life, and I have always been able to make people laugh. At times, the laughter came at another's expense.

I didn't fully realize what I was doing to the self-images of those around me, particularly one classmate of mine. Her name was Tracy, and she had a crush on me. Instead of nicely letting her know that I wasn't interested in her, I got caught up in trying to be funny, with her being the brunt of my jokes. I am ashamed now to think of how I treated her in seventh grade. I went out of my way to make things miserable for her. I made up songs about her, and even wrote short stories in which I had to save the world from Tracy, the evil villain.

That all changed about halfway through the year, however, when Mr. Greer, my PE teacher, came up to me one day.

"Hey, Mike, you got a second?"

"Sure, Mr. Greer!" I said. Everybody loved Mr. Greer, and I looked up to him like a father.

"Mike, I heard a rumor that you were going around picking on Tracy." He paused and looked me straight in the eye. It seemed like an eternity before he continued.

"You know what I told the person I heard that from? I told them it couldn't possibly be true. The Mike Powers I know would never treat another person like that. Especially a young lady."

I gulped, but said nothing. He gently put his hand on my shoulder and said, "I just thought you should know that." Then he turned and walked away without a backward glance, leaving me to my thoughts.

That very day I stopped picking on Tracy. I knew that the rumor was true, and that I had let my role model down by my actions. More importantly, though, it made me realize how badly I must have hurt this girl and others for whom I had made life difficult. It was probably a couple of months later before I fully realized the incredible way in which Mr. Greer handled the problem. He not only made me realize the seriousness of my actions, but he did it in a way that helped me to save some of my pride. My respect and love for him grew even stronger after that.

I don't think I ever apologized to Tracy for my hurtful words and actions. She moved away the next year, and I never saw her again. While I was very immature as a seventh-grader, I still should have known better. In fact, I did know better, but it took the wisdom of my favorite teacher to bring it out into the light.

Michael T. Powers

Stupidity

Keep true, never be ashamed of doing right; decide on what you think is right and stick to it.

George Eliot

He looked full-grown compared to the other children, and his arms and hands were constantly moving, as if he had no control over them. He talked curiously, in a language my second-grade ears could not decipher. He laughed like the rest of us, though perhaps a little louder and sometimes when there was nothing to laugh about. Other children called him "slow" and "retarded" and "stupid"—words I was only beginning to understand, and that made me uncomfortable, like toes trapped in shoes that are too small.

I have a stark memory of him that took place during the innocent time of day every student longed for, when the bell rang and herds of children stampeded out the door of the large, brick building called Central School and scattered like sheep on the playground to expend excess energy on swings or monkey bars, teeter-totters or sandboxes. I chose the swings that day, for I liked the way the wind lifted my hair like an opening umbrella, cooling my face and neck on my way up to the treetops, where I challenged myself to swing high enough to kick the leaves on the branches.

From my vantage point, I observed a large crowd of children gathering around the "stupid" boy, holding hands as they orbited around him, chanting something I could not make out from a distance.

Something about the scene was bothersome to me, and I jumped from the swing still in motion, stumbling to my knees in my haste to get to the scene in question. As I neared the crowd, I could see the large, clumsy boy in the center of the whirling children, laughing, drool spilling from his chin, his arms flopping up and down as he pranced on his tiptoes. The group was chanting "Gravy Train, Gravy Train." Someone invited me to join in the "fun," but the display paralyzed me as I looked on through eyes suddenly blurred by tears. The "retarded" boy didn't have the capacity to realize he was being made fun of, thinking instead that he was taking part in a game, making the taste of salty tears in my mouth all the more repulsive.

I silently vowed that day never to take part in making fun of others because they were "different."

I have seen the boy repeatedly over the years in the bodies of many people with cruel labels attached to their names—the brunts of hurtful jokes, the misfits, the nerds, the deformed, the shy, the helpless, the ugly, the friendless—and I have also experienced the humiliation of being the lonely one inside the circle of chanting "children."

I wish I could say I remained true to my vow and boast complete innocence to indifference and bigotry, but I have done my share of gossiping in the cafeteria behind the back of one who could not even defend herself. I have laughed at demeaning jokes and scoffed at someone's choice of clothing. I even feared for my safety because of the color of someone's skin. But more often than not, I quickly regretted it, haunted by the memory of a retarded boy, alone inside a moving circle of taunting children chanting "Gravy Train," and I am the one too "stupid" to not laugh.

Marjee Berry-Wellman

Waves of Good-Bye

In the highway breeze, Adie's hair whips her cheeks like a dozen inky horsetails. Most of her mane has fallen out of her upsweep, the strands flapping wildly around her face, around her exposed shoulders. Alongside our Jeep, the beach yawns, waking with its seagulls and surfers. Adie turns up the radio, and we belt out the chorus in our best high notes until our voices drown into the ocean air. It is senior ditch day, after all, and we have much rejoicing to do.

We were both Leos, and our manes, we reasoned, were direct extensions of ourselves. It sounded very sensible, even a little mystical, lending justification to our nicknames at high school: the two good witches. Adie and I would do everything imaginable to our locks: curling, straightening, knotting, weaving, teasing. Adie's hair was so much more alive with possibility: Her black hair cascaded lazily from her scalp, and when the sunlight hit it just right, it had a way of reflecting silvery pools in its loose waves. My hair, a kind of dusty orange, had an unmanageable thickness about it, a dull frumpiness that took a backseat to Adie's slicker twists and braids.

With her foot still planted on the gas pedal, Adie manages to stand up in the Jeep. Her head is peering over the windshield, high above the roll bars. Even in her rashness, she is graceful—a statuesque performer balancing upon the spine of a Lippizan.

"Adie!" I holler. "You're insane! Get down!"

"Come on and live a little," she sing-songs. "We're nearly done with high school! Can you believe it? I mean, can you beee-lieve it?"

Adie collapses back to the seat, exhilarated with her feat. She mutters something about trig class, only I am far away now. I glance to the seamless shore and think, for the first time, about *after* high school, and everything becomes the hollow sucking sound of the sea in a conch. Come fall, Adie will be at a university in San Diego, and I will be navigating my way around a campus in Santa Barbara. One shore, two separate cities, an entire world away.

Her hands come off the steering wheel and reach toward the sky in an utterly free stretch. My hands are suddenly curling nervously around my kneecaps.

We have our usual spot, between lifeguard stands 11 and 12, which we have methodically stalked out over four years, finding it to be the spot for the best-looking lifeguards. Our towels are unfurled, the radio antenna elongated, and the baby oil is at the ready.

"Adie?" I ask. She is dousing herself in oil, which gives her a ubiquitous sheen. "Have you thought about what college will be like?"

"Mmmmm, not really," she answers. The question seems to slide off her back like the oil itself. "I guess I'll just find out when it happens."

"Right, right," I say, half-assuredly. "That's how I feel." Only I don't. Horrific images of wandering, lost, in a sea of people—mature people with bills and rent—streak across my mind. I worry about the notorious bike paths I was warned of at orientation, about devilish seniors careening and forcing me off the road, and about who my roommate will be, and if she'll have lousy taste in music. "Isn't it funny how we know all of the same words to the same songs?" I ask.

"What? Are you day dreaming again?" Adie replies. "Here," she continues, handing me the baby oil, "can you coat my back?" With the sun striking her, she already appears perfectly bronze, a stark contrast to my pale skin mottled with freckles.

She is lying with her belly to the sun and a towel over her face. "You know," she says, removing the towel for a moment, "I bet you'll be the only one in your dorm with red hair."

As if I weren't self-conscious enough! No amount of good-witchery could mask the peculiarity of my hair.

"You're lucky," she continues. "It's what makes you, you," and the towel goes back over her eyes.

"I think it's time to flip," Adie announces. We roll over, repositioning ourselves perpendicular to the sun, when a deep voice overhead startles us.

"Hi ladies. Hard day at the office?" He is tall, almost unbearably tan, and his hair falls over one eye.

"The hardest," Adie responds, propping herself up on one arm. She usually takes the lead in these things, while I wait to chime in. Sometimes I wait eternities.

His hands are on his hips now, angling his torso and flashing ripples of muscle. I think about how I look. Should I lean on one arm? Is my stomach in? Am I showing cleavage? Do I even have cleavage? Adie seems to be doing everything right. Her body is relaxed and firm at once. I seem light-years behind. "Well," he says, "I'm headed out to catch some waves," and he heads toward the breakers.

"Now this," Adie mumbles, "is how I imagine college."

And then he turns around, looking straight at me. "You coming or what?"

Steve. It's an older name. A real guy name. The water is up to our chests, lapping haphazardly at our throats. When the sun hits, it blinds us temporarily, and then we laugh, trying to keep our balance in the ocean.

"So I take it you don't work," Steve questions. "How about school?"

I nod. This is uncharted territory.

"UCLA?" he asks. "No, wait, you look like a Pepperdine girl."

My nodding gets wilder.

"Which one?"

"Ummm. Neither."

"Oh, a private school, then."

Our high school *is* private, I reason, agreeing with him. And then his hands are about my waist.

"Watch this," he whispers, and then tosses me up out of the ocean, and I crash back in through the water, submerged with a deep sloshing of water. I force my way back up to the surface, gasping. "Pretty good," Steve boasts, only I have no idea about what's so good about any of this.

My eyes rove the shore and I see Adie there, and she sees me, giving an exaggerated wave. Maybe this *is* like college, I think, my being on my own—floating—and Adie somewhere further off, wondering where I've gone. It has always been me waving back at Adie, watching her flirt, wondering when she will come back to land, or if she will. Now, I am my own element of surprise. I wave back to her, just barely, unassuredly, holding up my hand like a hesitant bicyclist unsure of the proper signal.

"You seem close to your friend," Steve inquires. "Same school?"

Yes, I answer, but not for long. When I finally tell him that we are just two girls, two seniors, ditching school, he isn't as repulsed as I feared. In fact, he becomes a little too anxious to give advice about college, about the freedoms and the friendships, about the failing and forgetting, all of the "f's." "It comes in waves," he says, and then, smiling, he splashes water into my face. "Get it?"

This time I nod genuinely, I get it, and, with my body chilled from the coolness of the ocean or maybe just from the coolness of everything, head back toward the shore where my best friend is soaking in the sun, soaking in everything, still waving to me as I wander back to her.

Jennifer Baxton

When It All Changes

The moment of change is the only poem.

Adrienne Rich

I am reminded of the song we used to sing in Girl Scouts: "Make new friends, but keep the old; one is silver and the other's gold." I graduated from high school a year and a half ago, and post-graduation, the old seemed more like gold dust—it all just blew away. My friends and I went our separate ways and made different lives with people in our new worlds. I put away my old photos and shot new ones to go with my new furniture in my new apartment—in my new life. Once in a while I would call a friend at college or an ex back home and rehash the past. The conversation usually didn't exceed ten minutes because we didn't really know what to say to each other. Everything had changed.

I believe that in life we have chapters—phases, if you will. The many faces of youth are shocking. We change from day to day, hour to hour. We love and then stop. We have a best friend and then we have five. We love our parents and then hate them. We play soccer and then decide to take dance classes instead. Okay, so we're fickle—fickle like the latest fashion trend. "In with the new, out with the old," that's our motto. This way we never get bored and it's easier to move on after being hurt. The flip side is that there will be a point when we look back on the old and miss it, like we miss a pet that dies or a small house that isn't big enough for a growing family. Moving away from something is exciting, but it all looks different in the rearview mirror. While visiting my parents during Thanksgiving, I awoke to the backward mirror image of my forward life.

I called several of my high-school friends and suggested that we go out for coffee to catch up. Everyone agreed, and so we met downtown at a familiar café. We all looked a bit different—older, taller, thicker. We sipped our coffee drinks and chatted, talking mostly about high school, boyfriends and finals. We laughed and hugged and remembered. For some reason; talking and remembering made me feel pretty bad, and when there was nothing left to talk about, I realized that we hadn't really talked about anything. So much had happened in the last year with all of us that we couldn't possibly know where to start. I went home that night feeling really alone and confused, and frustrated with myself for . . . for what? Changing, I guess.

It took me about an hour to realize how ridiculous that sounded. I was feeling guilty for changing? I was confused because we had all endured another year and mastered new experiences. My guilt was short-lived. Sure, everything has changed because we have changed and will continue to change forever. We all care a little less about who wore what to the *MTV Awards* and what the latest toy trend is. (What's that scooter thing called again?) We have healed our hearts from the devastation of breaking up with our first loves. We are secure with the fact that no matter what happens, we will always have tomorrow. We have all changed in college, or in the University of Life. Some of us have jobs, and some of us have boyfriends. Next year, we will all have grown a little more, and then a little more the next year. We will have pain, and we will have joy. We will endure and we will accept, and then we'll be back to share or just to smile with each other and know that everything will be all right.

Rebecca Woolf

What's on the Inside

To measure the man, measure his heart.

Malcolm Stevenson Forbes

I can still remember that boy in perfect detail. He had beautiful blue eyes that lit up whenever he smiled. And when his mouth smiled, half of his face would light up with shiny white teeth. He was the first boy who gave me that feeling like my heart was going to stop. When he walked by, I could see him out of the corner of my eye and smell the detergent he used on his clothes. My body would freeze, and my brain would stop ticking. Then he would flash that big smile at me and my breath would stop. I can picture myself standing in front of him like a fool with my mouth gaping open and my eyes melting with lust as this beautiful boy charmed me.

There was no doubt about it, I was head-over-heels, madly in puppy love. I might have only been in third grade, but this was real or at least I thought it was. I was constantly thinking about him and ways I could get closer to him. "Eric" was scribbled all over my notebooks with messy little hearts drawn around them. I adored him, and he knew it.

Then one Saturday I got the chance to get closer to him. I was at a birthday party, and Eric showed up at the front door. The whole night I avoided him for fear that I would say something stupid.

As I was pigging out on potato chips, I turned around and saw him staring right at me. My stomach jumped and my cheeks blushed as he walked closer to me. He flashed his eyes at me and said, "Come here, Eleanor. I want to tell you something." My heart fluttered at the thought of being so close to him. Eric leaned closer and cupped his hand around my ear. He brought his face closer to mine, closer, closer. I moved my head away to give him more room, but he moved closer still. I felt his arm across my back and his hand warming my ear. But I didn't hear any words. I tilted my head away from him in an almost uncomfortable position and again his face moved closer to mine. I turned to look at him and there was his face, two inches from mine, with his eyes closed and his mouth pursed into a kiss. A wave of shock came over my face, and his expression copied mine as he opened his eyes.

"What are you doing?" he asked. He raised his eyebrows in a puzzled expression

"What are YOU doing?" I shot back. I could only imagine what Eric was thinking right now. I'm sure he was thinking, *This girl, Eleanor, is a dork!* I desperately hoped that wasn't what he was thinking.

He looked right at me and yelled, "Geez, Eleanor, I'm just trying to kiss you!"

What? He was going to kiss me? I missed my chance! My one and only chance to kiss this boy of my dreams, and I ruined it.

"Oh, sorry," I said, very embarrassed.

He gave me a small kiss on the cheek then scrambled off to a group of boys who were laughing hysterically.

Then he yelled at his friends. "I'm NEVER playing Truth-or-Dare again!"

At the sound of his words, my sensitive heart crumbled into pieces. *Tell me he didn't say what I thought he said.* But I knew it was true. I could feel a sob starting in the back of my throat, but I promised myself to hold it in. Then tears came, filling up my eyes and spilling over my bottom lashes. My lip started to quiver, and I knew a flood of tears was only seconds away. I flew out of the basement with my head in my hands and retreated to the bathroom to cry alone for the rest of the night.

As much as I would like to, I can't say that this experience was easily forgotten. That night, I realized Eric didn't like me as much as I liked him. The next week at school, I would hear groups of kids talking about the incident when they didn't think I was listening. But I heard them and my feelings were hurt each and every time. While my heart ached for a while, I actually recovered rather quickly. I got over it in a couple of weeks, and the gossip stopped long before that. I did learn a lesson, though, and it still helps me to this day. *There are a lot of cute boys out there, some even cuter than Eric, but just because a boy is cute doesn't mean he is necessarily nice.* I still get crushes on boys who are cute, but I find out what their personality is like before I let my heart get involved.

Eleanor Luken

And Still I Search . . .

Ah yes, it's all going to pay off, I used to think. *Once I ask her out, things will be simple.*

Well, that is, they would be simple . . . if the girl said yes. Fact of the matter is, I must not be attractive, because if I try to sit near them, they most certainly get up and walk away. They don't make it obvious or anything; almost as if they are just making a trip to the vending machines or to see another friend a few feet away. And then there are my feeble attempts at small talk. Whatever comes out of my mouth, something will come out of theirs that is calculated simply to end the conversation and shut me up so they can spy on the guys they actually do like. I have made up my mind that girls simply don't like me.

I've tried asking a girl out before, and boy did it go down in flames. It was a disaster beyond reasoning. You know, the sort of catastrophe you'd never see the likes of in a movie. It's always the same: Boy pines for beautiful, unattainable girl, hooks up with less-attractive girl next door at the end. Problem is, there's no girl next door for me. And since every other girl in my school qualifies as unattainable in comparison to the likes of me, Vegas oddsmakers will tell you I don't have a snowball's chance. And, you know, once a girl has made up her mind that she doesn't like you, that's it. Girls are a wonder to behold, but they are incredibly stubborn. The second she puts you in that "Out" box, forget all about her. Move on. She'll never set eyes on you again, so it's not worth your time to chase somebody who's already filed you away.

I don't know if I'll ever be in someone's "In" box. It might not happen until I meet new girls. Go to college. Enter the workforce. I can already tell she's out there somewhere, but she's certainly not here. The looks on these girls' faces when I walk around a corner or make eye contact don't exactly do wonders for my self-confidence. So I've given up on girls for now. They just don't seem to care. They will soon, though. Not these girls. Not at this place. Not now. Somewhere else I have yet to go. And that's one of the little things that makes life worth waiting for, you know? Thinking the journey's still in the future, still uncharted water, sort of helps me get through my day.

Oh, yes. This is supposed to be the part when I tell you that I've fallen in love with a great girl who really does like me, and I tell you never to give up. Nope. Hasn't happened yet. And I can safely assure you it never will at my high school. You might say, "Well, of course it won't with that attitude!" But an optimistic outlook wouldn't do any good, either. I used to be optimistic about it, but that got me nowhere.

However, there *is* a point to all this, and it goes something like this: She's out there. She's just not at your high school. So you're going to have to wait. Do some homework to occupy your time until then.

Brian Firenzi

The Single-for-Life Syndrome

The snow goose need not bathe to make itself white. Neither need you do anything but be yourself.

Lao-tzu

As my best friend so eloquently put it, we were "Rated PG," or platonically gifted. Always the shoulders for guys to cry on, we were the founders and co-presidents of the Never Been Kissed Club (in our area anyway; I'm sure there are other NBKCs out there), and were both still "proud" members at the ripe old age of nineteen. Both of us were intelligent, enthusiastic and active in clubs and sports. We had great senses of humor and were just as comfortable yelling at the refs from the stands as getting all primped to go out on the town.

Yet there existed a difference in our singleness. Melissa was single by choice. Granted, some of the guys who had pursued her were not exactly desirable, but the fact remains that they had pursued her. She had enjoyed a few minor almost-flings, but still claimed to be perpetually single. Now, when I say I hadn't ever had a boyfriend or even been pursued, this is not a "that-fling-with-the-guy-in-Ohio-last-summer-doesn't-count-because-we-won't-ever-see-each-other-again" statement. I didn't even have a kindergarten boyfriend. I had never been on a date, save for junior prom, which was an arranged thing—neither of us asked the other; someone just decided we should go together because our best friends were going together. It's not that I was antisocial or deathly afraid of boys; by the end of high school I hung out with about three times as many guys on a regular basis as girls. I was the eternal good friend whom any guy knew he could come to for advice on dating and how to snag the girl he wanted—it was just never me.

This was a source of longing, sadness, irritation, questioning and occasional misery for me. In most areas of my life I was quite stable, but for a few years every couple of months would yield a night of crying, generally catalyzed by a sappy movie or even just a song on the radio.

I came up with personal mottos such as, "If even the losers get lucky, then what does that make me?" and, "If nobody's going to be interested in you, you might as well be picky." While I constantly joked about my singleness, my insides were stinging. The sight of a happy couple on the street or in the mall would bring with it the knowledge that both of those people had found someone to hold, so why couldn't I? People I had graduated with were getting engaged, even married, but I couldn't get a date if my life depended on it. Testimonials from attached people who claimed to remember the deep despair I was experiencing did not make me feel better; rather they sent tidal waves crashing through the ocean of resentment building inside me.

After a few months at college, though, a funny thing happened. Even though my confidence in the relationship field did not improve, I began caring less and less.

My roommates, eerily similar to me in personality, were both in serious relationships, but instead of depressing me further, it helped me to think that maybe there was someone out there for me. My sophomore year I chose to live with the same two girls and another, also in a serious relationship, and everyone said it was *my* year—that Bec was gonna get some action on the dating scene. I wasn't so sure, but I didn't focus on it too much. College put enough on my mind without having to worry about being single for life. Besides, everyone told me love would find me when I wasn't looking for it.

So here I am, well into my sophomore year, *my* year, and here's where you're expecting me to start gushing about Mr. Right, the boyfriend I never thought I'd have—how he is the best thing that has ever happened to me and how I was silly to think I'd never get one because there really is someone out there for everyone. But no, this is not one of those "I got a significant other so you can, too!" musings that will just end up making someone more bitter. This is purely about a sorely needed attitude adjustment. I still have sporadic lonely nights, but I now know that I don't have to be alone to be lonely. I still love to torment my roommates and lay on the heavy guilt trips when they have date nights, or when I'm what I like to refer to as the "seventh wheel" on an outing with three couples and me, but this is mostly to see that look of amused frustration on their faces. I still make gagging noises when someone's being all lovey-dovey on the phone or talking about what her boyfriend did for her birthday. I still joke about being the first "gold plus" member of the NBKC. I still refuse to settle for less than what I want and deserve; perhaps I, too, am single by choice in that sense. I still haven't been kissed, but I'm okay with that. I live in hope.

Rebecca Ayres

Sweet-and-Sour Sixteen

If you can learn from hard knocks, you can also learn from soft touches.

Carolyn Kenmore

I was fifteen, soon to turn sixteen, and I felt pressured. I had never been kissed. I was certain I had to be one of the most backward, late-blooming teenagers there was, carrying around this terrible secret that might reveal itself at any moment—if I ever got a date.

My only consolation was that my best friend, Carol, was in the same predicament. She, too, feared the label "sweet sixteen and never been kissed."

We spent that summer plotting ways to absolve ourselves by meeting guys and getting dates. We even went so far as to sign ourselves up for corn detasseling. For three hot, sweaty weeks in humid Iowa, we walked up and down cornfields with a busload of teenagers, mostly guys, and picked corn. There were water fights, romps through the fields, heady compliments and serious flirtations—but no dates.

Carol had her sights set on one promising candidate (he

was at her side constantly), but when the last day of work came, he still had not asked her out. I think it was sheer frustration that drove her to tell him that she would be sixteen in two months and had never been kissed.

"You haven't?" he asked. "That's great! If you can go another two months without a kiss, you'll be sweet sixteen, not sour sixteen!"

So much for that candidate.

By the end of the summer, we had pretty much given up on our quest. We went out for pizza with a group of girls in another town. We were sitting there laughing and having a good time when two of the girls noticed a group of guys at a nearby table. Before long all the other girls had joined in and it was a full-on flirting party.

Carol and I became annoyed. Sure, the guys were cute. Sure, they were looking at us, but this was our last night of the summer! We weren't about to waste it on a group of guys who might send all kinds of positive signals then never make it to our table. We stomped outside to the parking lot to talk in peace. The guys followed us and asked if we knew the time.

They were even cuter close up. I tried not to stare at the one with dark, wavy hair and hazel eyes, but my eyes kept wandering back to him. His name was Cody.

The other girls soon joined us, and we talked with the guys as late as our curfews would allow. They arranged to meet us the next night at a park.

Somehow, the next night, we ended up paired off as couples. I found myself with Cody. He and I walked over to a monument in the park and sat down on it. Suddenly, anxiety overcame me. I realized that I was about to receive my first kiss, and I simply wasn't ready for it. I burst into tears. Cody put his arm around me and asked what was wrong. I blurted out the whole tragic story of being sixteen and having never been kissed. Then, realizing how lame this must have sounded, I went for broke. I blurted out every negative thing that had ever happened in my life. By the time I was done, I was convinced he must have thought I was a total nutcase.

He looked at me for a few moments from under those long, dark eyelashes, then slowly brushed his lips against mine. The kiss was soft, quick and moist. I was just glad when it was over—and that I was away from home. No one needed to know the embarrassment I had just put myself through. I never bothered to tell him how he could reach me again, and he never asked.

The next day, the phone rang and my mom answered. "It's for you," she said, a startled look in her eyes. As I walked over she whispered, "It's a boy!"

My heart went crazy. I managed to mumble a hello, and a male voice started talking. Cody! I felt as if my heart might burst out of my chest. Mom stared at me. I stared back. This was the first time that a boy who I cared about had called me.

I asked how he had gotten my number. He told me my girlfriend had given it to him and asked if I wanted to go out with him that weekend. He told me my girlfriend and his friend would be coming with us. "Would you like to go out with them?" he asked.

I'm not sure how I responded, but I know I accepted. I also said, "I never expected to hear from you again."

"Why not?" he asked.

"Well, after last night . . ."

"After last night, I think you're the sweetest girl I ever met," he said. There was a pause, then he added, "Someone has to sour you."

Ronica Stromberg

First Kiss

It's a beautiful day, the summer before I start seventh grade. For Dee, it's the summer before eighth grade.

I'm watching TV. *Jenny Jones* is on. The guests argue about their unfaithful husbands or wives, while their wives or husbands deny all of the accusations of infidelity. Suddenly, Dee plops down next to me on the couch, coming from the bathroom. She nuzzles very close to me and rests her head on my shoulder, complaining about how bony it is. I tell her to shut up. I feel very conscious of her head on my shoulder, and then I feel conscious of her staring at me. I look at her and smile.

"What's up?" I ask, confused.

"Nothing," she answers, shaking her head.

She nuzzles even closer to me, and I feel awkward. Her arm slides in between my arm and my body, and she clings to me. A billion thoughts race through my head and then all of a sudden . . . nothing. I feel her staring at me, the heat of her face close to mine. I look at her, and I see three eyes. She looks straight into my eyes, pinning me with her gaze, locking my eyes with hers.

"Don't you wanna kiss me?" she asks sweetly.

My mouth drops open, and I quickly close it, realizing

that it was not the right look to give. I start to sweat a little. What's worse, I feel her arms snake around my neck. I glance down for a second, sensing an awkwardness, like she doesn't know what she's doing. I look up again into her big green eyes. Her confidence suddenly blows me away, and I am intimidated. Time ceases to pass in minutes or even seconds . . . but in milliseconds. Actually, the only time that exists is measured by the small movements that she makes.

A smile slowly forms on her lips.

I start to blush, feeling my blood rush into my cheeks, and I feel stupid, like I don't know what I'm doing, which I don't. And in that moment I curse her for making me feel stupid; she knows what she's doing to me.

I have to do something. Her next move might be an embarrassing question, like, "Do you not know how to kiss or something?" or "Are you a prude?" or "What's wrong with you, boy?" She's too close to me. She's moving too fast for me. She's too close to my face! She's too intimidating. She's too . . . cute!

She stops smiling.

Oh no! What's she thinking now? I'm so stupid! I should've done something! She thinks I'm a prude! I am! So what?!?!? So, I'm a prude. Give me a break! Give . . . me . . . a break!

She wets her lips.

Whoa.

Her face inches closer.

Oh, man. Only a breath away from my face now, I see her lips form a smile before she presses hers to mine.

Slow, soft and sweet. Only her arms around me keep me from flying.

After what seems like a few minutes, she stops kissing me and looks up. Her emerald eyes sparkle, and she smiles. She giggles and says that I'm cute. I stare at her. She nuzzles back against me and watches TV. I sit there, staring at her, dumbfounded . . . with a stupid smile pasted on my lips.

Wow.

Ron Cheng

Changes and the Game "High School"

School is a battlefield for your heart.

Angela, *My So-Called Life*

In the still darkness of my bedroom, my mind wandered unrestrained by the four walls that created boundaries for my body. I could not see a single thing. My vision was blurred without my glasses, leaving only my mind to see things in focus.

For the past year my life had been spinning out of control. I was becoming disoriented in a world I had once seen with vision as clear as crystal. Everything was changing. My friends were being lost to boyfriends, crushes and obsessions. The world that revolved around me was being dismantled, smashed and demolished by the people who had helped make it. Everything was falling apart, and I couldn't stop it.

Things were changing. "High school is a place to grow, to experiment and to change," someone once told a scared, unsure eighth-grader on the fateful first day at a whole new game with rules unknown. I didn't want to ever change, and so I tried to make a square block fit into a circular hole. Needless to say, it did not work. I spent a whole year in lies—black destructive lies that I now regret and would rather forget. I tried to follow my friends in all that they did, positive that they knew better. At parties, I tried what everyone else did, but the next day I realized I had not had that much fun.

My friends were trying to help me fit into this mold, and it hurt to be prodded, poked and squeezed like a tube of toothpaste just to try to fit in. All of the things I had promised myself before entering high school just didn't seem to apply. I grew silly, obnoxious, like a crybaby or a little girl. I did not mature; I grew immature. I thought I was cute and likable. What I did not realize was that I was a fraud. I tried to be like everyone else. I started to dress in the same clone-like fashions, talk, write and even eat the same way.

Later that year a new girl arrived in high school. I decided to support her by being a life raft for a while. Little did I expect that she would start to copy me. Like everyone else, I pretended to know what I was doing. As she spent more and more time with me, I realized that little things like her choice of words, hand gestures and her attitude were all annoying. One gray, gloomy day, I had taped myself giving a speech and when I played it back, it did not sound like me. I could not recognize the voice on the tape for a while and then it hit me. The attitude and persona portrayed through my voice was like hers. I was the same. From that moment I detested myself. Through this hatred, a window opened and for a nanosecond I saw the girl who didn't care what everyone else thought, who always stood up for others and who had friends who loved her just the way she was. She was the real me. Full of determination, I started the long, perilous hike back to individuality. On the way up, I found pieces of myself that I had lost along the way. My life had become a long quest in which I was to search for priceless capsules holding my identity and to put them back in the treasury of my soul. The quest is undoubtedly not over, but I gain more freedom every day. I now surprise my friends and myself with values and morals I didn't know I possessed and I no longer just take others' words for truth anymore.

I realized high school is a game we all play. We are thrown into a big pool with no one yelling expectations, instructions or the objective. We are forced to sink or swim. Perhaps I have seen the light, the truth and the goal of high school. Or perhaps I have only opened my eyes to a bigger stage of shadows and illusions. Who really knows?

Adelene Wong

A Toast

Raise your glass to the sky
with hopes and dreams held high.
To the graduates I toast . . .

Here's to the friends we've lost and gained,
and the people we'll never know by name.
To the bonds that we've made and albums we filled,
memories that may fade but never be killed.

Here's to the phone calls filled with tears,
and to the hours spent talking away our fears.
To the people we thought deserved our hearts,
whom now we bash and rip apart.

Here's to the pictures in frames with stories to say,
that we will be sure to pack when we go away.
To the football games we have watched beneath the lights,
and our cheers and chants drifting into the night.

Here's to proms and dances,
and high-school romances.
To homecoming games,
with all the wins in our name.

Here's to late nights we've spent cramming for tests,
and mornings where coffee made up for our rest.
To the dances and events we took months to create,
the night before worries that came too late.

Here's to the tears we knew we'd cry,
to the people and places we say good-bye.
To the wild and bizarre things we've done,
that we will remember to be the most fun.

Here's to the letters we left unsigned,
may our identities be revealed all in due time.
To the relationships we wonder how we ever lived without,
and the crushes we look back on and laugh about.

So now it is time to place our glasses down,
put our caps on and turn our tassels around.
Listen for our names and let them echo through,
and realize how fast these four years just flew.

Sarah Watroba

12

LETTERS FROM READERS

To send a letter is a good way to go somewhere without moving anything but your heart.

Anaïs Nin

Bonding with Notebooks

Today could be the day that my mom realizes I'm growing up and gives me some more responsibility.

Jenny Gleason

Dear Chicken Soup for the Teenage Soul,

I have always been a real fan of your books and the important lessons of love and understanding that are shared in each of the stories. They have helped me to see things that were not so clear to me. I have received a great deal of comfort from reading many of the stories.

I had been going through some difficult times not so long ago dealing with the pressures of growing up and trying to communicate with my parents, particularly my mother. Our relationship had suffered because of this. When I would get frustrated or angry it seemed like we would end up in some sort of confrontation with each other and not talk about what we were really feeling. I feel like I have overcome those obstacles now, but not without a certain turn of events.

A while back I ran away from home so that I could be far enough away to vent my anger and release some of the pain bottled up inside of me. I stayed away for many hours, well into the night, before I finally decided to return home. When I walked through the front door of my house, I immediately saw all the pain, anger and disappointment on my parents' faces, especially my mother's. For days after the incident, my mom and I were on unfirm ground, to say the least. Everything we did or said was filled with tension until we both eventually snapped. We knew we desperately had to have a talk. We agreed to have breakfast together the next morning. That morning will remain etched in my memory forever. It was a turning point in both of our lives and our relationship.

We decided to go to a local café. On our way to the table I noticed that my mother had two notebooks and some pens. I asked her what they were for. She explained to me that sometimes it is easier to write down our feelings rather than try to talk about them. She then proceeded to hand me a notebook of my own and she kept one for herself. The "rules" for that talk were that she would pick a topic, and we would write down our feelings about the topic in the form of a letter. It could be as long or as short as we wanted. Our first topic was: "Why I am so angry." I had written a half page worth of stuff, and my mom filled up nearly three pages. I watched tears stream down her face as she wrote. I never realized anyone could hide so much anger and frustration. It could have been that I never paid much attention, either. Sometimes we think we are the only ones with problems, but I was reminded that morning that other people can be hurting just as much.

After she was finished writing we exchanged our notebooks and read what the other had written. As soon as I started reading my mother's words, I began to cry and so did she. When we were finished reading we discussed our feelings. Amazingly enough, it felt like all the anger I had welled up inside of me drained from my body. Our talk helped me realize so many things I had never thought of before, not only about my mother but about other people as well.

My mother and I continue to use our notebooks as a means of communicating our anger and frustrations, and our happiness also. We know that no matter how we feel about each other, our notebooks are a safe place to express it. We have made a pact that at the end of each letter we write, "I love you." Here are two of our more recent entries:

Dear Mom,

I just wanted you to know that some things I do are not meant to hurt or spite you. When I yell at you it's not because I hate you. And when I tell you I hate you, you should know that I really don't, although at times I feel like you hate me. Sometimes you just make me really mad and frustrated, and I don't know what to do with it. Like when you tell me you don't believe me even though I'm not lying, or when you do things that invade my privacy without my permission that you know I won't like. For instance, the other day you searched my room without me knowing or being there. I just wanted to hate you so much then. Then today you yelled at me, and it made me so mad. I really don't think there is much more to say right now. I love you.
Katie

And my mother's response to my letter:

Dear Katie,

I realize that you get mad and frustrated, but I do, too. I don't want you to think that since I am an adult I don't have feelings. As much as you think that I might

like it, I don't like yelling at you. I just wish you would help out a little more with the family and around the house. It would make things easier on me. Some things I do, like searching your room or not believing you, are not done to be mean. I only do those things if I have good cause. Sometimes you worry me, but it's just because I care. Although you might not think so, you yell at me as much as I yell at you. It hurts my feelings as well. Sometimes I just want to cry. I'm glad you told me how you felt about all those things. I'll try to work on my temper with you, and I'll try to be more patient if you will return the same courtesy to me and help me out a little around the house. If this is not okay, tell me and we can try to work something out. I love you.
Mom

We gained a special gift that day at the restaurant and we continue to be blessed with each other's everlasting love and patience. I am now a firm believer that we all need to express our feelings in order to live healthy lives. Thank you so much for letting me share this with you.

Sincerely,
Katie Benson

Life Is a Bumpy Road

Dear Kimberly,

Chicken Soup for the Teenage Soul was such a blessing for me. The quotes and stories really opened my eyes to all new perspectives in life. I am only twenty-three, and I have been incarcerated for seven years. This book has given me the courage to share my story with you.

When I was sixteen, I had my mind set on two things: having fun and being cool. One Saturday night, a friend and I knocked off from work at a local grocery store and could think of nothing better to do than ride around and get drunk. I never expected how drastically my life would change before that night ended.

After I was intoxicated, I came up with the "coolest" idea to show off in front of my older friend. "Hey man, let's go get my gun and find someone to scare by shooting at them." My friend didn't see anything wrong with the idea, so we went and got the gun. The alcohol, and now the gun, gave me all the "courage" I needed to show off. We finally passed a boy walking by himself along the road, and I just pointed the gun out of the window and started firing. He was fatally wounded and died right there on the side of the road.

I have now been paying for those actions for the past seven years as I sit in the Louisiana State Penitentiary serving a mandatory life sentence without parole. Like a lot of teens, I never worried about the consequences of my actions. I didn't care what happened tomorrow. I just wanted to have all the "fun" I could have today, but there was a price to pay. I'm afraid too many of us are making foolish decisions that come at such a high price, and we will never be able to clear ourselves of the consequences.

I am often asked what's the most important lesson I've learned, or what would I tell teens if I could only say one thing to them. It would be this: Life is a bumpy road with many regrets and very few second chances, so think before you act.

I have missed a lot of things in life. But reading all the stories in *Chicken Soup for the Teenage Soul* has taught me many things. I am thankful for the wonderful work y'all have done. Please keep up the awesome job. I can hardly wait for the new one to come out.

Thankfully yours,
Gary LeRoux

Learning the Hard Way

Dear Chicken Soup for the Teenage Soul,

My name is Kim, and I am from Ohio. I have really enjoyed reading your books. My friend Chelsea introduced me to them, and I've been reading them ever since.

I am fifteen years old—and five months pregnant. One subject I haven't read much about in your books is that of teenage pregnancy and its consequences. Girls and guys my age do not realize how serious it is to have sex. My mom always tried to warn me about making better choices for myself. She warned me about the serious things that could happen to me like getting pregnant, and contracting an STD or AIDS. But I never listened.

I've made a lot of mistakes. And now I'm pregnant. The father is not going to be in my life—or the baby's life, for that matter. I would give anything to be able to take it all back, but I can't. My only hope is that I can help to prevent it from happening to someone else by sharing with teens the extent of my remorse.

The stories in the book *have* helped me to do the right thing in other areas of my life. Last weekend my friends who had been drinking told me they would take me home.

But having read the story about a guy who was killed when he let his friends drive drunk, I decided to call my mom and ask her to pick me up. My friends didn't think I was a dork or anything, because I was just looking out for myself and my baby. I felt very positive about my decision. My mom was proud of me, too.

I hope your books continue to teach us lessons and open our eyes. It's hard to listen to our parents all the time. Sometimes it helps to be able to take our life lessons in the form of a story, rather than the bitter medicine of our parents' lectures. Thank you.

Sincerely,
Kim Lowery

My Magic Mirror

Dear Chicken Soup,

I haven't been as fortunate or as lucky as my friends when it comes to dating and relationships. Everyone else always seems to be able to "get the guy." One Friday night I was sitting at home without a date while all my friends were out with their boyfriends and I was inspired to write this poem:

My Magic Mirror

There is a mirror in my house,
It's on my bathroom wall.
Although I've met some other ones,
It's the friendliest of all.

It doesn't matter when I look,
It can happen any time.
A beautiful reflection it will show,
And then I'll see it's mine.

So how does it make me look so good,
At any time of day?
And why can't all the guys at school,
See me in my mirror's way?

If they could only see that girl,
Who greets me with a smile,
Then maybe I'd have a date, or two—
Hasn't happened in a while.

But do I want to date a guy,
Who'll judge by what he sees?
Or do I want to date a guy
Who will love and appreciate me?

He'll love me for my intelligence,
My humor and my taste.
He'll love me for my selflessness,
Which I haven't put to waste.

He'll love me for the things I do,
And how I get them done.
He'll love me with each breath I take,
And with each ray of the sun.

So then when will he find me,
And in my mirror see?
When will he come to fill the void,
That aches inside of me?

Will he show up on my front door,
When I'm about to give up hope?
Or will he come when I'm at peace within,
With the strength inside to help me cope?

Because I'm not just what's on the outside,
I am me down to my core.
And as I learn to love myself,
There will be a guy who loves me more.

A week later, I met a guy who I really liked. Unfortunately, that didn't work out, but I was okay with that because I believe in what my poem says about a guy loving you for *you*.

Since then, it's been like a lucky charm. Now that I finally allowed myself to have that kind of confidence, my teenage years are looking much better! I never used to believe it when teenage magazines would say that as soon as you have confidence, guys would pick up on it and take interest. After experiencing this for myself, however, I want to let everyone else know that it does work.

I hope my poem can help at least one person in the same way your books have helped me. So, for all those teenagers sitting at home on a Friday night: Stop waiting around, throw on a smile and lift your chin high!

Thank you,
Melinda Allen

It's Not What's on the Outside, but What's on the Inside

Dear Chicken Soup for the Teenage Soul,

I am writing to thank you for teaching me what to value in other people. Your books have taught me that it is a person's character and what's in a person's heart that matter the most—not what people look like or the clothes they wear.

Recently I fell hard for a guy at our school. His name is Nick. The first time I laid eyes on him I thought I had come face-to-face with an angel. He was absolutely the most beautiful human being I had ever encountered. When he walked down the hallways at school, every female within a six-foot radius would turn and follow him with their gaze. He was tall, dark and handsome—a regular Prince Charming. His eyes were a deep chestnut brown, and when directed toward me could send shivers down my spine and turn my knees to gelatin. Upon pointing him out to my closest friend, the obvious thing happened: She, too, fell head-over-heels for Nick.

The two of us followed him around school so often he

could have pressed charges against us for harassment. We sent him countless love letters and verses of bad poetry. Every day after school, we lingered by his car, waited for him to get in it and then watched him wistfully as he drove away. We were under his spell, and we had become stalkers.

As time passed, however, I noticed that even though Nick had a shiny, beautiful exterior, his interior needed a little work. His personality struck me as icy and self-centered. Following him so closely all the time gave me the chance to hear the rude comments he made to people, and it shattered my fantasy. My Prince Charming was turning out to be not so charming after all!

Eventually reality sunk in. Yes, Nick was beautiful on the outside, but inside he was made of stone. And even though I realized my knight-in-shining-armor was a fraud, I was not brokenhearted. Instead, I was grateful to him for showing me that I truly do care about more than superficial appearances. I now know that true beauty comes from the heart—not the face. Your books have reinforced that for me. Thank you for sharing these stories with us teens. Maybe one day even the Nicks of the world will read them and learn a thing or two about kindness and character.

Sincerely,
Caitlin Pollock

More Chicken Soup?

Many of the letters, stories and poems that you have read in this book were submitted by readers like you who have read *Chicken Soup for the Teenage Soul* and the other *Chicken Soup for the Soul* books. In the future, we are planning to publish *Chicken Soup for the Teenage Soul IV, Chicken Soup for the Teenage Soul on Love and Relationships, Chicken Soup for the Teenage Boy's Soul* and *Chicken Soup for the Teenage Christian Soul.* We would love to have you contribute a story, poem or letter to one of these future books.

This may be a story you write yourself, or one you clip out of your school newspaper, local newspaper, church bulletin or a magazine. It might be something you read in a book or find on the Internet. It could also be a favorite poem, quotation or cartoon you have saved. Please also send along as much information as you know about where it came from.

Just send a copy of your stories or other pieces to us at this address:

Chicken Soup for the Teenage Soul
P.O. Box 936
Pacific Palisades, CA 90272
e-mail: *stories@iam4teens.com*
Web site: *www.iam4teens.com*

Who Is Jack Canfield?

Jack Canfield is a bestselling author and one of America's leading experts in the development of human potential. He is both a dynamic and entertaining speaker and a highly sought-after trainer with a wonderful ability to inform and inspire audiences to open their hearts, love more openly and boldly pursue their dreams.

Jack spent his teenage years growing up in Martins Ferry, Ohio, and Wheeling, West Virginia, with his sister Kimberly (Kirberger) and his two brothers, Rick and Taylor. The whole family has spent most of their professional careers dedicated to educating, counseling and empowering teens. Jack admits to being shy and lacking self-confidence in high school, but through a lot of hard work he earned letters in three sports and graduated third in his class.

After graduating college, Jack taught high school in the inner city of Chicago and in Iowa. In recent years, Jack has expanded this to include adults in both educational and corporate settings.

He is the author and narrator of several bestselling audio- and videocassette programs. He is a regularly consulted expert for radio and television broadcasts and has published numerous books—all bestsellers within their categories—including more than twenty *Chicken Soup for the Soul* books, *The Aladdin Factor, Heart at Work, 100 Ways to Build Self-Concept in the Classroom* and *Dare to Win.*

Jack addresses over one hundred groups each year. His clients include professional associations, school districts, government agencies, churches and corporations in all fifty states.

Jack conducts an annual eight-day Training of Trainers program in the areas of building self-esteem and achieving peak performance. It attracts educators, counselors, parenting trainers, corporate trainers, professional speakers, ministers and others interested in developing their speaking and seminar-leading skills in these areas.

For further information about Jack's books, tapes and trainings, or to schedule him for a presentation, please contact:

The Canfield Training Group
P.O. Box 30880 • Santa Barbara, CA 93130
phone: 800-237-8336 • fax: 805-563-2945
e-mail: *speaking@canfieldgroup.com*
Web site: *www.chickensoup.com*

Who Is Mark Victor Hansen?

Mark Victor Hansen is a professional speaker who, in the last twenty years, has made over four thousand presentations to more than two million people in thirty-three countries. His presentations cover sales excellence and strategies; personal empowerment and development; and how to triple your income and double your time off.

Mark has spent a lifetime dedicated to his mission of making a profound and positive difference in people's lives. Throughout his career, he has inspired hundreds of thousands of people to create a more powerful and purposeful future for themselves while stimulating the sale of billions of dollars worth of goods and services.

Mark is a prolific writer and has authored *Future Diary, How to Achieve Total Prosperity* and *The Miracle of Tithing.* He is the coauthor of the *Chicken Soup for the Soul* series, *Dare to Win* and *The Aladdin Factor* (all with Jack Canfield) and *The Master Motivator* (with Joe Batten).

Mark has also produced a complete library of personal empowerment audio- and videocassette programs that have enabled his listeners to recognize and better use their innate abilities in their business and personal lives. His message has made him a popular television and radio personality with appearances on ABC, NBC, CBS, HBO, PBS, QVC and CNN.

He has also appeared on the cover of numerous magazines, including *Success, Entrepreneur* and *Changes.*

Mark is a big man with a heart and a spirit to match—an inspiration to all who seek to better themselves.

For further information about Mark, please contact:

Mark Victor Hansen & Associates
P.O. Box 7665
Newport Beach, CA 92658
phone: 949-759-9304 or 800-433-2314
fax: 949-722-6912
Web site: *www.chickensoup.com*

Who Is Kimberly Kirberger?

Kimberly is an advocate for teens, a writer for teens, a mother of a teen, and a friend and confidante to the many teens in her life. She is committed to bettering the lives of teens around the globe through her books and the outreach she does for teens on behalf of her organization, Inspiration and Motivation for Teens, Inc.

Kim's love for teens was first expressed globally with the publication of the bestselling *Chicken Soup for the Teenage Soul.* This book was a true labor of love for Kim, and the result of years of friendship and research with teens from whom she learned what really matters. After the success of the first Teenage Soul book, and the outpouring of hundreds and thousands of letters and submissions from teens around the world, Kim went on to coauthor the *New York Times* #1 bestsellers *Chicken Soup for the Teenage Soul II* and *Chicken Soup for the Teenage Soul III, Chicken Soup for the Teenage Soul Journal, Chicken Soup for the Teenage Soul Letters* and *Chicken Soup for the College Soul.* Kim's empathic understanding of the issues affecting parents led her to coauthor the recent release *Chicken Soup for the Parent's Soul.*

In October 1999, the first book in Kim's *Teen Love* series was released. *Teen Love: On Relationships* has since become a *New York Times* bestseller. Her friendship and collaboration with Colin Mortensen of MTV's *Real World Hawaii* produced the much-loved *Teen Love: A Journal on Relationships* and *Teen Love: On Friendship.* She recently released *Teen Love: A Journal on Friendship.*

Her nonprofit organization, Soup and Support for Teachers, is committed to teens and teachers having available to them inspiring and supportive reading materials.

When she is not reading letters she gets from teens, Kim is offering them support and encouragement in the forums on her Web site, *www.iam4teens.com.* She also enjoys nurturing her family, listening to her son's band and hanging out with her friends.

For information or to schedule Kim for a presentation, contact:

I.A.M. 4 Teens, Inc.
P.O. Box 936
Pacific Palisades, CA 90272
e-mail for stories: *stories@iam4teens.com*
e-mail for letters and feedback: *kim@iam4teens.com*
Web site: *www.iam4teens.com*

Contributors

Several of the stories in this book were taken from previously published sources, such as books, magazines and newspapers. These sources are acknowledged in the permissions section. However, some of the stories were written by humorists, comedians, professional speakers and workshop presenters as well as kids. If you would like to contact them for information on their books, audiotapes and videotapes, seminars and workshops, you can reach them at the addresses and phone numbers provided below.

The remainder of the stories were submitted by readers of our previous *Chicken Soup for the Soul* books who responded to our requests for stories. We have also included information about them.

Becka Allen is a fifteen-year-old sophomore. She has always enjoyed writing and this is her first published story. She can be reached at *tallen@central.net.*

Melinda Allen is a seventeen-year-old senior in Goffstown, New Hampshire. She holds a black belt in American Kenpo Karate and currently works as a karate instructor. Melinda is also an avid snowboarder and plans to continue both hobbies at Assumption College in the fall.

Dr. Eric Allenbaugh is a management consultant, a national keynote speaker and bestselling author of *Wake-Up Calls: You Don't Have to Sleepwalk Through Your Life, Love or Career.* Eric has been a guest on nearly 300 television and radio talk shows regarding leadership and life issues. His seminars are frequently described as "life changing." He can be reached at Allenbaugh Associates, Inc., in Lake Oswego, Oregon, at 503-635-3963 or via e-mail at *eric@allenbaugh.com.*

Adi Amar is a graduate of Verde Valley School in Sedona, Arizona and currently an Outdoor Education student at Garrett College in Maryland. Born in Israel, Adi (whose name means "jewel" in Hebrew) is passionate about rock climbing, hiking, sailing, journaling, and yoga. She has received considerable acclaim for her innovative photography. Her mother, Lana Grimm, coproduced and costarred in the award-winning video *The Spirit of Yoga* in Sedona, just three months before the near-fatal crash. Her mother's miraculous recovery inspired Adi to develop a new appreciation for life, and she plans to build her future career on a combination of her outdoor skills, photographic talents and genuine love for nature.

Rebecca Ayres received a psychology degree from Santa Clara University and currently volunteers full-time. She plans on earning a master's in social work to become a counselor. Her story is dedicated to her wonderfully supportive friends, her ex-roommates and their significant others, her family and NBKC members everywhere (especially Melissa). She can be reached by e-mail at *RebeccaLA@yahoo.com.*

Greg Barker is currently the pastor at Grace Lutheran Church in Victoria, British Columbia, Canada. He enjoys communicating the grace of God to people of all ages, especially to his confirmation class of seventh and eighth grade students. Greg and his wife, Teresa, are enjoying their first baby, Christopher. Greg can be reached at 1273 Fort St., Victoria, British Columbia, Canada V8V 3L4 or e-mail: *glc@islandnet.com.*

Andrea Barkoukis wrote her story while in high school at Gilmour Academy in Cleveland, Ohio. She loves to read, be with friends and write. She has always wanted to be a writer and hopes to pursue writing as a career. She can be reached via e-mail at *Heaven675@aol.com.*

Libby Barnes is a freshman in high school in Minnesota. She enjoys writing poems, songs, music, stories and also loves to sing. Although she has never been published before, she hopes that it's not the last opportunity she gets to share her writing. Libby dedicates "China's Story" to her friends, whom she loves with all of her heart. She wants to thank them for sticking with her through thick and thin.

James D. Barron is the author of *She's Having a Baby—And I'm Having a Breakdown, She's Had a Baby—And I'm Having a Meltdown,* and *She Wants a Ring—And I Don't Wanna Change a Thing.* He can be reached at *jdbarron6@aol.com.*

Jennifer Baxton is a writer currently living in a "weird" suburb of Los Angeles. An alumni of AmeriCorps, she has been trained as a red-carded firefighter and a national park ranger. Currently, Jennifer teaches writing compositions at too many community colleges in Southern California. She can be reached at *goobiesun@yahoo.com.*

Eugene E. Beasley enjoys reading, traveling, biking, walking and communicating with people and nature. After thirty-nine years of teaching communication arts, he is now presently writing, teaching drivers education, religious pursuits and gardening. There is much Eugene has learned through experience that he wishes to share. Thus, he writes and examines. At the moment, he is preparing a memoir for his children and grandchildren to explore after he goes on to the "greater" adventure.

Michele Bender is a freelance writer in New York City. She has written for many publications, including the *New York Times, Glamour, Jump, Cosmopolitan, Cosmo Girl, Ladies' Home Journal, Fitness* and *Marie Claire.* She can be reached via e-mail at *Mbender878@aol.com.*

Marjee Berry-Wellman is a Christian author and proud mother of Jeff, Josh and Julie, as well as her angel baby, Melanie. Writing is Marjee's passion, and she hopes to leave readers with something solid to digest. Born and raised in Sterling, Illinois, Marjee currently resides in Clarion, Iowa. She welcomes feedback at *mrjwell@goldfieldaccess.net.*

Amanda Bertrand attends Cook College at Rutgers University in New Jersey. This is her first published work, and she is extremely excited. She would like to thank her family and friends for always being there for her. She dedicates this work to Ken R. Brams. She can be reached at *RutgersAngel@aol.com.*

Bryony Blackwood is a Kenyan-born British citizen living in Virginia. He spent two years in a boarding school overseas before returning to the states for college. Change and adjustment have become recurring themes in his life. The most important lessons those changes have taught him are that you are free to choose your own path in life and to shape that life to fit your dreams. Life really is what you make of it.

Chris Blake teaches English and communications at Union College, a Seventh-day Adventist college in Lincoln, Nebraska. Chris is the former editor of *Insight* magazine and the author of *In Search of a God to Love* (to be released in 1998.) He loves God.

Hannah Brandys is twenty-two years old and lives in Toronto, Canada. She wrote "The First" when she was fifteen, and she is thrilled to have the chance to share it with others. Hannah's hobbies include reading, writing, skiing, kickboxing and traveling. She can be reached at *hannahbran@yahoo.com.*

Stacy Brakebush is eighteen years old and is starting college in the fall. She plans to major in psychology at Saddleback Community College and transfer wherever God leads her. She is a leader in AWANA's at her church to third and fourth grade girls. She dedicates her story to her grandfather, James Smith, who passed away. He was a true example of human compassion and kindness and a soldier for Christ.

Jessie Braun is currently a sophomore at Pomona College in Claremont, California. She feels privileged and honored to have been given the opportunity to work on both the first and second volumes of *Chicken Soup for the Teenage Soul.*

Eva Burke is a student at Central Florida Community College and plans to transfer to the University of Central Florida to finish her degree in social work. Eva has been writing since she was a child, and her first love in writing has always been poetry. She can be reached at P.O. Box 14787, Gainesville, FL 32604.

Cambra J. Cameron is a sophomore at Lubbock Christian University where she is involved in Kappa Phi Kappa and Acappella Chorus. She is grateful to God, her family and her friends for their continuing to help and encourage her. And to "David" who will always hold a special place in her heart. Her e-mail address in *jcameron@itl.net.*

Michelle Wallace Campanelli is a national bestselling author. She was born on the Space Coast of Florida where she still resides with her husband, Louis. She is a graduate of Melbourne High School, Writers' Digest School and Keiser College. She is the author of *Hero of Her Heart,* by Blue Note Books and *Margarita,* by Hollis Books. She is also a short-story author in several nationally distributed anthologies published by Simon and Schuster's *Chocolate For a Woman's Heart* series. She has always enjoyed writing and painting as outlets for artistic expression. Currently, she is working on the sequel to *Margarita.* She can be reached via e-mail at *MCAMPANELLI@juno.com.*

Martha Campbell is a graduate of Washington University School of Fine Arts, and a former writer-designer for Hallmark Cards. Since she became a freelancer in 1973, she has had over two thousand cartoons published and has illustrated ninteen books. You can write her at P.O. Box 2538, Harrison, AR 72602 or call 870-741-5323.

Nathen Cantwell is a high-school student in Aberdeen, South Dakota. He lives with his parents and little brother, and he enjoys drawing, writing, hunting, fishing and golfing. He wrote the story "Angel" for his mother for a mother's day gift in 1998.

Dave Carpenter has been a full-time cartoonist since 1981. His cartoons have appeared in a variety of publications, including *Reader's Digest, Barron's, Harvard Business Review,* the *Wall Street Journal,* the *Saturday Evening Post, Better Homes and Gardens, Good Housekeeping, Forbes, Woman's World,* as well as numerous other publications. Dave can be reached at P.O. Box 520, Emmetsburg, IA 50536.

Don Caskey writes a column for the *Gwinnett Daily Post* in Lawrenceville, Georgia, and develops training and performance support systems for Synesis Corporation in Roswell, Georgia. For more of Don's stories and columns, visit *www.nbdigital.com.* Letters are welcome at 2180 Pleasant Hill Road A5-271, Duluth, GA 30096 or *caskey@nbdigital.com.*

Terri Cecil has always been driven by challenges and that is how she looked at the car accident in 1983 that left her unable to walk. Since that injury, Terri has graduated from the University of Louisville, maintained full-time employment, served as a community volunteer, competed on the 1996 Paralympic Fencing Team and earned the national title of Ms. Wheelchair America for 1998. She enjoys traveling and speaking on the joy of diversity, the triumph of the human spirit and the need to eradicate what Terri considers to be the strongest handicap of all—prejudice of any kind. Terri can be reached at 596 Plymouth St., Apt. 1, Wilkes-Barre, PA 18702 or by calling 717-820-3272 or by e-mail: *TerriMWA98@aol.com.* She can also be reached at Pride Health Care, Inc., at 800-800-8586.

David Coleman is known nationwide as "The Dating Doctor." He received the 1997 National Lecture Entertainer of the Year from the National Association for Campus Activities and the 1996 and 1997 Reader's Choice Lecture Program of the Year from *Campus Activities* magazine. He was nominated for six straight years and is currently the number-one ranked entertainer in America by *Campus Activities* magazine. David received his bachelor's degree from Bowling Green State University, Ohio. He is the author of a self-syndicated column on relationships and a book entitled *101 Great Dates.* He is currently working on two more books: *Prescriptions from the Dating Doctor: Answers to the Most Common Relationship Questions* and *When the Heart Is Unavailable: Putting a Stop to Revolving Door Relationships* (with Richard Doyle). David can be reached at *www.datingdoctor.com* or by calling 513-583-8000. He is represented in the college market by Umbrella Productions, Inc. at 407-649-6448.

Melissa Collette is most happy when she is spending time with her friends, listening to music, writing poetry and acting. She hopes to one day become an actress and work her way up to directing and producing. She lives by the saying, "Everything happens for a reason."

Noah Campana is an English and psychology major who gives talks to teens about sex and relationships. He enjoys running, climbing and sleeping. He knows karate and seventeen other Japanese words and is best known for spontaneously singing, "Play that Funky Music White Boy." This and everything else he does is dedicated to God—"you rock!" He can be reached at *lord-biohazarrd@hotmail.com.*

David Cooney's cartoons and illustrations are published in a variety of magazines including *USA Weekend, American Legion, Mutual Funds* and the *Chronicle of Higher Education.* Through the scientific journals that feature his work, his cartoons are seen in over fifty countries. David's cartoons are also published in *The New Breed,* a cartoon feature distributed by King Features Syndicate. His cartoons run in numerous newspapers under the title *Twisted View.* David lives with his wife Marcia and two children in the small Pennsylvania town of Mifflinburg. His Web site is *www.davidcooney.com* and he can be reached via e-mail at *david@davidcooney.com.*

Liz Correale is a New Jersey native who currently attends college in New England. She is a psychology major with high hopes of a career in governmental intelligence. Liz attributes much of her inspiration to her deep faith and her mother's lively sense of humor. She remains happy by writing, running and guessing what color her sister's hair will be this week—fuchsia or royal blue?

Emily Crane is a student at Kansas State University. She is majoring in advertising and is a member of the Alpha Kappa Chapter of Alpha Xi Delta. Her poem is dedicated to her cherished sisters of the pink rose and written for Josh. She can be reached via e-mail at *crane_emily@hotmail.com.*

Nick Curry III was born in Korea and then adopted by an American family when he was four years old. This all-American boy was president of his class, played soccer and baseball, and "will golf for food"! He attends school in Orlando, Florida.

Leesa Dean is a recent graduate from Mount Baker High School in Cranbrook, British Columbia, Canada. She is planning to further her education in order to one day teach high-school English. Her hobbies include reading, writing, traveling, going on outdoor adventures and talking to people. Her life goals include having fun, saving the Earth and making a difference! She can be reached via e-mail at *leesadean@hotmail.com.*

Jason Dorsey is one of America's leading young speakers. Each year he reaches over 100,000 people of all ages, backgrounds and aspirations. His first book, *Graduate to Your Perfect Job,* and integrated curriculum are used across America. You may reach him by phone at 512-442-5170 or at *www.jasondorsey.com.*

Brian Firenzi is a sophomore in high school in California. He enjoys creating videos with his friends, writing screenplays and snowboarding. Brain aspires to work in journalism or filmmaking. He can be reached at *bfirenzi@earthlink.net.*

Sydney Fox was born on November 1, 1982 in Tulsa, Oklahoma. Her parents' ministry to the homeless and the poor moved the family to the Washington, D.C. area. Helping the needy sparked her writing desires. It transformed daily journal entries into inspirational anecdotes about poverty's struggles. She works in a camera store and hopes to couple photography with her writings. She loves drama, plays the violin and cello and sings. She's planning her future and college major.

Carol Gallivan lives in East Hartford, Connecticut, with her husband, Kevin, and their two teenage daughters, Kelly and Tracy. The greatest joys in her life are her relationships with God; her family; her niece and nephew, Renee and Eric; her dear friends; and the teenagers in her neighborhood.

Joanna Gates is a senior at Columbine High School and will graduate in May 2000. She lives in Littleton, Colorado with her parents, brother and a variety of pets. Joanna is an aspiring artist and writer and plans to major in visual arts in college. She also enjoys spending time with friends, singing and basketball. She can be reached via e-mail at *jgates123@yahoo.com.*

Zan Gaudioso is a freelance writer whose stories have appeared in newspapers across the country. Zan earned her degree in special education for the deaf and went on to teach sign language, as well as teaching deaf children and adults. She became part of a landmark program that was the first to utilize sign language in order to foster verbal language skills in autistic children. From there, with additional training, she went on to become a surgical nurse. With writing as an integral driving force in her life, she continued to write and be published in newspapers and in family medical journals. She currently lives with her fiancé and their dog, Delilah, in Pacific Palisades, California. She can be reached via e-mail at *justzan@usa.net.*

Randy Glasbergen has had more than twenty-five thousand cartoons published in magazines, books and greeting cards around the world. He also creates *The Better Half,* which is syndicated to newspapers by King Features Syndicate. You can find more of Randy's cartoons online at *www.glasbergen.com.*

Kristy Glassen is a student at Penn State University. As a senior graduating in December, she wanted to take this opportunity to say thank-you to those people who have stuck by her side through it all. They know who they are. To her family, Mom, Dad and Ryan, she thanks them for believing in her and giving her the courage to chase her dreams. Her love goes out to them. This quote sums up how she looks at life, "I am not afraid of tomorrow. I have seen yesterday, and I love today." She can be reached at *psukristy21@hotmail.com.*

Danette Julene Gomez is currently pursuing a career in the fashion industry, however writing remains her true passion, one she indulges in whenever possible. This piece was inspired by the joy and unconditional love she has shared with the two people who mirror her soul: her sisters, Darlene and Desiree. She resides in Los Angeles, California and this will be the first time her work has been published. She can be reached via e-mail at *DGomez6457@aol.com.*

Andrea Gonsalves is a student in her final year of high school in Ontario, Canada. She plans to study English literature at a university and become a novelist. She enjoys writing daily, finding it to be an effective medium for making sense of a confusing world. She hopes to use her writing to help and inspire others. Andrea can be reached via e-mail at *gonsalvesa@usa.net.*

Lisa Gumenick is a fifteen-year-old freshman in Pacific Palisades, California. She lives with her mom, dad and sister. Her older brother attends Brown University. Lisa loves friends, talking, dancing and drawing.

Nicole Hamberger is a sixteen-year-old optimist who loves to give back to her community. Aside from her passion for writing, she volunteers at Saint Barnabas Hospital twice a week, working in both the emergency room and the Child Care Development Center. She also teaches religious education and enjoys spending time with her friends.

Alison Hamby is a senior in high school, where she plays on the varsity basketball team and is drum major in the band. She enjoys writing in her free time.

Kelly Harrington is studying psychology at the University of Southern California. She is a member of Psi Chi, a national honors society in psychology, and teaches elementary education at a local battered women's shelter. She has many passions, all of which are reflected in her writings. Her poetry is published in *Mystical Night* and *America at the Millennium.* From the psychology perspective, she will witness her dreams, as well as the dreams of many others, come to life. She can be reached via e-mail at *kellz94@aol.com.*

Barbara Hauck is currently a sophomore in high school and enjoys her cat, athletics, music, math, computers, writing and drawing. A polo enthusiast, Barbara hopes to attend a college where she can play polo competitively.

Claire Hayenga was born in Forth Worth, Texas. Since then she has lived with her mother, father and younger sister in four different locations in the area. The arts greatly interest Claire, who is sixteen years old.

Andrea Hensley has worked for the Salvation Army Camps, a program that reaches out to children, for five summers. Currently, Andrea works as a substitute teacher in the Renton School District. Andrea can be reached at 12037 64th Ave. South, Seattle, WA 98178.

Amy Hilborn is an honors English student at Redeemer University College in Ancaster, Ontario, hoping to pursue a master's degree in creative writing. She has been published at her university and the Poetry Institute of Canada. Written when seventeen years old, this story is dedicated to her family and her boyfriend, Colin.

Ashley Hiser is a seventeen-year old senior in high school in Morristown, New Jersey. She is involved in many activities through her school such as president of the French Club, member of the French Honor Socdiety, secretary of the Junior Statesmen of America, coeditor in chief of her school newspaper and manager of her cross-country team. Ashley has achieved perfect attendance throughout her three years of high school and has also been on the honor roll. She volunteers through her church's youth ministry and she makes a trip to Appalachia every summer. Ashley also works part-time at GapKids twelve to fifteen hours per week.

Ashley Hodgeson, age fifteen, began her writing career with a winning personal hero essay in fifth grade. Her writing achievements sparked ambition in other areas: academics (4.0 GPA), speech, track (she has run since sixth grade) and science projects.

Amy Huffman is a seventeen-year-old student in high school in St. Louis, Missouri. Her favorite pastime is horseback riding, but she also enjoys writing, reading, listening to music, and spending time with her friends and her boyfriend. She gives many thanks to her family and friends for their continual support and belief in her and her dreams. And special thanks to "Buddy," who has made many of those dreams realities.

Jim Hullihan is an internationally recognized film producer and leadership retreat designer whose motivational media assemblies programs annually appear before 4 million people. As the creator of America's first CD-ROM magazine for teens entitled *Sweet! Digizine*, Jim is the leading motivation expert in U.S. secondary education. He can be reached at 148 S. Victory, Burbank, CA 91502, or by calling 818-848-1980.

Robin Hyatt was eighteen years old when she went to Camp Virginia Jaycee for the first time. She learned a lot from that experience and was also given a wonderful chance to broaden her horizons. It was the first time that she had ever worked with people of any mental handicap. She volunteered three more times at Camp Jaycee until she graduated from Lynchburg College in 1996 with a Bachelor of Arts degree. Each time she went she looked at the world a little differently. She is currently working as the special events coordinator at the Alexandria Chamber of Commerce.

Amanda Johnson is sixteen years old and a junior in high school in Placerville, California. This is her first published work but she has been writing poems and children's stories for years. Aside from writing, she also takes Jazz and Ballet and performs in school and community theatre productions. Amanda loves children.

Bret Anthony Johnston is a writer in northern Michigan. This story is dedicated to his brother, Bill.

Molly Karlin is currently a high-school senior in Connecticut. She is class valedictorian, drama club vice president, student council secretary, reporter for the school newspaper and an active member of chorus and the National Honor Society. She aspires to write and star in a successful film or play. She would like to dedicate her story to the friends who have stayed by her through hard times (you know who you are). She can be reached via e-mail at *Sky1414@aol.com.*

Cassie Kirby lives in Livonia, Michigan. She is currently in college, studying to be an elementary-school teacher. She would like to thank her family, her boyfriend and her best friends for their unwavering support and constant laughs. She can be reached at *KirbAngel@aol.com.*

Tom Krause is a motivational speaker, teacher and coach. He is the founder of Positive People Presentations and speaks to teenagers, teaching staffs, any organization dealing with teen issues and business organizations in the area of motivation and stress reduction. He is the author of *Touching Hearts—Teaching Greatness,* "Stories from a coach to touch your heart and inspire your soul," a motivational book for teenagers and adults. He can be reached via e-mail at *justmetrk@aol.com.*

Thad Langenberg is a student in Shawnee Mission, Kansas. His poetry has been published by *Indian Lore* and by the Kansas State Poetry Society's *Sunflower Petals.* His poem demonstrates how a single act of warmth and kindness can preserve life. It is dedicated to people who think they mean nothing to the world. He can be reached via e-mail at *langy999@earthlink.net.*

Jason Leib is twenty years old and an upper junior at Yeshiva University. He was born and raised in the Chicagoland area. He is legally blind. Despite the vision problem, he played six years of Little League. He also attends the Special Olympics where he competed in several different sporting events and won gold, silver and bronze medals in the events he played in. He attended Ida Crown Jewish Academy for high school where he played one year of junior varsity basketball and two years of varsity basketball. He received the Sportsmanship trophy award as well as an award from B'nai B'rith for basketball. Jason played basketball in the Maccabee games and won a silver medal. He also participated in intramural softball all four years of high school. Jason can be reached at 4000 Enfield, Skokie, IL 60076 or by calling 847-329-7078.

Melissa Lew is a seventeen-year-old high-school senior in Fountain Valley, California. She lives with her parents and her older brother, Chris. She looks forward to graduating this year, but until then she is kept busy as the FVHS Colorguard Captain. She can be reached via e-mail at *MissaStar@aol.com.*

Kim Lowery is a fifteen-year-old freshman. She loves animals and playing softball with her friends Chelsea and Andrea. She likes giving advice to her friends, as well as receiving it. She has learned so much from her mistakes and hopes to help others make the right decisions. After high school she wants to attend college. She greatly appreciates the help and support from her friends and family, especially her mother. She can be reached by e-mail at *TigBittiez15@aol.com.*

Eleanor Luken is an amateur high-school writer from Louisville, Kentucky. She can be reached at *ellieluken@aol.com.*

Anna Maier is a first-year college student in Michigan. She is working toward a degree in education with hopes of teaching the hearing-impaired. She submitted her piece as part of a final exam in her high-school English class. Anna can be reached at *Brainsync2@aol.com.*

Nailah Malik is a multicultural storyteller, literacy advocate and young-adult librarian of the Los Angeles Public Library. Having triumphed over formidable personal challenges, she brings a warmth and passion to her presentations that inspire and empower others. Her emphasis on stories that have practical applications for learning and living has made her a highly sought-after trainer and weaver of tales, and a powerful motivational speaker for students and educators of grade schools, colleges and universities in California. She has earned a B.A. in drama and an M.L.S. from the University of Southern California, and a B.A. in Economics from the University of California, Santa Barbara. Nailah can be reached at P.O. Box 6026-282, Sherman Oaks, CA 91413, or by calling 213-857-8089.

Chance Margheim is a high-school student from Blacksburg, Virginia. He enjoys writing in his leisure time and takes much pride in his work. He plans to attend a college in the near future and major in the field of communications, where he will work in the area of public relations. He can be reached via e-mail at *chance@bburg.net.*

Selina E. Matis is a native of southwestern Pennsylvania, and was born in December 1984. She wrote the poem "Ability" for an English assignment when she was thirteen years old. Her inspiration for "Ability" came from her English teacher and classmates. Selina is currently a high-school freshman, planning to graduate with the class of 2003.

Meladee McCarty is a program specialist for the Sacramento County Office of Education in California. She works to find educational support for students with severe disabilities. She is coauthor, with her husband, of four best-selling books, including *A 4th Course of Chicken Soup for the Soul,* which has sold over 1.5 million copies, as well as *Acts of Kindness: How to Make A Gentle Difference.* She can be reached at Learning Resources, P.O. Box 66, Galt, CA 95632, or by calling 209-745-2212, or by faxing 209-745-2252.

Kate McMahon resides in South Orange, New Jersey with her parents, Vincent and Elizabeth and her brother, Luke. She is a senior in high school, where Olive O'Sullivan instructs her in English. Kate is interested in pursuing studies in creative writing as well as sociology.

Shelly Miller is a freshman studying electrical engineering at UM-Rolla. She really enjoys being a sister in Kappa Delta sorority and is the founder of the Society for the Antidisestablishment of Fairy Pressing! Check it out on her homepage at *http://www.umr.edu/~michele/.*

Sierra Millman's teenage years form a collage of creative expression in academics and arts at the Branson School and Stanford University, where she pursues her passion for theater, dance and writing. An honor student, National Merit Finalist and member of the Cum Laude Society, Sierra's first play, *Eccentricities,* won grand prize at the Rocky Mountain Playwriting Festival; she has published essays and articles, with stories in development, a children's book out with an agent and new ideas percolating. She can be reached via e-mail at *smillman@leland.stanford.edu.*

Chick Moorman is the director of the Institute for Personal Power, a consulting firm dedicated to providing high-quality professional development activities for educators and parents. His latest book, *Where the Heart Is: Stories of Home and Family,* celebrates family strength, love, tolerance, hope and commitment. It can be ordered for $14.95 from Personal Power Press, P.O. Box 5985, Saginaw, MI 48603, or by calling 1-800-797-4133.

Brooke Mueller is seventeen years old and has been a resident of Anchorage, Alaska, all her life. At age eight, she began writing, along with her other hobbies of drawing and playing the piano. She also enjoys the many experiences life in Alaska has to offer, such as moose and caribou hunting, fishing, and skiing.

Amy Muscato is a high school student in New Jersey. She has varied interests including theater, singing, politics and forensics. After her graduation in June 1999, she looks forward to attending college. Amy has aspirations of a career in either politics or television news.

Laura O'Neill is a freelance writer in Ellicott City, Missouri. She is sixteen years old and attends Mount de Sales Academy. She is very involved in her parish's youth ministry program and hopes to pursue a career as a youth minister. Laura can be reached at *squeakylaughter@hotmail.com.*

Jennifer Orendach is a sixteen-year-old high school student in Allentown, Pennsylvania. She is extremely happy to have been given the opportunity to display her work to such a large amount of people. Her life has always revolved around using her writing to help others better understand her feelings. She would like to dedicate this piece to her family, her many friends, and the kind people at *Chicken Soup for the Soul.* She can be reached at P.O. Box 4065, Bethlehem, PA 18018.

Peer Resources is a leading authority in peer helping services, programs, and resources for children, teens and adults. They can be contacted by e-mail at*helping@islandnet.com* or visited at *www.islandnet.com/~rcarr/peer.html.* Write to 1052 Davie St., Victoria, BC V8S 4E3 or call 800-567-3700.

Rochelle M. Pennington is a nationally recognized author of poetry, drama and nonfiction. She is also the originator and author of the midwestern newspaper column, *Insight and Inspiration.* As a quotations specialist, Rochelle has worked with several bestselling authors providing quote recommendations to enhance their books, including H. Jackson Brown (*Life's Little Instruction Books*) and Jack Canfield (*Chicken Soup for the Soul*). She is currently coauthoring Mr. Brown's next book, *Life's Little Instruction Book à la mode*. Rochelle, who resides in rural Wisconsin with her husband and their children, spends her free time actively involved in Christian education and in volunteering Hospice Hope care to the terminally ill. Rochelle can be reached at N1911 Double D Rd., Campbellsport, WI 53010 or by calling 920-533-5880.

Alexei Perry is a fifteen-year-old girl with a passion for writing. She has delighted in playing with words since she was two years old. If you should chance to see a young girl scribbling on a piece of candy paper, table napkin, feather or birch bark it is likely to be Alexei. In her poetry, she documents the pain and promise of life. She can be reached at P.O. Box 51, Site 2, RR#1 Elora, Ontario, N0B 1S0, Canada.

Caitlin Pollock is a fifteen-year-old aspiring author. She lives in British Columbia, Canada with her parents and older brother. Aside from writing fiction and nonfiction stories, Caitlin is an avid artist, scholar, musician and poet. She is thrilled to have a piece of her writing published in the *Chicken Soup for the Teenage Soul* series. Caitlin can be reached by e-mail at *cjpollock@hotmail.com*.

Michael T. Powers, whose writing appears in many inspirational teen books, is a high-school girls' coach, youth director and the author of his own book, *Straight from the Heart*. For a sneak peek or to join the thousands of worldwide readers on his daily inspirational e-mail list, visit *www.HeartTouchers.com*. He can also be reached at *MichaelTPowers@aol.com*.

Susan Record is currently a student at Brigham Young University studying humanities, music and art history. She works as an editorial assistant for the BYU Faculty Center and plans to graduate in April of 1999. She and Justin Record were married in November 1996. In her spare time she enjoys writing and working in the garden.

Danielle Rosenblatt is a sixteen-year-old student who enjoys theater, dancing, running, writing and laughing with her friends. She plans to pursue writing as a career and hopes to publish her own book one day. Danielle would like to thank her family and friends who have filled her life with love and encouraged her to reach for her dreams.

Lisa Rothbard is a seventeen-year-old senior in high school. She has been involved with the *Chicken Soup for the Teenage Soul* series since she was thirteen. She can be reached via e-mail at *Rothie99@hotmail.com*.

Meredith Rowe is currently a member of the class of 2002 at Stanford University. However, she calls McKinney, Texas, home, and graduated in May 1998 from McKinney High School. Meredith has been writing since she was seven years old and loves to contribute to the Internet, especially by designing Web pages. She would like to thank all those who made her publication possible by adding their input. She can be reached via e-mail at *cardinal02@hotmail.com.*

Jodi Rudin is a high-school senior. She enjoys reading and writing short stories. She facilitates The Pacific Institute's curriculum *Increasing Your Causative Power,* which is a self-help program for teens. This story is in memory of Mary Scharlach. She can be reached at *rudi_07@hotmail.com.*

Amanda Russell is a resident of Tennessee, who enjoys writing poems and short stories. She is pursuing a Bachelor of Science degree in theater education at Middle Tennessee State University. This story is dedicated to her best friend, Kristen Hrusovsky. She can be reached at *meow_kitten@hotmail.com.*

Harley Schwadron is a self-taught cartoonist living in Ann Arbor, Michigan and worked as a journalist and public relations writer before switching to cartooning full-time in 1984. His cartoons appear in *Barron's, Harvard Business Review, Wall Street Journal, National Law Journal* and many others. He can be reached at P.O. Box 1347, Ann Arbor, MI 48106 or call 313-426-8433.

Talina Sessler-Barker, age twenty-three, graduated in 1998 from the University of Texas where she was a member of the Longhorn Cheerleading Squad. She currently teaches language arts and coaches cheerleading at Leander Middle School, while seeking her masters of education degree from Southwest Texas University. Her goal is to help young people realize that true beauty lies within themselves. She resides in Leander, Texas with her husband Donny.

Jamie Shockley currently attends high school in Spring, Texas. She actively participates in band, tennis and student council. She enjoys reading and outdoor activities. Jamie hopes to attend University of Texas at Austin or A&M University at College Station after graduating high school. She plans to major in business or engineering.

Patty Anne Sluys is an eighteen-year-old Christian homeschool graduate residing in Chilliwack, British Columbia. She enjoys hockey, people, photography, hairdressing, desktop publishing and especially writing. She has put out a teen magazine called the *Penpal Scene* for three years. (It features inspirational articles, poems, stories, advice and more. Send $1 for sample issue.) Patty can be reached at 49950 Patterson Rd., Chilliwack, BC V2P 6H3, Canada.

Bobbi Smith is partner in a Baha'i-inspired socioeconomic development project based on Vancouver Island, British Columbia. Her story is dedicated to Norman and Toni Smith, Erika Hastings Adlparvar, the Smiths, the Sabripours and all those who have enabled her to serve. She can be reached at *ilikebikes1234@yahoo.com.*

Marc St. Pierre is a seventeen-year-old high school senior. He enjoys listening to music and hanging out with his friends. Thanks, Aunt Linda.

Sara Strickland is an amateur writer. She enjoys writing short stories and writing poetry. She is a student and a model. This story is dedicated to Kyle, the most important lesson she ever learned. She can be reached via e-mail at *SJStrickland@webtv.net.*

Ronica Stromberg has written for many publications and is the author of the young adult mystery, *The Glass Inheritance* published by Royal Fireworks Press. She is currently at work on a teen series to be published by Moody Press. She can be reached at *ronicak@yahoo.com.*

Andrew Tertes authors enchanting books, stories and poetry intended to inspire passion for one's own personal journey. For news on Andrew's upcoming books for adults and children, write to Unicorn News, P.O. Box 3164, San Rafael, CA 94901, or call 888-434-6789.

Allison Thorp is a freshman at West Virginia Wesleyan College majoring in music education and English. She enjoys playing the piano, especially for the college jazz ensemble. She is secretary for her class and is active in Kappa Phi, a Christian woman's organization. She can be reached at *a_thorp@wvwc.edu.*

Julia Travis is a high-school junior in Livonia, Michigan, where she is class president and a member of the soccer team. Her work has been published in *A Celebration of Michigan's Young Poets—1999.* She would like to thank the friends who have always been there for her. She can be reached via e-mail at *Julesorama@aol.com.*

Becky Tucker is eighteen years old and leads an active life in her hometown of Lebanon, Oregon. She believes in God and thanks him for all the inspiration he has placed within her.

Micah Twaddle lives in Maryville, Missouri, with her mother, father and three brothers. She is currently a freshman. "Voices" is her first published writing. The past two years she has struggled with anorexia and, although she still has her days, she is slowly getting a hold on it. Her experiences with anorexia are what initially inspired her writing. She can be reached via e-mail at *mtstars_@hotmail.com.*

Kathryn Vacca is a seventeen-year-old senior in high school in Boulder, Colorado. She is the opinion editor of her high-school newspaper, as well as the captain of the dance team and the debate team. Dance is her first passion, but she enjoys writing and is looking forward to a career in journalism.

Glenn Van Ekeren is a dynamic speaker and trainer dedicated to helping people and organizations maximize their potential. Glenn is the author of *The Speaker's Sourcebook, The Speaker's Sourcebook II* and the popular *Potential*

Newsletter. Glenn has a wide variety of written publications and audio and video presentations available. He can be reached at People Building Institute, 330 Village Circle, Sheldon, IA 51201, or by calling 1-800-899-4878.

Danni Villemez loves riding her horse Cal-o-Kashif, also known as Marshmallow because he is so fat. She only likes to ride him bareback because he is so comfy. When she rides she has lots of thoughts come to her and she makes sure she writes them down afterward. It drives her trainer crazy seeing sheaves of paper all over the tack room. Riding helps her to relax and is a great opportunity for her to reflect and pray.

Sarah Watroba is a freshman at Oswego State University. She is majoring in broadcasting and plans to pursue a career in the television or radio industry. Her poem is dedicated to the class of 2001 of North Tonawanda High School. It was read to all of the graduates on their final day in high school at an assembly dedicated to taking the next step in life. The class of 2001 was her inspiration for writing this poem. She will never forget the memories they shared and the lessons that she learned during those unforgettable four years. Best of luck to all future graduates. She can be reached at *Sarah5416@aol.com.*

Whitney Welch is thirteen years old and in the eighth grade in Prineville, Oregon. She loves writing, especially poems and reading. In addition to cross-country running and track, she is active in tap and jazz dance. She travels as much as possible with her family and to date has been to twenty-eight states and Washington D.C. She plans to have a career as a teacher.

Digby Wolfe had a writing career of fifty years that has been divided equally between theatre and the media. British-born Digby Wolfe is perhaps best known for being the co-creator of the landmark television hit, *Laugh-In.* A multiple Emmy nominee and winner, Digby is now the tenured Professor of Play and Screenwriting at the University of New Mexico in Albuquerque.

Adelene Wong is currently a senior in the International Baccalaureate program. She wants to thank her mother and sister for all the support they've given over the years. She wishes to share this thought: *A closed mind is a good thing to lose. Be open, honest and empathetic. You will get a lot further than you think!*

Rebecca Woolf is a freelance writer and photographer who has written for *Chicken Soup for the Teenage Soul II* and *III, Teen Love: On Relationships, Teen Love: On Friendship, Teen Love: A Journal on Friendship, 19* (the popular UK magazine) and more. Keep your eyes out for Rebecca's first solo book of poetry titled, *Through Broken Mirrors: A Reflective Memoir.* Rebecca is the program director and newsletter editor for Lead the Star, a creative company devoted to inspiring creativity and strength of identity in young adults. She can be reached at *rebeccawoolf@hotmail.com.*

Kelley Youmans is a junior at Michigan State majoring in English education. This is her first publication, but she has been on *YM's* news team and writes daily. She dedicates this story to her family and friends for their support and to her sister Sarah. She can be reached at *KellJuneBug@hotmail.com.*

Permissions *(continued from page ii)*

Inside. Reprinted by permission of Melissa Collette. ©1998 Melissa Collette.

Lost Love and *Love and Belonging.* Reprinted by permission of Theresa Jensen Lacey. ©1998 Theresa Jensen Lacey.

David's Smile. Reprinted by permission of Cambra J. Cameron. ©1998 Cambra J. Cameron.

One of Those Days. Reprinted by permission of Cassie Kirby. ©2000 Cassie Kirby.

Experience Is a Teacher. Reprinted by permission of Julia Travis. ©2000 Julia Travis.

Living Without You. Reprinted by permission of Kristy Glassen. ©2000 Kristy Glassen.

Kiss. Reprinted by permission of Emily Crane. ©2000 Emily Crane.

He Finally Said, "I Love You." Reprinted by permission of Jennifer Orendach. ©2000 Jennifer Orendach.

My Childhood Sweetheart. Reprinted by permission of Leesa Dean. ©2000 Leesa Dean.

Late-Night Talk. Reprinted by permission of Nicole Hamberger. ©2001 Nicole Hamberger.

I Had to Let Him Go. Reprinted by permission of Andrea Barkoukis. ©2000 Andrea Barkoukis.

Please Sign My Yearbook. Reprinted by permission of Stacy Brakebush. ©2000 Stacy Brakebush.

My Knight on His White Horse. Reprinted by permission of Rebecca Woolf. ©2000 Rebecca Woolf.

The First. Reprinted by permission of Hannah Brandys. ©1999 Hannah Brandys.

The Love I'll Never Forget. Reprinted by permission of Tim Madigan. ©1999 Tim Madigan.

Donna and Claudia. Reprinted by permission of Carol Gallivan. ©1998 Carol Gallivan.

I Need You Now. Reprinted by permission of Becky Tucker. ©1998 Becky Tucker.

The Tragic Reunion. Reprinted by permission of Amy Muscato. ©1998 Amy Muscato.

My Fairy Tale. Reprinted by permission of Kathryn Vacca. ©2000 Kathryn Vacca.

When Forever Ends. Reprinted by permission of Molly Karlin. ©2000 Molly Karlin.

Falling Out. Reprinted by permission of Melissa Lew. ©2000 Melissa Lew.

My Best Friend. Reprinted by permission of Lisa Rothbard. ©2000 Lisa Rothbard.

My Star. Reprinted by permission of Zan Gaudioso. ©1999 Zan Gaudioso.

Have a Seat upon a Cloud and *Forgive.* Reprinted by permission of Danielle Rosenblatt. ©2000 Danielle Rosenblatt.

Tinfoil and a Hair Ribbon. Reprinted by permission of Cheryl Costello-Forshey. ©2002 Cheryl Costello-Forshey.

Saying Good-Bye. Reprinted by permission of Kathryn Litzenberger. ©2000 Kathryn Litzenberger.

I Hope. Reprinted by permission of Laura O'Neill. ©2000 Laura O'Neill.

Losing My Best Friend. Reprinted by permission of Amanda Russell. ©1999 Amanda Russell.

My Friend Andrea. Reprinted by permission of Laura Loken. ©2000 Laura Loken.

The Secret of Happiness and *From Crutches to a World-Class Runner.* Reprinted by permission of Glenn Van Ekeren. ©1994 Glenn Van Ekeren.

Smile. Reprinted by permission of Barbara Hauck. ©1996 Barbara Hauck.

Mrs. Link. Reprinted by permission of Susan Daniels Adams. ©1996 Susan Daniels Adams.

A Gift for Two. Reprinted by permission of Andrea Hensley. ©1996 Andrea Hensley.

Kids Who Are Different. Reprinted by permission of Digby Wolfe. ©1996 Digby Wolfe.

McDonald's. Reprinted by permission of Shelly Miller. ©1998 Shelly Miller.

A Valentine for Laura. Reprinted by permission of Donald Caskey. ©1998 Donald Caskey.

My Friend Charley. Reprinted by permission of Robin Hyatt. ©1998 Robin Hyatt.

Losing an Enemy. Reprinted by permission of Patty Anne Sluys. ©1998 Patty Anne Sluys.

Forgive.

Someday When I'm Older. Reprinted by permission of Andrea Gonsalves. ©2000 Andrea Gonsalves.

Dear Child—A Sister's Message. Reprinted by permission of Danette Julene Gomez. ©2000 Danette Julene Gomez.

Finger Paints and Crayons. Reprinted by permission of Cheryl Costello-Forshey. ©2000 Cheryl Costello-Forshey.

The Stranger Within. Reprinted by permission of Amy Hilborn. ©1997 Amy Hilborn.

One Single Rose. Reprinted by permission of Amanda Bertrand. ©2000 Amanda Bertrand.

The Graduation Dance. Reprinted by permission of Linda Chiara. ©1999 Linda Chiara.

Mary. Reprinted by permission of Jodi Rudin. ©2000 Jodi Rudin.

May I Help You? Reprinted by permission of Bobbi Smith. ©1997 Bobbi Smith.

My Big Brother. Reprinted by permission of Lisa Gumenick. ©1996 Lisa Gumenick.

The Champ. Reprinted by permission of Nailah Malik. ©1996 Nailah Malik.

I Love You, Dad. Reprinted by permission of Nick Curry III. ©1996 Nick Curry III.

Role Reversal. Reprinted by permission of Adi Amar. ©1998 Adi Amar.

My Most Memorable Christmas. Reprinted by permission of Reverend Robert Schuller. ©1998 Reverend Robert Schuller.

There Is an Oz. Reprinted by permission of Terri Cecil. ©1998 Terri Cecil.

The Perfect Family. Reprinted by permission of Marc St. Pierre. ©1998 Marc St. Pierre.

Ghost Mother. Reprinted by permission of Michele Bender. ©2000 Michele Bender.

Dear Diary . . . Reprinted by permission of Liz Correale. ©2000 Liz Correale.

A Birthday Gift. Reprinted by permission of Thad Langenberg. ©2000 Thad Langenberg.

My Real Father. Used with permission. Author wishes to remain anonymous.

Angel. Reprinted by permission of Nathen Cantwell. ©2000 Nathen Cantwell.

My Little Brother. Reprinted by permission of Christine Walsh. ©2001 Christine Walsh.

My Sister, My Enemy, My Friend. Reprinted by permission of Allison Thorp. ©2000 Allison Thorp.

Always There for Me. Reprinted by permission of Kelley Youmans. ©2000 Kelley Youmans.

The Bigger Man. Reprinted by permission of C. S. Dweck. ©2002 C. S. Dweck.

Challenge Days. Reprinted by permission of Andrew Tertes. ©1996 Andrew Tertes.

The Bat. Reprinted by permission of Bryony Blackwood. ©1998 Bryony Blackwood.

Lessons in Baseball. Reprinted by permission of Chick Moorman. ©1996 Chick Moorman.

Terri Jackson. Reprinted by permission of Sydney Fox. ©2000 Sydney Fox.

My Most Embarrassing Moment. Reprinted by permission of Rochelle M. Pennington. ©1998 Rochelle M. Pennington.

Firmer Ground. Reprinted by permission of Diana L. Chapman. ©1998 Diana L. Chapman.

What I Wish I'd Known Sooner. Reprinted by permission of Meredith Rowe. ©1998 Meredith Rowe.

A Wider Classroom. Reprinted by permission of Kate McMahon. ©1998 Kate McMahon.

Children's Eyes, Mark's Choice and *Inspirations.* Reprinted by permission of Tom Krause. ©2000 Tom Krause.

China's Story. Reprinted by permission of Libby Barnes. ©2000 Libby Barnes.

Accent*uating Difference.* Reprinted by permission of Daphna Renan. ©2000 Daphna Renan.

Eternal Light. Reprinted by permission of Anastasia. ©1998 Anastasia.

One Final Lesson. Reprinted by permission of Noah Campana. ©2000 Noah Campana.

The Bus Stop. Reprinted by permission of Anna Maier. ©2000 Anna Maier.

Tomorrow Came Again. Reprinted by permission of Ashley Hiser. ©1998 Ashley Hiser.

It Happened to Me. Reprinted by permission of Joanie Twersky. ©1998 Joanie Twersky.

I Am Not Alone. Reprinted by permission of Sara Strickland. ©2000 Sara Strickland.

Visionary. Reprinted by permission of Jason Leib. ©1998 Jason Leib.

The Mom I Never Had. Reprinted by permission of Becka Allen. ©1998 Becka Allen.

Train Tracks. Reprinted by permission of Alison Hamby. ©2000 Alison Hamby.

Let's Go Dancing in the Rain. Reprinted by permission of Claire Hayenga. ©1999 Claire Hayenga.

Emergency 911. Reprinted by permission of Danni Villemez. ©2000 Danni Villemez.

11:21 A.M. Reprinted by permission of Joanna Gates. ©2000 Joanna Gates.

Building Bridges. Excerpted from *Teens with the Courage to Give,* copyright ©2000 by Jackie Waldman, used by permission of Conari Press.

Fire and Rain.

Owning the World. Reprinted by permission of Mary Pat Alarie. ©2000 Mary Pat Alarie.

Voices. Reprinted by permission of Micah Twaddle. ©2000 Micah Twaddle.

I Just Wanted to Be Skinny. Reprinted by permission of Laura Bloor. ©2000 Laura Bloor.

Inner Sustenance. Reprinted by permission of Michelle Wallace Campanelli. ©2000 Michelle Wallace Campanelli.

I Am Not Alone. Reprinted by permission of Sara Strickland. ©2000 Sara Strickland.

Four Kisses. Reprinted by permission of Kate Reder. ©2000 Kate Reder.

Ability. Reprinted by permission of Selina E. Matis. ©2000 Selina E. Matis.

Mark's Choice. Reprinted by permission of Tom Krause.

The Leader. Reprinted by permission of Tony Overman. ©1996 Tony Overman.

Turning Up Your Light. Reprinted by permission of Eric Allenbaugh. ©1995 Eric Allenbaugh. Excerpted from *Wake-Up Calls: You Don't Have to Sleepwalk Through Your Life, Love or Career.*

The Most Mature Thing I've Ever Seen. Reprinted by permission of Chris Blake. ©1997 Chris Blake.

Broken Wing. Reprinted by permission of Jim Hullihan. ©1996 Jim Hullihan.

To Track Down My Dream. Reprinted by permission of Ashley Hodgeson. ©1996 Ashley Hodgeson.

The Power of a Smile. Reprinted by permission of Susan Record. ©1998 Susan Record.

Joe Camel. Reprinted by permission of Meladee McCarty. ©1998 Meladee McCarty.

Anything Is Possible. Reprinted by permission of Jason Dorsey. ©1998 Jason Dorsey.

A Challenge That I Overcame. Reprinted by permission of Arundel Hartman Bell. ©1998 Arundel Hartman Bell.

Minimaxims for My Godson. Reprinted by permission of Arthur Gordon. ©2000 Arthur Gordon.

No Longer a Child. Reprinted by permission of Hilary E. Kisch. ©2000 Hilary E. Kisch.

Finding a Vision. Reprinted by permission of Talina Sessler-Barker. ©2000 Talina Sessler-Barker.

No More What Ifs. Reprinted by permission of Chance Margheim. ©2000 Chance Margheim.

All the More Beautiful. Reprinted by permission of Marc Gaudioso. ©2000 Marc Gaudioso.

Return to High School. Reprinted by permission of Sierra Millman. ©2000 Sierra Millman.

Growing. Reprinted by permission of Brooke Mueller. ©1996 Brooke Mueller.

The Two Roads. Reprinted by permission of Whitney Welch. ©2000 Whitney Welch.

Image Isn't Everything. Reprinted by permission of Jamie Shockley. ©1998 Jamie Shockley.

Hi There, Ugly! Reprinted by permission of Greg Barker. ©1998 Greg Barker.

Just Me. Reprinted by permission of Tom Krause. ©1996 Tom Krause.

Winner. Reprinted by permission of Amy Huffman. ©2000 Amy Huffman.

So I Am Told. Reprinted by permission of Alexei Perry. ©2000 Alexei Perry.

Finding a Vision. Reprinted by permission of Talina Sessler-Barker. ©2000 Talina Sessler-Barker.

No More What Ifs. Reprinted by permission of Chance Margheim. ©2000 Chance Margheim.

Return to High School. Reprinted by permission of Sierra Millman. ©2000 Sierra Millman.

The Days of Cardboard Boxes. Reprinted by permission of Eva Burke. ©1996 Eva Burke.

The Need for Speed. Reprinted by permission of James D. Barron. ©2002 James D. Barron.

On Shame and Shadowboxing. Reprinted by permission of Bret Anthony Johnston. ©2001 Bret Anthony Johnston.

Spare Change. Reprinted by permission of Alyssa Morgan and C. S. Dweck. ©2002 C. S. Dweck.

The Rumor Was True. Reprinted by permission of Michael T. Powers. ©2000 Michael T. Powers.

Stupidity. Reprinted by permission of Marjee Berry-Wellman. ©2001 Marjee Berry-Wellman.

Waves of Good-Bye. Reprinted by permission of Jennifer Baxton. ©2002 Jennifer Baxton.

When It All Changes. Reprinted by permission of Rebecca Woolf. ©2000 Rebecca Woolf.

What's on the Inside. Reprinted by permission of Eleanor Luken. ©2001 Eleanor Luken.

And Still I Search . . . Reprinted by permission of Brian Firenzi. ©2001 Brian Firenzi.

The Single-for-Life Syndrome. Reprinted by permission of Rebecca Ayres. ©1999 Rebecca Ayres.

Sweet-and-Sour Sixteen. Reprinted by permission of Ronica Stromberg. ©2001 Ronica Stromberg.

First Kiss. Reprinted by permission of Ron Cheng. ©1999 Ron Cheng.

Changes and the Game "High School." Reprinted by permission of Adelene Wong. ©1999 Adelene Wong.

A Toast. Reprinted by permission of Sarah Watroba. ©2001 Sarah Watroba.

Bonding with Notebooks. Reprinted by permission of Katie Benson. ©2001 Katie Benson.

Life Is a Bumpy Road. Reprinted by permission of Gary LeRoux. ©1998 Gary LeRoux.

Learning the Hard Way. Reprinted by permission of Kim Lowery. ©2000 Kim Lowery.

My Magic Mirror. Reprinted by permission of Melinda Allen. ©2001 Melinda Allen.

It's Not What's on the Outside, but What's on the Inside. Reprinted by permission of Caitlin Pollock. ©2000 Caitlin Pollock.

Collect them all

Code #9594 • hardcover • $19.95